P9-CQR-217

Mondale

Finlay Lewis

Mondale

Portrait of an American Politician

HARPER & ROW, PUBLISHERS
NEW YORK

Cambridge London
Hagerstown   Mexico City
Philadelphia   São Paulo
San Francisco   Sydney
1817

To the memory of my mother and father

FIRST EDITION

Designed by C. Linda Dingler

Library of Congress Cataloging in Publication Data

Lewis, Finlay.
    Mondale: portrait of an American politician.
    Includes index.
    1. Mondale, Walter F., 1928–   2. Vice-Presidents
—United States—Biography. 3. Legislators—United
States—Biography. 4. United States. Congress.
Senate—Biography.
E840.8.M66L48   1980   973.926'092'4 [B] 79–1672
ISBN 0-06-012599-3

---

80 81 82 83 84 10 9 8 7 6 5 4 3 2 1

Contents

Illustrations follow pages 60, 158, and 232.

Preface

"You in America should trust to that volcanic political instinct which I have divined in you"
—GEORGE BERNARD SHAW

Politics and politicians have always fascinated me. In part, my curiosity can be attributed to growing up the son of a newspaperman. As a reporter, editorial writer and editor, my father spent a lifetime as a bemused and discerning observer of the public scene. He not only cared deeply about issues but he loved the richness, the grandeur, the tragedy, and triumph of individual struggles that were part of the larger drama unfolding in front of his typewriter.

In time, I, too, discovered how to get paid for watching politics. Since being hired by the Minneapolis *Tribune* in early 1966, I've covered county boards and congressional debates, school board races and national campaigns, inaugurations and impeachments. One of those whom I met along the way was Walter Mondale of Minnesota, a U.S. senator at our first acquaintance. There was much about him that intrigued me: his roots in Minnesota's exuberant political tradition, the unique way he emerged from obscurity into national office, his skillful adaptation of a liberal political philosophy to the constantly evolving mood of a constituency living in a dynamic world of tough choices. Mondale's election as vice president in November, 1976, offered me the opportunity to deal with a serious political subject on a much broader scale than anything I had ever attempted.

Statistically, Mondale now occupies the most advanta-
geous position in American politics, short of the presidency. Seven men have been president since Franklin
Delano Roosevelt died on April 12, 1945, and four of them
—Harry Truman, Lyndon Johnson, Richard Nixon, and
Gerald Ford—advanced to the Oval Office after first serving as vice presidents. That trend alone suggests the importance of knowing something about those politicians who,
on a moment's notice, may be thrust out of history's
shadow and onto center stage. Ultimately, of course, no
one can anticipate how any human being will respond once
entrusted with the incredible powers and responsibilities of
world leadership. However, that does not diminish the importance of understanding what we can about those who,
by accident or design, might occupy the office that FDR
once described as "preeminently a place of moral leadership." My purpose in writing this book is to illumin-
ate Walter Mondale's political career, and his possible
strengths and weaknesses as a national leader.

There are many to thank for helping bring the project to
completion. Charles Bailey and Frank Wright, the *Tribune*'s
senior editors, were obliging, sympathetic, and tolerant,
since my preoccupation with the book was of little help to
them in putting out a daily paper.

Similarly, my workmates in the *Tribune*'s Washington Bureau, Al McConagha and Eric Pianin, cheerfully took up the
slack and were generous in contributing insights and criticisms. Anne Elliott, the bureau's news assistant, gave un-
stintingly of her time and boundless energy.

To my cousin, Bruce Ingersoll, a reporter in the Chicago
Sun-Times' Washington Bureau, a special debt is owed. A
talented editor, Bruce spent an enormous amount of time
reading and sharpening the manuscript.

Two close friends, Eugene Eidenberg and Ted Marmor,
took time neither could conveniently afford to read the

manuscript. As critics, they were very well-informed and extremely helpful.

My brother, Piers Lewis, and his wife, Kathy, went over the book word by word, applying their rigorous standards as writers and teachers. I did my best to meet everyone's suggestions. The book's failings are therefore a reflection on me alone.

Steve Schofel and Beth Miller, two able researchers, dug through newspaper morgues, historical society files, various public records, and so on. These thankless tasks they performed with diligence and great thoroughness.

Others intervened at particular times when I was most in need of their help—Mortimer Caplin, Arthur Naftalin, John Haynes, Kent Kobersteen, David Lebedoff, Norman Sherman, Mel Elfin, Noomane Kacem, Heidi Berry, Helen McMaster, Ken Allen, and my sister, Georgiana Anderson.

My research encompassed over 150 separate interviews; directly and indirectly, each helped shape the book.

The constant support, advice and good judgment of Alan Barth, an important figure in American journalism, was enormously encouraging. As my agent, Leona Schecter was patient and resourceful. Perhaps the biggest break came when the manuscript wound up on the desk of Amy Bonoff at Harper & Row. Amy is a most sensitive and painstaking editor. To her, to her boss, Simon Michael Bessie, and to my copy editor, David Frederickson, I'm especially grateful.

As for the Mondales, I found the entire family—including children, brothers, half-brothers, et al.—courteous, helpful, and good humored, despite my frequent impositions on their privacy and spare time. Although this is by no means an authorized biography, Vice President and Mrs. Mondale indulged what must have seemed like an unending series of interview requests and specific questions with good grace and great civility. That was likewise true of the Mondale staff. Dick Moe, Jim Johnson and Michael Berman cheerfully put up with endless quizzing, much of it on pure trivia. Maxine Isaacs, Bess Abell, Bert Carp, David Aaron, Gail Harrison, Bill Smith, Denis Clift, Susan Holloway, Bob McNeely, Mike Hill, Ann Stock, Nancy Beck—all were accessible, pleasant, and helpful, indeed.

A special word about Al Eisele. For years a formidable—perhaps too formidable—competitor, he is now a fine press secretary. He made my job infinitely easier by sharing files he had accumulated as a reporter and by offering tips from his own experiences as an author of an excellent joint biography of Hubert Humphrey and Eugene McCarthy.

Finally, my wife, Willee, and our son, Ingersoll, showed pure patience. I hold her responsible for giving me the idea and incentive to write the book in the first place.

1

Carter's Choice

The twin-engine Cessna circled the grass landing strip. Passengers shifted in their seats, anxious to get on with the next phase of their journey. Looking down, Walter Mondale caught his first glimpse of Plains, a sleepy-looking village carved out of the red-clay soil of southern Georgia. Six hundred and eighty-three citizens lived there, but at the moment only one mattered to Mondale. The Democratic senator from Minnesota could see a cluster of men with cameras and microphones standing near the field's lone hangar, topped by a torn wind cone that hung limply in the still, muggy air. Dressed in a garish assortment of T-shirts, Levi's, bermuda shorts, bib overalls, and rakish hats, the waiting reporters were an unofficial reception committee.

Mondale had been silent and withdrawn during most of the forty-minute flight from Atlanta, and the others in the five-seat aircraft had been careful not to disturb his reverie. In his lap were some briefing papers and notes, but mostly he gazed out at the bright early July morning, his sharp-edged, owlish profile a study in reflection.

And now, as Mondale pried himself from his seat, no one needed to tell him that he was approaching a turning point in his career. He was followed by his attentive wife, Joan, a tall, slender, well-scrubbed woman with alert dark eyes and an expressive, sensitive face. Unlimbering, Mondale was peppered by half-jesting questions ("Welcome to the South, Senator. How do you feel about busing, now?") that he would have been crazy to answer.

Mondale grinned at the reporters, most of whom he knew, and looked around for the car Jimmy Carter's aides had said would be waiting. It hadn't arrived yet.

"Do you suppose he's trying to tell me something?" Mondale wondered aloud.

The delay was mercifully brief—it was not yet nine in the morning but the day was already oppressively hot. Within moments of leaving the airstrip, their driver was turning into the shaded drive leading to the red-brick rambler belonging to Plains's most famous citizen. As the car pulled to a stop beside the house, Jimmy Carter, a sandy-haired figure in a brown short-sleeved shirt and light brown slacks, moved through the trees towards them.

"Hi, Fritz," said Carter as Mondale got out of the car, his light-gray suit jacket across his arm. Mrs. Carter soon joined them while a mob of photographers jostled to record the event.

Mondale could recall having met Carter on only a couple of prior occasions. Both encounters were inconsequential —certainly nothing like this. But then, who would have thought that Carter, a once-obscure Southern politician, would be the Democratic party's presumptive nominee for president in 1976? Their first meeting had been in Atlanta when Carter was governor of Georgia and Mondale was assessing his own chances of running for president. They next met in the winter of 1976, when Carter dropped into Mondale's Senate office for a courtesy call. Carter was just beginning a roundup of national convention delegates that would propel him to the threshold of national power. The nomination now in his grasp, Carter had summoned Mondale to his ancestral home to be screened as a potential vice-presidential running mate. It was July 8; Carter would announce his decision on the final day of the Democratic National Convention one week later.

For the past several months, Mondale and his people had been pondering the implications of Carter's growing strength. While a number of important figures in the Democratic party were hatching schemes to block Carter, Dick Moe, Mondale's top Senate staff aide, was writing a memo analyzing Carter's vice-presidential needs and assessing how those needs might affect his boss's political future. Moe was convinced that Carter would eventually have to turn to Mondale—or someone like him—to balance the presidential ticket. With that in mind, Moe's memo advised Mondale to "prepare for the session with Carter" and to consider "the kind of arrangement you would want to have with him if elected."

Mondale followed Moe's advice. He crammed for the interview—comparing Carter's autobiography with his own book about politics and government. He had studied the Georgian's speeches and campaign papers for possible conflicts and then had gone on to list the ways in which he could strengthen Carter politically. And, though it seemed presumptuous, he had developed a description of his proposed role in the Carter administration as vice president.

Now the moment anticipated in Moe's memo was at hand. Once inside Carter's house, it was clear the two men were to be left alone. Joan Mondale and Rosalynn Carter went into the living room, while their husbands walked through the dining room and took seats out back. There, in the patio's sun-dappled shade, they talked, swiping futilely at gnats swarming around their heads. Otherwise, the two men were comfortable with each other. Though probing, Carter's questions were asked in a friendly, conversational tone—his lilting southern accent free of challenging or hostile overtones. Mondale's replies were delivered in a voice that was both respectful, unapologetic, and candid. When Carter asked what kind of role Mondale aspired to play as a potential vice president, Mondale said he would want to be an activist. That would mean having a degree of presidential access few—if any—vice presidents had ever enjoyed. Mondale said he understood the fate of others who had held that office, but he, for one, would not be happy as a figurehead. He offered that last assertion with particular emphasis. Carter's inquiries about their respective records were answered forthrightly. With succinct detail, Mondale noted specific issues on which they differed, but suggested that the books they had written were evidence of an overriding commitment to reforming and improving government—to purging it of its occasional lawless tendencies and to making it a better servant of human needs.

Politically, Mondale was the more liberal of the two. His career, after all, had blossomed under the sponsorship and tutelage of Hubert Humphrey, but, as Mondale talked, Carter could see that his visitor might be right—that this could be a useful alliance. Even Mondale's reputation as one of the Senate's most outspoken defenders of school busing could be reconciled with Carter's own stance as a Southern moderate. It was also pretty clear that this man would not be an embarrassment in other ways. If there was ever a Mr. Clean in American politics, it was Walter Frederick Mondale. A minister's son, Mondale was one of the poorest men in the Senate; his net worth at the end of 1975, estimated at $77,000, was about 10 percent of Carter's. No scandal there. The Mondale family's only substantial asset was a relatively modest house where they had lived for ten years. His personal life was impeccable, but what about his health? That was a potential problem. As they talked, Mondale handed Carter a letter from a physician. Since 1970, Mondale had been receiving medication for hypertension —high blood pressure—but the doctor described the condition as "moderate" and not an impediment to Mondale's career.

Then there was the business of Mondale quitting the

presidential race before it even got started. Something
Mondale had said at the time bothered Carter. "Basically,
I found I did not have the overwhelming desire to be president which is essential for the kind of campaign that is
required," Mondale admitted on November 21, 1974, in
shelving his presidential ambitions. "I don't think anyone
should be president who is not willing to go through fire."
Was Mondale a quitter? Now Mondale was telling Carter
that the real reason for his aborted candidacy was his real-
ization that he had no chance and that the country was
down on Washington politicians in general. It was a question of emphasis. After fifteen months of exploratory campaigning, Mondale had dropped out for two reasons—his
distaste for the rigors of the presidential race and the absence of tangible support that would have made the ordeal
tolerable. Carter, of course, had brooked no discourage-
ment and he might well have challenged Mondale's explanation, which stressed only the second of those reasons.
Carter's own standing was far less than the Minnesotan's in
late 1974. How could Mondale have known where the
country was headed? Wasn't it after all a question of being
tough enough to stick it out? But Carter let the matter pass.

Afterwards, Carter gave no hint of how he was leaning,
although Mondale felt certain he had made a good impression. However, he prudently concealed his elation from the
reporters, deflecting their questions with a quip. "We were
about to get to the question of who he wanted as vice
president," Mondale told the press. "Just as he was about
to tell me, time ran out."

After leaving the house, Carter and Mondale walked
along the Plains main street towards the green-and-white
railway depot that had been converted into a campaign
office. Standing in the shade of a loading dock next to the
station, Mondale heard Carter tell reporters, "I don't think
there'd be any philosophical incompatibilities that would
prevent us running as a harmonious ticket."

Turning to Mondale's short-lived pursuit of the presidency, Carter said he was confident Mondale would be a hard-working running mate. When it was his turn, Mondale joked, "I said I didn't want to spend all my life in Holiday Inns, but I've checked and found they've all been redecorated and they're all marvelous places to stay."

Mondale left Plains that afternoon, only an hour or so before his place was taken at the interview table by Sen. John Glenn of Ohio. They both had been preceded by Sen. Edmund Muskie of Maine. Mondale returned to Washington and four days later flew to New York, the scene of the 1976 Democratic National Convention.

When Mondale set up his staff command post at the Statler Hilton Hotel, across the street from Madison Square Garden, the convention site, the city was awash with rumor. The vice-presidential nomination was all that entered people's minds. With Carter's nomination locked up, there was nothing else to talk about. Carter fed the gossip mill by continuing to interview candidates in his suite at the Hotel Americana. Sens. Frank Church of Idaho, Adlai Stevenson of Illinois, and Henry Jackson of Washington came and went, each one holding a joint press conference with Carter before disappearing. Rep. Peter Rodino of New Jersey, the plain-spoken, unpretentious congressman who had become a folk-hero as the chairman of the impeachment investigation of President Nixon, had his moment with Carter, too. Later, he asked Carter to scratch his name and to choose Mondale instead.

As the tension and excitement mounted, speculation increasingly centered on two men, Mondale and Muskie, the first two candidates to be interviewed in Plains. Mondale was not surprised at Muskie's emergence as a major vice-presidential possibility. There were strong arguments in favor of picking the Maine senator, not the least of which were anxieties among Democratic party professionals about Carter's possible problems as a Southern Baptist in attracting urban, heavily Catholic, ethnic voters. As a Polish Catholic, Muskie had ideal credentials as a bridge-builder to blue-collar voters whose support in past elections had been the backbone of Democratic strength. Mondale thought his own strong ties to Humphrey and the labor wing of the party—cemented by a near-perfect voting record on issues favored by the AFL-CIO—might also ease the problem. Others agreed, but Muskie had a powerful supporter in Charles Kirbo, possibly Carter's closest friend and confidant. In conversations with leading Democrats during convention week, Kirbo, an Atlanta lawyer, worried over primary results in several Northeastern states where Carter seemed weak with traditional Democrats.

The Muskie boom continued to build during convention week with the publication of a poll commissioned by the New York *Times* and CBS showing Carter running behind the landslide margins scored by many past Democratic candidates with Catholic voters. The poll bolstered those who thought the problem, magnified by Carter's equivocal statements on abortion and his evangelical enthusiasm as a born-again Christian, dictated Muskie's selection. Carter's staff members, meanwhile, were as much in ignorance about their boss's thinking as everybody else. The staff, including several members of Carter's own family, preferred Mondale, according to one survey. Kirbo's pragmatic support of Muskie put him at odds with two others close to Carter. Campaign manager Hamilton Jordan and Press Secretary Jody Powell were in Mondale's corner. Both felt that Carter's problem with the urban ethnic vote was only partly religious. They drew support for that view from surveys by Patrick Caddell, which showed that only about 10 percent of the nation's Catholics would base their vote on the abortion issue. Jordan described the whole debate as "exaggerated" and argued that the decision on the vice-presidential nomination should be based on a broader strategic view of the campaign.

There was nothing for Mondale to do under the circumstances but wait. Minnesota Gov. Wendell Anderson told his state's delegation, "Senator Mondale can't be here. He's sitting by the phone and doesn't want to leave. Please don't call him. He wants to keep the line open."

Mondale himself told a visitor that the suspense was "unnerving."

"It's a peculiar feeling because there's nothing you can do. You hear these rumors that you're being seriously considered and you don't know what life will be like two days from now. You have this eerie feeling that things might change abruptly and it might be the beginning of a whirlwind or it might be returning to life as a senator from Minnesota."

At one point, Mondale startled a group of visitors by throwing open a window in his suite and shouting, "Hey, Jimmy, it's me, Fritz. I'm over here."

Then, on Wednesday, July 14—twenty-four hours before Carter was to announce his decision—Mondale canceled an interview on ABC's *Good Morning, America* program and disappeared from view. The media focus had been intense and unrelenting. Mondale was acutely aware that the matter was out of his hands and that he could do nothing to strengthen his case. But he could weaken it. A slip of the tongue could dash his hopes and send him back to Washington empty-handed. Even if he said his lines perfectly every time he talked to a reporter, Carter still might get the impression that he was trying to influence the decision through the media. Mondale knew that blatant self-promotion was not the way to sway Jimmy Carter. With all that in mind, he and Joan secluded themselves in the Carlyle Hotel's penthouse suite, where John Kennedy used to stay. Their whereabouts was kept secret, until a few reporters figured it out.

If Mondale's hands were tied, others were active in his name—if not with his blessings. The key man was his old friend and political mentor, Hubert Humphrey.

They had first met thirty years earlier when Humphrey was running for reelection as mayor of Minneapolis. Mondale, an eager college freshman, enlisted as a campaign volunteer and then went on to pursue a political career uncommonly blessed with good fortune. Humphrey once said that Mondale was the one politician who could arrange to be appointed president. At forty-eight, Mondale had certainly been one of the luckiest men in American politics —and also one of the most skilled. He was never out of position. The pattern began in 1960, when Gov. Orville Freeman appointed Mondale from the ranks of Minnesota's Democratic Farmer-Labor (DFL) party to a vacancy as the state's attorney general. It was his first public office. He was then reelected twice in his own right by landslide margins, establishing himself as a power in state politics, second only to Humphrey himself. It happened again in 1964 when President Kennedy's assassination a year earlier set in motion a chain of events that swept Humphrey to the vice presidency. Karl Rolvaag, then the governor, named Mondale to fill the vacant Minnesota seat in the U.S. Senate. In 1972, George McGovern approached Mondale about signing on as McGovern's running mate in the coming campaign against President Nixon. Mondale declined. He was up for reelection to the Senate that fall. Accepting McGovern's offer would have required forfeiting his seat—thus greatly increasing the risk of a premature end to a promising political career. Now—in 1976—Mondale seemed on the verge of another exciting development.

With the generosity of spirit that had become his trademark, Humphrey had begun a drumbeating campaign for Mondale as early as mid-June, when he told a group of black newspaper publishers, "Mondale's my man, and he's yours. I've been your friend over the years and you've been mine. Now I have one last favor to ask of you. Give Fritz Mondale the favored-son treatment."

Humphrey was also on the telephone to old friends in the labor movement, giving them the same message—men like I.W. Abel of the Steelworkers, Lane Kirkland of the AFL-CIO, Leonard Woodcock of United Auto Workers and Bob Georgine of the Building Trades.

Humphrey also talked twice to both Carter and Kirbo. "I wanted Governor Carter to know that if Fritz Mondale was put on the ticket, I'd be mighty pleased," Humphrey told a visitor in his hotel room midway through the convention. Then, discussing Carter's potential problems with some of the party's traditional interest groups, Humphrey added pointedly, "I've got a lot of friends who might not be Governor Carter's friends—now. But they could be. I like Carter but I'm also Hubert Humphrey and I'm only human. If he picks my friend, I'll probably like him a little better."

Humphrey then recalled having made the motion in the Senate Democratic caucus some time earlier when Carter received its endorsement. "Quite honestly, I didn't think this would hurt Mondale," Humphrey said.

Virtually every group contacted by Humphrey—the black newspapermen, the labor leaders, and others—eventually made Carter aware of their support for Mondale.

Mondale, meanwhile, discovered that he had more mundane and immediate problems. His anxiety level rose sharply at the discovery that many incoming calls from people who knew his number were getting fouled up at the switchboard.

"Our standard joke was that Carter would call and get a recording, 'Sorry, this number is temporarily disconnected,' " recalled Dick Moe. The only solution was to install a special line, bypassing the source of the trouble.

That done, there really was nothing left to do but sit and wait.

On Thursday morning—decision day—Mondale was up at six-thirty to continue work on an acceptance speech, just in case the telephone were to ring with the right message.

About an hour later, he was joined by Moe, who, at thirty-nine, was a highly regarded political professional. A Williams College graduate and a lawyer, Moe had taken over the leadership of the DFL after its unity and morale had been smashed by an unsuccessful palace revolt in 1966 against Governor Rolvaag. Moe's task was to revive the DFL—an ironic assignment, since he had been one of the chief anti-Rolvaag conspirators. As state chairman, he inherited a party that held only one of six statewide constitutional offices and three of eight U.S. House seats. By 1972, the situation was almost exactly reversed. The DFL had picked up a fourth House seat, was about to take control of the state Legislature, and held all but one of the state offices, including the governorship and the attorney general's post. Moe moved to Washington in late 1972 to help direct Mondale's destinies.

As soon as Moe entered the Mondales' Carlyle suite, he walked over and picked up the telephone to check for a dial tone.

"I just did that," Mondale said. The two men laughed.

Others soon joined them. A couple of trusted Senate aides were on hand to do typing and smooth out personal arrangements, along with several close friends. People talked, drank coffee, and moved around the suite, but their attention was focused on the telephone with four plastic buttons in its base.

Mondale, dressed in rumpled khaki slacks, a sports shirt, and tennis shoes, was working over a speech draft with Moe when a telephone button blinked on, indicating that a call was coming in on the newly installed line. A split second later, the telephone itself rang, breaking the tense silence. Bounding across the room, Moe snatched up the receiver, removing his second cigar of the day. After listening silently for a moment to an unfamiliar voice, he murmured, "Just a moment, please," and beckoned to Mondale.

It was 8:26 A.M.

"Hi, did I wake you?"

Carter, who had been nominated for the presidency the night before, laughed at his own question. The call placed by Carter aide Greg Schneiders was the first of six that were made that morning to waiting hopefuls. Seconds into the conversation—it seemed like an eternity to Moe and the others—Mondale turned and vigorously jerked his thumb upwards. He was it.

He would be nominated that night by the Democratic National Convention to run with Carter against the Republicans in the fall as the vice-presidential candidate.

Suddenly, everyone in the room was slightly giddy. Before hanging up, Carter admonished Mondale to keep the news of his good fortune to himself until Carter could personally reveal his decision at a 10:00 A.M. press conference.

For the next ninety minutes, Mondale, Moe, and the others guarded the secret, not daring to venture out of the room for fear of saying or doing something that would give it all away. Moe, who has the usually reliable poker face of a political pro, toyed with the thought of going to the lobby to treat himself to an expensive cigar. But, knowing that reporters had sniffed out Mondale's hideaway, he held back, not confident that he could maintain his stonyface in a state of high excitement. Then, shortly before ten, Mondale called his waiting children in Washington—Teddy, eighteen, Eleanor Jane, sixteen, and William, thirteen—and told them simply to stay on the line but also to watch television because "something interesting is about to happen."

Meanwhile, down in the lobby, a strange little charade was being acted out. At precisely nine-thirty Jerry Parr strode into the lobby, fourteen years a Secret Service agent and every inch a professional. Only this time, he displayed none of the outward badges of his service. He and his partner were operating under cover to protect Carter's secret. Their presence in the lobby of Walter Mondale's supposedly secret hotel would have been a dead giveaway. Trying to look casual, the two agents strolled to the front desk to ask for clearance past the hotel's security guards in order to get to Mondale's room. The assistant manager looked at them narrowly and told them firmly that they would have to be cleared first by someone with Mondale. With a sinking feeling, Parr watched the man dial the room number. There were too many people nearby for him to risk letting the hotel in on the truth, and he was sure no one on the other end of the line would know who Jerry Parr was. By sheerest coincidence, Moe, who picked up the telephone, recalled being told by Norman Sherman, Hubert Humphrey's vice-presidential press secretary, that a man named Parr had headed the Humphrey security detail and might well draw the Mondale assignment in the event of the nomination. Minutes later, Parr and his partner walked into the Mondale suite.

During their telephone conversation that morning, Carter told Mondale, "Over the last month or so, even though I've changed my mind several times, my ultimate decision evolved to where I wanted you to run with me. The same movement took place among my family."

Certainly he didn't have to convince his mother, Miss Lillian. That sprightly woman was on Mondale's side from the start.

"He's the one I wanted from the very beginning. At first because he was so good looking and next because he was so gentle to the people at home, so affable and friendly. Everybody liked him when he visited Plains," she said.

The process was a little more complicated for her son. He began thinking about how to pick a running mate once the momentum in the middle primaries—a trend accelerated by his victory in Pennsylvania—made the nomination seem a likelihood. Working from an initial list of several hundred names, Carter and his staff soon narrowed the possibilities to about two dozen. Carter and Kirbo then contacted thirty or forty major public figures and opinion leaders for their thoughts about specific candidates. In late May, Caddell, Carter's pollster, and Jordan devised a sampling to measure how the top fourteen prospects would affect a ticket headed by Carter. Mondale turned out to be the least well known. As Carter and his top advisers—mainly Kirbo, Jordan, and Caddell—began to focus on his political needs in the fall, Carter was drawn to Church, a popular Westerner in a region where Carter was weak. Once Carter clinched the nomination by winning the Ohio primary on June 8, he began looking at data assembled by Caddell showing that Glenn, an American space hero, would make an attractive partner. Later that month, however, Carter began thinking about his urban ethnic problem and how Ed Muskie might help establish the base he would need in the heavily populated industrial states of the Northeast and Middle Atlantic regions. For much of the time, Mondale was a hazy figure in the middle distance, whom Carter included because almost everybody had nice things to say about him despite his relative public obscurity. But in addition to Mondale's unwillingness two years earlier to undertake an uphill struggle for the presidency, Carter also had to be concerned about the Minnesotan's reputation as a do-gooder on supposedly knee-jerk issues like abortion, busing, and child-care. That, too, was troubling to a presidential candidate who could not afford to alienate a Southern power base.

But, for obvious reasons, Carter was anxious to avoid the kind of hasty, offhand, last-minute decisions that in the past had awarded vice-presidential nominations to Spiro Agnew and Thomas Eagleton. As the screening process began, Mondale came into sharper focus and Carter decided that his earlier views were wrong. Meeting with reporters a few hours after announcing his selection, Carter said his fears about Mondale's possible "lassitude" and his supposed fixation on "peripheral" issues had vanished, and the "movement towards Senator Mondale was almost inexorable."

Although he didn't say so, the most compelling arguments in Mondale's favor were undoubtedly political. There never was much mystery about the grand design of the Carter campaign. Brilliant in concept and execution, Carter's prenomination strategy, by its very success, created problems that might later doom him. The quintessential outsider, Carter had more credibility in 1976 than perhaps even George Wallace when he preached antiestablishment politics. In speech after speech, Carter's love-and-compassion rhetoric merely softened the impact of his strident thrusts against the political "bigshots" who had become entrenched in positions of government power.

In a way, the system had been unwittingly rigged for somebody like Carter. The Democratic party's proportional formulas for awarding delegates on the basis of each candidate's relative strength virtually guaranteed that Carter would get a share of national convention votes wherever he mounted a campaign. And he campaigned in almost every state. On top of that, the new campaign-financing law neutralized the advantages of well-heeled candidates like Henry Jackson and Lloyd Bentsen. It did so by putting limits on the amounts they could spend, while funneling subsidies to Carter, who probably could never have financed his effort as a political unknown if forced to rely on the fat cats of elections past. Finally, the haphazard maze of primary elections and state conventions permitted Carter to plot a strategy that would always keep him on the move, always able to minimize a poor showing in one place by holding out the expectation of a better performance someplace else. Carter never stood still long enough for any of his opponents to take aim.

But what all this meant was that Carter came to the convention with an odd-lot assortment of delegates won as a result of his guerrilla, hit-and-run tactics. They covered all shades of the political spectrum. Tallied up, they were enough to clinch the nomination. That, however, was about all. Carter's was a fragmented, diverse constituency. The primary campaigns had engaged the attention of a very minor fraction of the nation's eligible voters. But the nature of Carter's campaign, with its antiestablishment bias, had aroused the suspicion of those traditional power centers that alone could produce the votes to win a national election.

From the moment Mondale was chosen, it was understood he would play the conciliator's role. He would be the chief emissary to the union bosses, the big-city Democratic chieftains, the leaders of the ethnic blocs, the intellectual cadres in the universities—all of whom would now be needed if Carter was to win in November. By accepting the vice-presidential nomination, Mondale mortgaged his own credentials as a political liberal in order to assure Carter's credibility.

The convention was an auspicious beginning. Quelling butterflies, Mondale stepped to the podium to accept the vice-presidential nomination. About twenty degrees to his left was the Minnesota delegation, the bastion of his support and the base of his political career. And, by a happy coincidence, the Georgia delegates were seated directly in front of the Minnesota contingent. The standards of the two states had become intertwined during the course of the evening, providing a colorful counterpoint to the themes of political and sectional reunification that ran through Mondale's acceptance speech. "I could see it in their eyes," Mondale confided later. "They seemed to be saying, 'Mondale, we're going to make you succeed in spite of yourself.' " Unlike the debacles of recent Democratic history, the final tableau was not one of intramural strife. The convention was adjourned moments after the Rev. Martin Luther King, Sr., delivered a stirring benediction and the delegates joined hands in singing "We Shall Overcome." The differences that in the past had split the party seemed to have been washed away by the rhetoric and symbolism of those final moments. The question was whether that ephemeral feeling of sunny optimism and unity could be sustained through the gray-cold weeks to follow.

There were plenty of reasons to feel good about Democratic prospects. The Republicans, having controlled the White House since 1969, had been ravaged by Watergate. Richard Nixon, Humphrey's conqueror in 1968, had resigned in disgrace, only to be pardoned for any possible Watergate crimes by his successor, Gerald Ford. Ford's decision, a month after taking office, to let Nixon off the prosecutor's hook turned out to be a self-inflicted political wound, and the new president's standing in the country never recovered. His administration was also belabored by a host of other problems. A plan to Whip Inflation Now, complete with WIN buttons, was widely ridiculed. Ford himself was forever being photographed bumping his head or tripping or doing something equally maladroit. The economy had been in a recession. Ford's perceived weakness as a candidate drew former California Gov. Ronald Reagan into the competition for the 1976 GOP presidential nomination. The contest was bitter, closely fought, and the outcome still unresolved by the time the Democrats harmoniously closed ranks behind Carter. All of these factors contributed to giving the Carter-Mondale ticket an overwhelming thirty percentage point cushion in the public opinion polls over any opposition the Republicans might offer.

From New York, the Mondales flew back to Washington, now encumbered by an entourage of Secret Service agents, staff aides, and news crews. Acquired overnight, this retinue would become a permanent part of their lives. At Washington's National Airport, a waiting motorcade whisked the family to a welcome-home party in front of

their Lowell Street house in the Cleveland Park neighborhood. A thunderstorm had preceded them, uprooting
trees, flooding basements, snuffing out electrical service.
Even so, their friends and neighbors seemed gaily oblivious
of the rubble-strewn streets and steady drizzle. Joan and
Fritz found their house and yard festooned with newly
minted white-on-green Carter-Mondale posters. One fan,
using borrowed press credentials, had snitched them from
the convention floor and rushed back to Washington to
help arrange a proper greeting. Buckets filled with iced
beer and champagne were everywhere, and the sidewalks
seemed alive with bobbing umbrellas. It was Mondale's first
campaign crowd.

By Labor Day, however, the Mondale campaign had
logged several shakedown, nation-spanning trips and was
ready for the real thing. Stretching in front of Mondale
were eight weeks of hectic days and one-night stands in
sterile, plastic motels. Twenty months after he had re-
nounced his own presidential ambitions, partly because he
couldn't abide the campaign lifestyle, Mondale was about
to commit himself to days of unremitting pressures that
would numb his mind and exhaust his body. But there was
this difference: Jimmy Carter had not allowed himself to be
deflected by self-doubt or personal discomfort from his
quest. By signing on as a junior partner for the long
march's last lap, Mondale was risking nothing. Victory
could move him, relatively effortlessly, across the threshold
of national power. Defeat would send him back to the Senate, where it would be easy to accept the outcome gracefully, especially if he had acquitted himself honorably in the
party's service.

That was Mondale's frame of mind when he took off from
Washington on a lovely, clear Labor Day morning for
coast-to-coast campaigning in front of working-class audiences that were to become his specialty. It was not exactly
a glory road. From time to time, it would take him to cities

like San Francisco, Seattle, Denver, and Los Angeles. More often, his targets were the grimy, blue-collar neighborhoods of Akron, Gary, Newark, Toledo. It meant embracing—however tentatively—disgraced politicians like Rep. Henry Helstoski in Bergen, New Jersey, whose followers were thought to be loyal still despite his indictment in an immigration scandal. It also meant chomping on a six-foot hero sandwich in a New York street market, being heckled by students at the University of Illinois, listening to rambling political speeches late at night when he yearned for bed, and enduring the inevitable snafus that would wrench schedules out of kilter and jeopardize the campaign's investment in an entire state.

Indeed, there were days when nothing seemed to go right. One Monday morning, eight days before the election, Mondale stumbled from bed about 5:30 A.M. in West Mifflin, Pennsylvania, outside Pittsburgh. The entourage had come in late the previous night after a series of mishaps that began when it became briefly lost in northern Ohio. More time had been lost in a post-game traffic jam outside the Cleveland Browns football stadium. The day had been capped as the campaign plane landed at the wrong Pittsburgh area airfield. Leaving the local Holiday Inn with only a couple of hours' sleep, Mondale was driven to the main gate of the huge U.S. Steel plant in Duquesne, Pennsylvania, where a well-staged media event had been planned. The gimmick was timely because local unemployment was high and more layoffs were expected.

However, when Mondale pulled up to the gate, he discovered that his advance party had misjudged the driving time. The incoming workers were already at their jobs. The going-home crew had disappeared into the predawn darkness. All Mondale could do was stand in the chilly rain, gazing down an empty street. Recognizing that the situation was beyond repair, Mondale beat a hasty retreat to the motorcade—with about forty minutes to kill before the next scheduled event. The caravan—two press buses, and about ten staff, Secret Service, and police cars—lurched into the street and then, inexplicably, circled back into the parking lot, where the reporters piled out and surrounded the candidate's car. Mondale emerged to confront the shivering press under the eerie glow of a mercury vapor light in the otherwise deserted parking lot. He waved his hand commandingly at the television crews.

"All right," he said, with the faintest trace of a smile. "I have a statement. Turn on the cameras."

After pausing to let everyone get ready, he said, "This campaign is getting off to a very good start. We feel we're up ahead of everyone else. At least there's no one else around here. As a result of careful calibration, we were able to get up very, very early and arrive at the Duquesne plant five minutes after the shift changed and everyone went into the plant.

"As a result, we were able to see the landscape unfettered by potential voters. We're on our way, things are picking up, they can't get worse, and we're very, very happy."

He concluded on a note of mock seriousness, saying, "I'll accept no questions." He then slid back into his car, only to reappear moments later at the side window, his face creased by an impish smile as he gazed out at the half-drenched reporters standing in the late October drizzle. It was the performance of a man whose sense of the absurd remained undiminished. It was also a media masterstroke. Improvising to avert disaster, Mondale transformed a clichéd, routine campaign event into a warm vignette. And the networks featured it on the evening news.

The plant gate was not the only flub that day. An hour later, Mondale walked into a local restaurant where he was to breakfast with some of the unemployed. The management had set places for about sixty at three long tables. But when Mondale showed up, about half of one table was filled. Otherwise, there were only empty places as television cameras scanned the room. Finally, the frantic advance crew rounded up enough union officials—all employed—to fill the remaining spaces at the one table. With that, Mondale proceeded as best he could.

Earlier in his career, Mondale would have been enraged at those foulups, and somebody would have paid. But in later years, he had softened and become more tolerant. Partly it was because the caliber of his staff had improved, but, more importantly, he had matured. Having shot down his own presidential balloon two years earlier, he seemed to find it easier to accept the shortcomings of others. Despite the futility of that early morning in Duquesne, he kept his perspective. Advance arrangements for the plant-gate visit had been in the hands of Gael Sullivan, a large, good-humored man who had worked loyally, ably—and futilely —for Mondale in 1974.

"I suppose I should get mad at Gael," Mondale said. "But, you know, I just can't. I just love that guy."

He still drove his staff. Occasionally, he would snap or lash out—particularly if tired. The early stages of the campaign had been particularly rough. Unsure of himself, Mondale was excessive in his praise of Carter. As he grew more confident, references to Carter diminished, and his campaign became more of an independent enterprise. Scheduling or other logistical snafus bothered him less, even though the pressure was growing.

His self-deprecating humor helped to make it bearable. About to leave a campaign event, Mondale turned to a local worker and said, "I sure hope you'll be out here helping us election day."

"I certainly will be—if it doesn't rain," the worker replied.

Turning to Sullivan, Mondale muttered, "Well, they're really strong for me out here."

After he had droned through one deadly dull speech to a group of businessmen in West Palm Beach, Florida, Mondale was asked to assess his performance.

"I don't know," he replied. "I fell asleep halfway through."

The mood aboard the campaign plane—a leased, elongated 727 dubbed the *Minnesota Fritz*—was often antic, sometimes rowdy. One day in mid-October, Mondale had been heckled during campaign rallies in San Jose and Portland by a splinter group of the U.S. Labor Party, chanting, "We want jobs, not hot air." Late that night, a group of reporters improvised by shouting from the rear of the plane, "We want news, not hot air." After enduring this for a few minutes, Mondale materialized at the door separating his quarters from the aft section. Wearing a drooping, wide-brimmed hat and looking like a jowly sheriff in a two-bit western, Mondale removed a thick cigar from his mouth and shouted, "Bullshit, bullshit," in a perfect parody of the cadenced taunts public officials routinely had to endure during the Vietnam War.

Mondale's willingness to disagree with Carter on certain issues distinguished him from Republican Sen. Robert Dole, President Ford's running mate. Dole once defined his role on the ticket by explaining, "The president winds me up and says, 'Go.' " When Carter criticized decisions of the U.S. Supreme Court under its late chief justice, Earl Warren, for expanding the rights of criminal defendants, Mondale took issue, saying he had consistently supported those rulings. The two halves of the Democratic ticket also disagreed over the Nixon pardon, with Carter taking the position that it was not a helpful issue for the Democrats. In his acceptance speech at the convention, however, Mondale attacked the pardon as a perversion of American justice. He returned to the issue in a passionate speech October 5 before a law school audience in Kansas City, calling it a "mockery" and saying, "No act more perpetuated Nixon's own dangerous doctrine that the president is somehow above the law."

Mondale could be touchy about being pressed too hard on points of more extreme ideological sensitivity. After giving hazy answers to a series of questions about housing and school desegregation in Northern cities, Mondale one day turned sarcastic. "I know what you're trying to get me to say," he remarked testily to Robert Shogan, the political writer for the Los Angeles *Times*. "You want to know how many blacks I want to move into Polish neighborhoods."

After all, Carter had not picked Mondale as his running mate so he could lose votes in Democratic strongholds. Their partnership was unique in Mondale's career only because it involved such high stakes. But few men in American politics were as experienced as Mondale at adapting personal ambition to the interests of someone else who happened to be in the forefront.

"On the fundamental question of being the junior partner, he was schooled beyond anyone else in American politics probably," said James Johnson, operational head of Mondale's campaign-plane staff and a young Minnesotan.

Working under Johnson were two press aides whose judgment and temperament made up for their mutual lack of any prior national campaign experience. One was Francis O'Brien, who had worked earlier as a top administrative aide to Congressman Rodino during the impeachment investigation two years earlier. O'Brien's reputation for resourcefulness quickly spread, and Mondale hired him as campaign press secretary shortly after the convention. O'Brien's assistant was Maxine Isaacs, an unflappable young woman from Mondale's Senate staff. Their civility under constant pressure, as well as their general savvy, won them the respect and affection of the traveling press corps, and undoubtedly played a role in earning Mondale favorable coverage throughout most of the campaign.

Mondale was determined to avoid friction at any level with Carter and his staff. Mondale's earliest important campaign decision was to integrate his people with Carter's in

Atlanta, instead of establishing a separate organization in Washington or Atlanta. That meant from the beginning that Moe, Mike Berman, another top member of Mondale's Minnesota mafia, and others were absorbed into the Carter campaign organization. Beyond question they strengthened it. For example, Berman, a thirty-seven-year-old expert in the intricacies of the nation's election laws and a wizard at campaign mechanics, had skills unmatched by anyone else in Atlanta.

Mondale's most important contribution was his ability to translate Jimmy Carter into the lingo of lunch-pail Democrats. As Humphrey's protégé and ally, Mondale was perfect for the role. The themes came to him naturally, reflecting values formed during boyhood on the sweeping prairies of southern Minnesota. His impoverished father moved several times to serve Methodist churches in small towns struggling under the Great Depression. Hard times, coupled with his father's admiration for Franklin Roosevelt and the New Deal, made a powerful impression on young Mondale. Indoctrinated by his father's dinner-table sermons, Mondale became committed to the notion that government had a duty to act as an equalizer in an uneven battle between working folk and the captains of capitalism. The calling of the politician was to see that the powerless got an even break. Speaking at a Democratic rally in Albuquerque the day after Labor Day, you could hear the son speaking in the cadences of a minister father: "It's one thing to look at the statistics of unemployment—7.8 percent, 7.9 percent. . . . It's another thing to stand and talk with someone with a family and kids and with love and hope and dreams and who tells you he can't make it and is losing confidence in himself and has had to give up his health insurance, his life insurance, his car, and sometimes his home—and even his family—and not know what's ahead. Those are the voices of America that our leaders must hear. . . . We want a government that honors work, that honors

the skill and energy of our people as its most priceless asset
. . . that realizes when a child fails, we all fail; when an
American fails to get work, we all fail; that seeks to restore
that lost sense of concern and compassion for others where
the greatness, the wealth and strength of Americans, is
found in our acts of justice and decency for those among
us who don't have a chance."

As repeated from stump to stump along the gritty vice-
presidential campaign trail, that message became the core
of a standard speech with just enough flexibility to adjust
to the topical, regional, ethnic, or ideological interests of
each audience. But basically, the format was like an old suit
that he could comfortably wear, with a few alterations, in
front of farmers in Wichita, Greek-Americans in Chicago,
steelworkers in Steubenville, or blacks in Cleveland. It was
also pure Mondale—a mixture of piety, bleeding-heart liberalism, partisanship, and humor.

For comic relief, he loved to quote Harry Truman on
Republicans: "They stand four-square for the American
home but not for housing; they are strong for labor but
they are stronger for restricting labor's rights; they favor
the minimum wage, the smaller the minimum, the better
. . . and they admire the government of the United States
so much they would like to buy it."

He would also mock Ford's campaign promises to provide the American people with more jobs, housing, and
parks, saying it reminded him of his father's experiences
with repentant sinners: " 'During my career I've heard a lot
of deathbed conversions,' " Mondale recalled being told by
his father. " 'The trouble is, they sometimes get well. And
they almost always forget.' " At that point, Mondale would
raise his fist and shout, "Mr. Republican President, it's too
late for you to be converted. We know your record."

Allowing for Mondale's personal touches, it was
nonetheless standard Democratic electioneering. And it
seemed to be effective. A Lou Harris poll early in the fall

showed Mondale leading Dole by fourteen points in the six
largest states, as compared to a five-point edge for Carter.
And while Carter was bogged down in controversy over his
confessions to *Playboy* magazine of lustful fantasies and
over a gaffe about tax reform, Robert Strauss, chairman of
the Democratic party, was able to detect a ray of hope for
the ticket. "Mondale is doing fine," he told a group of
reporters hounding him with questions about Carter's er-
ratic performance.

Ultimately, Mondale's niche in the history of the 1976
campaign would be determined on October 15, when he
and Dole were to meet in Houston's Alley Theater for the
first televised debate in history between two vice-presidential candidates. He could go down as a goat or a hero.

As the date approached, Mondale broke off campaigning
and returned to Washington. He began preparing like a
hybrid prize-fighter–trial-lawyer. His top issues experts
were summoned from Atlanta, thick black briefing books
tucked under their arms. When he wasn't cramming, Mondale would run laps around the St. Alban's School athletic
field, play tennis against Jim Johnson, and then run more
laps.

Finally, there was a mock debate in his office. Three staff
members posed as a panel of newsmen. A young staff lawyer, Roger Colloff, played Bob Dole. After it was over, John
Reilly, one of Mondale's top political advisers, voiced a
verdict shared by others in the room.

"Colloff won," Reilly declared.

So it appeared he had. Colloff, tall, witty, well-educated,
had made a careful study of Dole's record and slashing
campaign style. From the beginning, he kept his boss off
balance with sharp verbal thrusts at Mondale's record as a
big-spending liberal, at the party's platform and congressional record, and at Carter's reputation as a politician who
took fuzzy or shifting positions on issues. While Colloff
successfully put Mondale on the defensive, he also suc-

ceeded in his larger assignment: He showed Mondale what
to avoid. He and his staff agreed that the important thing
was to be himself. Watching Colloff, Mondale realized that
Dole's style was self-destructive. There was no need to
out-Dole Dole.

Once Mondale arrived in Houston, things seemed to go
right. Dole was in an irritable mood, nursing a cold and
oddly defensive about his role on the ticket. Indeed, Moe
got the strong impression during the predebate negotiations that Dole gladly would have skipped the whole thing.

As the debate opened, Mondale seemed wooden and
nervous, but soon Dole's slashing style opened him to
effective counterpunches. A jibe at Carter about his tax
deductions enabled Mondale to point out that the Democratic candidates had opened their tax returns to public
inspection; the Republicans hadn't. Dole's assertion that
Mondale had never met the exiled Russian author Alek-
sandr Solzhenitsyn was false and permitted Mondale to
make an indignant rebuttal. But all along, Mondale was
waiting for the opportunity to land one telling blow without
having to flail like an alley fighter. Finally, Walter Mears of
the Associated Press asked Dole whether the Nixon pardon
wasn't an appropriate campaign issue.

"It's an appropriate topic, I guess," Dole replied. "But
it's not a very good issue any more than the war in Vietnam
would be or World War II or World War I, or the war in
Korea, all Democrat wars, all in this century. . . ."

Mondale did not miss: "I think Sen. Dole has richly
earned his reputation as a hatchet man tonight. . . . Does
he really mean to suggest to the American people that there
was a partisan difference over involvement in the war to
fight Nazi Germany? I don't think any reasonable American
would accept that."

Like a wave cresting, the Mondale campaign was carried
from Houston on a rising tide of excitement and expectation. The critics' reviews were mostly favorable; some were

raves. Mondale and his own staff were elated with a shared gut feeling that the victory had clearly been theirs. The campaign had turned a corner and, win or lose, everyone would know that Mondale had performed his role well.

The ultimate accolade came from Carter, who now turned his selection of Mondale into a campaign issue by drawing an invidious comparison with Ford's choice of Dole. That ploy was buttressed by national public-opinion polls following the debate, showing that Mondale had strengthened Carter, while Dole had weakened Ford.

Beginning with a noisy rally the next day at a shopping center outside of St. Louis, the crowds now seemed larger, more enthusiastic about Mondale, more responsive to what he had to say. Mondale acted crisper, more sure of himself. Putting aside his inherent caution, he became almost free-wheeling in his attacks. At an airport press conference in Los Angeles on October 18, Mondale told reporters that Gen. George Brown, chairman of the Joint Chiefs of Staff, wasn't fit to be named sewer commissioner because of disparaging remarks the general had made about the Israeli armed forces. Two days later, he took aim at Dole, saying, "Someone who voted against health care shoudn't be elected dog-catcher." The next day, Mondale assailed Ford before a Norwegian ethnic audience in Everett, Washington. Noting the large proportion of elderly in the audience, Mondale denounced a Ford administration budget proposal, claiming it would increase medical costs of those over sixty-five by $1.5 billion.

"The cruelest thing you could do in America is to raise the medical costs of senior citizens. That's about as mean-spirited as you can be. . . . That kind of person would steal crutches."

By now the campaign was in its final phase. The polls had begun picking up a Republican surge that seemed to threaten the Democratic lead. The pressure was excruciating. Mondale returned to Washington October 22 after a seven-day western swing that had started the day before the debate. Exhausted, Mondale insisted over mild objections from the Atlanta headquarters on taking a break.

On October 24, the *Minnesota Fritz* was again airborne and Mondale's goal was clear. The election would be won or lost in the Northeast, assuming Carter held the South. Moe's own projections ceded the Republicans every Northern state west of the Mississippi except Missouri. But the Carter-Mondale ticket would still be safe, assuming the old Democratic coalition held firm. The final itinerary made sense only to someone like Moe, whose mind calculated the distance between two points not in terms of miles but of electoral votes. The result was a logistical nightmare. Starting in Ohio, Mondale made stops in Cleveland, Lorain, Mayfield Heights, and Independence. He spent the night outside of Pittsburgh. Then on to New Jersey—to Teterboro, Paramus, Wayne, Morristown, and West Orange. The next day was spent in Elizabeth, New Jersey, Wilkes-Barre, Pennsylvania, Albany, New York, and Philadelphia. Then it was Camden, New Jersey, and Dayton and Akron. From there it was back and forth between the Middle West and the East Coast several more times, with many stops in between. Mondale was in and out of Cleveland so many times that Anthony Garofoli, Cuyahoga County Democratic chairman, wondered aloud whether the Minnesotan was running for county commissioner. In all, Mondale visited thirteen Ohio cities by the end of the campaign.

The symmetry of the campaign's first six weeks had been discarded. It had become a sprint in and out of obscure factory towns—a series of zigs and zags undertaken in a frenetic burst of energy. Nothing could be taken for granted. Carter's midsummer lead of over thirty percentage points in the public-opinion polls had steadily dwindled through the fall. Now, in the final days, the pollsters agreed the election was too close to call.

Mondale made no effort to hide what an ordeal it was.

"You know, I want to tell you the truth," Mondale told the Polish-American Club in Camden early one morning. "I've been campaigning eighteen hours a day now for two months, and when I got up this morning, I said, 'I just can't make it any more, I'm so tired.'" His voice sounded tired, although he told the crowd, including some plump women in bright ethnic costumes, that "in just fifteen minutes you've made me feel so good I'm ready to go full-out for the rest of the campaign." In a very literal way, he had described the alternating cycles of despondency and exhilaration, exhaustion and renewal he had felt since Labor Day. It had been an emotional roller coaster.

By the final day of campaigning, Mondale was continuing to reach out to voters and political leaders in the smaller and humbler neighborhoods east of the Mississippi River where Carter was still perceived as a political aberration from the redneck South. Democrats in upstate New York, led by Joe Crangle, longtime boss of the Erie County machine, gave Mondale perhaps his most tumultuous welcome of the campaign when he stopped in Buffalo. Earlier that day, Mondale struck political gold in Philadelphia when Mayor Frank Rizzo promised Mondale something he wouldn't personally promise Carter: The local organization would not sit on its hands on election day.

The campaign culminated in an emotional rally in Flint. Mondale and Carter were reunited for one final appearance before nine thousand screaming Democrats. Joan Mondale and Rosalynn Carter were there, too. Afterwards, the Carters flew off to Georgia, while the Mondales headed for Minneapolis. It was all over but the waiting.

2

"I'm Planning on Going into Politics . . ."

The land was an equalitarian master. It treated everyone equally—and generally harshly, at that. The fact that the Mundal family owned substantial amounts of mountainous, rocky, unyielding Norwegian soil assured Walter Mondale's forebears of some respectability, a lot of hardship, and a sense of mystical well-being that had nothing to do with the vagaries of a rural Scandinavian economy. For the survivors of its rigors, the environment nurtured qualities of physical endurance, courage, shrewdness, and moral hardiness that would later be transplanted to the American frontier. Those were among the legacies passed from generation to generation by the Mundal/Mondale clan. Above all, Mondale's ancestors were tough, physically and mentally. They had to be. Their survival depended on it.

There was certainly a primitive toughness in the political dealings of one branch of the Mondale family, reputed to stem from the dim and martial days of the Viking warlords. This bloodline is said to include a seventh-century chieftain who consolidated his power by inviting all the neighboring nobles to a banquet in a hall built especially for the occasion. The timber structure had one door and no windows, and, after the guests had become quite drunk, the host walled up the entrance and set the place on fire. He became known as the Deceitful One.

That marauding spirit had receded into legend by the time Walter Mondale's great-grandfather, Frederik, was born in 1824 in a village on the shores of Sogne Fjord, Norway's longest, widest, and deepest relic of the glacial age. Taking their names from the villages where they lived, Mondale's ancestors farmed for centuries in a setting of snowcapped peaks, huge fir forests, and a spectacular, cascading waterfall. Once important landowners, the family was financially ruined in the aftermath of the Napoleonic wars. After several years of trying to eke out a living from a forbidding and rocky terrain, Frederik set out in 1856 with his young family from the village of Mundal for the rich, tillable soil described in reports from America. He eventually settled in southern Minnesota in 1864.

Twelve years later, Mondale's father, Theodore, was born. The family name—Mundal—had become Anglicized, but the frontier environment remained harsh and primitive. As a child, Theodore endured family scorn because he seemed "slow" mentally and clumsy physically. When he showed signs of being left-handed, his parents used a mitten to break him of the tendency. As he grew older, the family was chagrined to discover that he would break into a stutter when excited. Theodore learned to live with his limitations. In a frontier society that valued sturdy, self-reliant frontiersmen who could work bare-handed miracles with the raw materials of nature, he fell short. However, there was a deeper sense of humanity stirring within Theodore Mondale, as well as a good-humored tolerance that made life within a harsh and arbitrary society not only bearable but enjoyable. In 1902, he married Jessie Larson, the prettiest girl in Redwood County, and went about the business of raising a family using his meager talents as a farmer.

Like agriculture, religion was a constant element of life on the Minnesota frontier. Theodore had been raised in a strict Norwegian Lutheran church at a time when predestination was a burning issue. He would never forget a family confrontation during his youth with the minister, a stern, mechanistic believer in the awesome and frightening doctrine that salvation could come only to those who were destined by God to be saved. When the minister demanded that all in the congregation who believed in the heretical—but liberating—doctrine of free will identify themselves, Theodore's father stood up and stalked from the church.

About the time of his marriage, Theodore took his own step towards a religious commitment based on human compassion and social concern. He joined the Methodist church. By 1911, he was ready to join that church's ministry as the result of a mystical experience during spring plowing. What actually happened—and why—is unclear. Evidence of a spiritual transformation was an important step in winning acceptance to the ministry. Theodore doubtless saw a preacher's life as his deliverance from the uncertain rigors of farming and an assurance of a degree of bourgeois respectability. He was thirty-five at the time, the father of two small boys—Lester and Clifford—and ready for a change in career. Whatever the experience, his testimony about a personal moment of great repose and universal harmony helped him win acceptance to the ministry.

One of his first undertakings was to follow an evangelist friend to the Deadwood region of South Dakota's Black Hills to do missionary work among the brawling silver and lead miners there. After six months, he returned, discouraged but not defeated, with an ugly head wound from having been mysteriously knocked unconscious. He never discussed the incident. There followed a series of assignments to small rural churches, such as the one in Jeffers, Minnesota, where he and his wife, Jessie, adopted the daughter of a man who had killed himself by swallowing carbolic acid. It was 1916 and suicides were regarded as beyond the pale. None of the other churches in the area, even the man's own Lutheran church, would perform the funeral services. The exception was Reverend Mondale. Later that year, Jessie gave birth to their third son.

World War I by now had engulfed Europe. The dramatic events unfolding thousands of miles away generated an era of unprecedented prosperity for American agriculture. These were also fat years for Theodore, who had kept his original farm as an investment and purchased another one for the same purpose. He dressed well, enjoyed the respect of the communities where he preached, and seemed confident of a solid, if unspectacular, career within the Methodist church. In 1920, he moved his family to St. James, Minnesota, a town of 2,673 and, as it turned out, the pinnacle of his career. Soon after arriving there, however, the family's luck worsened as Reverend Mondale suffered a series of setbacks that were to leave him widowed, financially ruined, physically drained, and professionally diminished. Those were years that could have turned a lesser man to self-hatred and a corrosive, self-destructive, misanthropic cynicism. That did not happen. He did become politically radicalized. However, those who knew Theodore Mondale felt he drew strength from the adversity of that period. They recall a man of quiet dignity and generous good humor, who devoted himself to his family and his ministry with a renewed sense of compassion and humility.

The first blow was financial. A sharp drop in farm prices after World War I wiped out the value of Theodore Mondale's two farms, and foreclosure followed. He was now left with no resources except a meager church salary. About this time, Jessie became fatally ill with encephalitis. Death came slowly. While Theodore had the funds, he hired both a day and a night nurse, but after six months he could no longer afford nighttime help. For the final year of her life, there was no night assistance at all.

"Dad had to assume the total burden of lifting mother around and seeing that she was bathed and so forth. And it left him stooped for the rest of his life," recalled Lester

Mondale, Jessie and Theodore's oldest son.

Shortly after Jessie died, Reverend Mondale contracted lockjaw—a dread and usually fatal frontier disease—after a kitchen-table tonsillectomy. At first, he could barely get soup between his clenched teeth. But he painstakingly, and painfully, worked at prying apart his clenched jaws by jamming a device, shaped like a top with a screwlike thread, between his teeth and twisting. After about a year of stoical and determined effort, he could open and close his mouth normally again.

It was also about this time that his church in St. James burned and had to be rebuilt. Theodore undertook this task amidst his other troubles. When it was completed, the new church was acclaimed as an even grander and more appropriate place of worship than the one that burned.

Just as he had rebuilt the church—and in the same spirit that had impelled his grandparents to abandon Norway's rocky soil—Theodore set about regaining control of his life. He started to court Claribel Cowan.

In fact, it was Jessie, a generous and caring woman, who helped bring the two together. Jessie remembered having met Claribel years earlier. Jessie also recalled that Claribel had expressed an open and innocent admiration for Theodore, whose Norwegian brogue and occasional stutter did not exactly endow him with eloquence. As she lay on her deathbed, Jessie worried about who would care for her family. At her suggestion, Theodore began to correspond with Claribel. Gradually, the stiffness and formality of the initial overtures ripened into a warm and intimate relationship. They married on June 19, 1925. Thirteen months later, a son, Clarence, was born.

Shortly thereafter, Reverend Mondale was assigned to Kasson, a somewhat smaller and less important community than St. James. If not a demotion, the move clearly indicated to him that he was being shunted aside in favor of younger men.

In desperation, Reverend Mondale hired an outside evangelist to stir up the community's religious zeal and to help build a congregation that would catch the Methodist hierarchy's eye. The move backfired. The evangelist, a man of mercurial temperament and brimstone rhetoric, turned on Reverend Mondale and tried to discredit him in the eyes of the congregation. The emotionally charged schism embarrassed the church establishment, and within a year Reverend Mondale was banished to Ceylon, a dot on the Minnesota map, a few miles north of the Iowa border. That was where Walter Frederick Mondale—soon to be nicknamed Fritz—was born on January 5, 1928.

During Fritz's early years, there were two political heroes in the Mondale household. One was Franklin Delano Roosevelt, although Theodore and Claribel cast "dry" votes in 1932 for Norman Thomas, because FDR, a political "wet," was advocating repeal of Prohibition. The other fabled figure was Floyd B. Olson, a charismatic, self-proclaimed radical who dominated Minnesota politics as governor from 1930 until his death in office from cancer in 1936.

Olson had come to power carrying the banner of the Farmer-Labor party—an ideological descendant of a variety of agrarian protest movements that began gathering momentum in Minnesota politics shortly after the Civil War. Initially, at least, the political ferment in the state's farm belt had little appeal for Theodore Mondale. In 1900, he shunned the Populist-backed candidacy of William Jennings Bryan and cast his first presidential-election ballot for President McKinley, the epitome of Main Street Republicanism.

The desperate conditions in the Minnesota countryside during the 1920s—coupled with his own troubles—shaped Theodore Mondale's political transformation. He now took his political text from that rich tradition of Populist protest that would become part of the soul of Hubert Humphrey's and Fritz Mondale's Democratic Farmer-Labor party. It was a tradition rooted in the experience of thousands of nineteenth-century immigrants—like those from Mundal, Norway—who, looking for lives of prosperity in the New World, discovered instead only bleak hardship. There had to be an explanation. In stark black-and-white terms, political reformers described the yeoman farmer as the exploited victim of impersonal and manipulative forces operating beyond the horizon under the murky rubric of Wall Street. There could be found the greedy capitalists who were crushing the cherished Jeffersonian ideal of a society built on the bedrock of the self-sufficient family farm.

It was Floyd Olson who became the political personification of the discontent that was spreading from the farms to Minnesota's cities after World War I. Gradually, the militancy of the more politically active and radical unions began winning converts among the more cautious elements of the state's labor movement. Economic circumstances and a shared sense of powerlessness drove prairie Populists and blue-collar organizers into temporarily laying aside their often conflicting goals and joining hands in a collaborative political effort—the Farmer-Labor party. However, Olson's death in 1936 triggered a power struggle within the Farmer-Labor party, pitting a cadre of Communists and nonmarxist radicals against more traditional liberals, Progressives and Populists. The internecine warfare destroyed Olson's party as a cohesive, statewide force but did not significantly diminish the emotional content of Farmer-Laborism and the powerful constituency it could command. Its earlier successes in electing Olson to the governor's chair and Henrik Shipstead to the U.S. Senate and others to lesser offices loosened the monolithic grip of the Republican party, which had ruled the state with few interludes since Territorial days. The question was whether the movement's political potency could ever again be harnessed.

While he lived, Olson's stature and the political attitudes
he inspired reflected the devastating impact of the Depression that had become a fact of life for the impoverished
preacher and his young family. However, Walter would
later recall that he grew up largely unaware of the family's
poverty, since everyone else was in the same straits. If everyone was poor, no one was poor. Nonetheless, by the
time he arrived in Ceylon, Theodore Mondale already bore
the imprint of hardship on his lined face, in his threadbare
wardrobe, and on his prematurely bent body. There were
times when the small community, bending under the Depression's weight, could not pay his salary, and he had to
ask the parishioners individually for financial help. The
situation was no better in Heron Lake, Reverend Mondale's
next assignment and an equally insignificant community,
where his youngest son, Mort, was born in 1934. In lieu of
full wages, farmers contributed produce and meat to the
family larder. To hold down heating bills, Theodore and
the boys—Pete, as Clarence was nicknamed, and Fritz—
would scrounge loads of corncobs to burn in place of coal.
By this time, the children of his first family were mostly
grown.

Reconciled to his status as a back-country preacher who
would never be assigned to a more prominent pulpit, Reverend Mondale moved his young family in 1937 to Elmore,
a town of about 950 souls only a few miles north of the Iowa
border. Reverend Mondale was sixty-one at the time. For
the next nine years, the Mondales lived in a modest white
frame house with two outbuildings and a large backyard
lot, which, together with another plot of land, was immediately seeded with vegetables—mainly corn and cabbage.
The boys learned to tend the garden and hawk the produce, either in Elmore or the nearby county seat of Blue
Earth.

That was one way of supplementing the family's income.
Claribel also helped out by giving piano lessons, as she had

done almost from the day she and Theodore were married. A sturdy woman of Scotch ancestry, Claribel worked hard for everything she ever had in life, including a college degree in music—a rare distinction in those days for a daughter of a poor farming family. In later years, she trained Fritz well enough so that he won a few singing contests. Together, they were in demand at social events like weddings and funerals. She also played the organ on Sundays, led the choir in church, and organized an ecumenical singing group from other congregations which had a moment of triumph when it won a standing ovation from a statewide convocation of Methodist clergymen.

While the circumstances of Reverend Mondale's own life and that of his neighbors helped refine his political attitudes, he was careful to keep politics out of his sermons. At home, however, Pete, Fritz, and Mort were imbued with their father's social-gospelist notions about the mutual responsibilities of church and state in seeking the maximum well-being—spiritual, economic, and social—of those they serve. Without charity and compassion, Reverend Mondale felt, religion and politics would wither into dry, meaningless abstractions.

Having come to terms with his own shortcomings, he sought to instill in his sons an appreciation of human worth unencumbered by materialist trappings. "I never saw a wealthy man die happy," he told Fritz.

One day, during the Second World War, Fritz received a stern reprimand from his father for having made a disparaging remark about the "Japs." "We're not fighting the Japanese people or the German people," Reverend Mondale said. "It's their governments we're fighting. They are individuals under God just like us."

Occasionally singing groups from black colleges in the South came to town on fund-raising tours. The Mondales would invariably take several of the visitors into their home for the night—as many as the house would handle—and find room elsewhere in the town for the rest. His parents' commitments took root, and by the time Fritz was in high school he would passionately join in discussions about racial equality and civil rights, taking the position that he would be happy if his half-sister, Eleanor, should choose to marry a member of a different race.

Theodore and Claribel raised their family according to a strict moral and religious code which forbade the use of liquor or tobacco. The worst transgression of all was deceit. Punishments were devised to fit the offense. Smoking, for example, was one thing: When Fritz was caught experimenting with a cigarette, Theodore took him behind the shed and made him puff on cigars until he retched. Another time, Fritz came home trembling in dread after having been kicked out of summer Bible school for misbehaving. His fears of physical punishment were unfounded. Calmly, but sternly, Reverend Mondale doubled the number of hours of study that would be required before Fritz would be allowed to run free with his friends. Lying, cheating, or stealing were sins of a different magnitude. Retribution was swift after Fritz and some friends were caught pilfering pennies from the Sunday collection plate. Reverend Mondale marched his son into the brush, let him pick a keen switch, and then whipped him until blood appeared.

Reverend Mondale tolerated dissent and forgave much human weakness. When Lester—Fritz's oldest half-brother —became a Unitarian minister, a humanist, and a free-thinker, Theodore Mondale cheerfully conceded that no mortal could claim ultimate knowledge of life's eternal mysteries. Perhaps because of an awareness of his own shortcomings, he practiced restraint in dealing with the foibles of his congregations, as well. In Ceylon, Reverend Mondale chose not to crusade against the gambling and bootlegging that had won the town a local reputation as a miniature Las Vegas. One of his favorite sermons would make the point that virtue, pursued with excessive or inconsiderate zeal, could become sinful. To illustrate the message, he chose the example of a mother whose obsession with neatness would compel her to ship her children to the neighbor's to play. As one whose casual attitude towards personal grooming caused his children to wince during their self-conscious teenage years, Reverend Mondale would invariably remark with gentle self-mockery that he, at least, would not be guilty of the sin of excessive neatness.

While religion pervaded almost every aspect of family life, it was a happy and optimistic faith that allowed the three Mondale children to live comfortably with the fact that they were preacher's kids. Neighbors and passersby would often hear laughter and song on a summer night through the open windows and doors of the Mondale house. From his very early years, Fritz, as a normally high-spirited and mischievous boy, was never in much danger of being stamped as a parsonage sissy. As a small boy in Ceylon, he was caught building a bridge across a street with hymnals from his father's church.

In Sunday school, Fritz was boisterous and exuberant—more interested in talking about sports than religion. Elmore's Main Street also included a pool hall where the kids were permitted because liquor was taboo. Fritz could often be found there, a hat pulled low over his face and slouched over the table to escape his parents' notice.

As a youngster, the future politician never seemed far beneath the surface of Fritz Mondale. Among companions his age, he was often the one who organized things—pickup games of baseball or basketball, and, on Halloween, tipping over outhouses and messing up corncribs.

Later on, Gene Kelly would remember how he, Fritz, and another Elmore youth went to a Methodist Youth Fellowship camp. Somehow Mondale managed to get himself and Kelly elected to a camp council. The following year there was an election for the organization's board. Kelly recalled being told by Mondale that it would be a good idea if one of them could wind up as an officer.

"Fine, I'll back you all the way," Kelly said.

The next thing Kelly knew, the ballots had been counted and Kelly had been elected treasurer—the most time-consuming and important job on the board.

Ed Emerson's grocery store, where Fritz worked after school, was not only a center of commerce in Elmore but also a gathering place for those who wanted to discuss sports, the crops, the weather—or politics. Everyone knew where Emerson stood. He was a staunch Republican. It wasn't long before it was equally clear which side of a political question Walter Mondale would choose. After enduring their running debate for some time, Emerson had this advice for his young helper: "Why don't you take up something where you can get ahead, like music, instead of this politics?"

There were others around Elmore who also got the idea that Mondale was a smart-alecky kid headed in a hurry for a larger, more exciting world somewhere beyond the rim of rural southern Minnesota. George Garmann learned to sympathize with Emerson one summer at Homer Enterline's poultry-processing plant. After enduring a steady stream of wisecracks from Fritz, one of his summer employees, Garmann became irked enough to snap back. A few minutes later, Mondale left his station where he was tying the legs of scalded chickens together and put his hand on Garmann's shoulder.

"I'm sorry, George, I didn't mean any harm," Mondale said. "But I'm planning on going into politics someday, and I've gotta learn how to get people's hackles up."

Incidents like that made it difficult to know how seriously to take Mondale. As the inscription beneath his senior-class picture in the 1946 high-school yearbook said: "A little nonsense now and then is relished by the best of men." His list of achievements showed that he had been elected president of the junior class. What the fine print didn't reveal was that he lost the race for senior-class president to Ed Naumann because some in the class got the idea that he had run things long enough.

There is no way of knowing what Fritz had in mind when he talked of a career in politics. His father's religious idealism doubtless contributed to some fuzzy notions about helping people, but the real influence of his parents was likely felt at a deeper level where it couldn't be articulated with precision. Their values became his values and, perhaps more importantly, their example of decency—often maintained in the face of considerable adversity—became the model for his life. In ways that repeated themselves too often to be coincidental, Mondale during subsequent stages of his life would find himself working on behalf of —and learning from—senior politicians, each of whom had confronted adversity in some form and had emerged with a grip on a set of values that would have commanded Reverend Mondale's respect. These relationships also yielded political inheritances that would minimize the risk and struggle in Walter Mondale's own career.

In their own way, Theodore and Claribel Mondale were anxious to prepare their sons for the wider world outside the confines of Elmore. Thus one summer morning in 1938, the parsonage's neighbors looked out of their windows to see a bizarre contraption parked in the Mondales' yard.

Despite his notorious incompetence with a hammer and saw, Reverend Mondale had laboriously constructed a plywood structure which he had placed atop an ancient flatbed trailer with off-sized wheels. The entire rig—looking like a prop from the movie set for *Grapes of Wrath*—had been painted the color of shiny aluminum. Inside was stored a month's supply of canned goods, a pile of mattresses, a walnut dresser, and a stove. With the odd trailer hitched to their 1935 Ford, the Mondales were ready to take off on a trip that would take them to Washington, New York, and

Canada. It was to be a perilous journey.

En route, they stopped at Warsaw, Missouri, to visit some relatives. There, major problems developed in the rear axle. The repair bill came to $30, leaving $100 to spare for the balance of the three-and-a-half-week trip to the East Coast. The trailer looked and handled like a small boxcar, but it survived the trip. The odd-sized tires didn't, and every flat forced Reverend Mondale to an extensive search for replacements.

In Washington, the family camped near the Potomac's banks in an area known as Hains Point. They materialized in Senator Shipstead's office one morning in hopes of shaking the hand of a real senator, even though Reverend Mondale was sorely disappointed in Shipstead's decision to renounce the Farmer-Labor party and to move into the Republican fold. Having stated their mission, they suddenly panicked when a secretary left to call Shipstead off the Senate floor.

"What on earth do we have to say that's important enough to have him called away from his duties?" worried Reverend Mondale.

"Ask him about foreign affairs," whispered Pete in desperation as the senator loomed in the doorway.

"Well, what can I do for you?" Shipstead inquired, looking as though he had been cast by Hollywood for the role of senator.

"I'd like to know your position on foreign affairs," blurted Reverend Mondale to the famous and outspoken isolationist who seven years later would cast one of the two Senate votes against ratification of the United Nations Charter.

With a chuckle and a pat on the back, Shipstead changed the subject, and graciously led his visitors to the Senate dining room, where Fritz tried to tuck his bare feet inconspicuously under the table while eating spaghetti and gaping at famous faces. Once at the table, Theodore Mondale recovered his composure and took Shipstead to task for damaging the political legacy of Floyd Olson.

Afterwards, during a tour of the Capitol, Reverend Mondale made a point of guiding his family to the statue of Sen. Robert LaFollette, the great Wisconsin Progressive, a reformer and crusader. "He was a great man, a man of the people," he whispered in an awed voice.

Outside, they stopped in front of the National Gallery of Art, which had been financed in part by the great fortune amassed by the Mellon family in Pittsburgh. Pointing his finger at the building, Reverend Mondale said in an outraged tone, "Do you see that? That was built out of the sweat of working men."

And, visiting Ford's Theater, he led his sons to a display of President Lincoln's Bible and of the pistol that assassinated him. "Don't ever forget—that is what Lincoln lived by and made him great," said Reverend Mondale, his finger jammed against the glass a few inches from the Bible. Then, indicating the pistol, he added, "And this is the evil that killed him."

There were other family trips as well. One summer, the Mondales visited Yellowstone; other years, Reverend Mondale would lead them on camping expeditions. By Mondale's senior year of 1945–46, he had seen enough of the world to have grown restless and anxious to embark on the next stage of his life. The year was crowned with notable athletic accomplishments. As co-captain and left halfback, he led the football team to five victories, against two losses, and earned himself the nickname "Crazylegs"—after a famous running back at the University of Wisconsin. He also was the captain of the basketball team and an all-conference guard, as well as a sprinter on the track team.

But he also knew it was time to put boyhood things behind him when his father suffered a major heart attack that year. Reverend Mondale recovered sufficiently to move with Claribel to a larger community a few miles away, where he lived until his death of a stroke in 1948. As a teenager, Mondale had shouldered his share of the family's financial responsibilities by working after school and summers. There had been a newspaper route for the Mankato *Free Press* and then Ed Emerson's store. Later, he helped a local veterinarian castrate calves, vaccinate hogs, and clean the afterbirth from cows at calving time. As he approached college age, he worked as a pea-lice inspector for a large vegetable cannery in Blue Earth—a job that would win a laugh from political audiences in future years when he described his qualifications for higher office. The job entailed going out into the pea fields and inspecting plant stems for lice infestations.

He also picked corn in the height of summer, working shoulder to shoulder with migrants who followed the harvests northward. Years later, Mondale would champion the interests of this deprived labor force, but even in those precollege years his sympathies were clear. In his youthful enthusiasm, Mondale helped foment an abortive strike that taught him an important lesson about the realities of economic, political, and social power.

"We'd pick corn all day, getting paid by the ton," Mondale recalled. "We had some really bad weather conditions, and the trucks were bogged down most of the time. There was no way to make any money, so we went on strike. The Mexicans especially couldn't make a living because they spent all day trying to get the trucks out of the mud. And because they went on strike, the bosses loaded them up and sent them back to Mexico.

"End of strike."

The ease with which the bosses crushed that pitiful little rebellion enhanced Mondale's sympathy for the plight of his coworkers. In one form or another, the problems encountered by those migrants would occupy his attention for years to come. While high-school graduation would formally close a chapter in his life, his mind was already filled with thoughts of the prospects and challenges that awaited him.

Meanwhile, other things apparently seemed less important.

Running the 220-yard dash during the final track meet of his high-school career, Mondale was about 20 yards from the finish line when he abruptly pulled up short.

"I said, 'What the hell, there's no point in this—I'm not interested in this.' And I just quit," Mondale recalled.

It may have been a simple act of immature boyish impulsiveness or an expression of impatience with a phase of his life that he was anxious to end. Whichever, the conclusion of his high-school athletic career perhaps foreshadowed a trait that puzzled Jimmy Carter and occasionally vexed others. Whether it involved working on legislative issues that commanded no support or running for president in 1974, Mondale would sometimes reach a point of no return. To continue would entail risks, sacrifice, uncertainty—perhaps a waste of time or, worse, a humiliating defeat. Either because of a loss of interest or a prudent concern for political reality, he would stop and go on to something else.

3

Starting Out with Humphrey

Walter Mondale would never forget his first encounter with Hubert Humphrey. It was at a rally in a dreary, sour-smelling union hall tucked away in a Minneapolis working-class neighborhood. The purpose of the event on that cold, clear night in late 1946 was to unify Democrats and Farmer-Laborites behind Humphrey's campaign the next spring to win reelection as mayor of Minneapolis. There were also rumors of Humphrey's aspirations for even higher office—a prospect that made victory-starved Democrats tingle with excitement.

Humphrey was only a vague personality to Mondale at the time, but Fritz showed up at the rally anyway, looking like a well-groomed Boy Scout, his sideburns cropped high and his hair slicked back in a pompadour. Mondale had been brought there, all the way from St. Paul, by his political-science instructor at Macalester College—a short, dark, intense woman named Dorothy Jacobson.

The term "Twin Cities" seemed a misnomer in those days: To cross the Mississippi River from St. Paul to Minneapolis—or vice versa—required an act of will. It wasn't that the distance was so great (it wasn't) or that the streetcar connections were so complicated (they were). It was that the cities were so different. They didn't encourage visits back and forth. St. Paul was older, stagnant, smaller,

Catholic, conservative, tradition-bound. Minneapolis was growing, exciting, changing, dynamic, Lutheran, Scandinavian. St. Paul was darkly suspicious of its neighbor. Minneapolis, when it bothered to notice, glanced back across the river with contempt.

Fritz Mondale's college was not exactly a hotbed of political activism. Nonetheless, the attitudes of Macalester's administrators had become more daring during the war years. In 1943, the school hired Humphrey to a yearlong visiting professorship. It was a move out of keeping with the staid, Presbyterian image so carefully cultivated by Macalester since admitting its first students in 1885. Although Macalester was a Protestant school and St. Paul a Catholic blue-collar community, the college and the city had grown comfortable with each other. St. Paul had outlived a raucous adolescence to become a straitlaced, dull town, dominated by the church and a few elite families who prided themselves on their gentility. As a river port in frontier days, St. Paul had been dominated by hard-driving robber barons and disreputable outcasts like Pig's Eye Parrant, whose extraordinary ugliness and crude manners impressed those who patronized his waterfront saloon in the 1840s. During most of the Prohibition era, the city was a haven for hoodlums, who finally outstayed their welcome by kidnapping prominent local citizens. After the FBI cracked down, the crooks moved over to Minneapolis to become inviting targets for crusading politicians like Humphrey, who earned a reputation as a crime-busting reform mayor.

Macalester was bordered on the north by Summit Avenue—a broad boulevard that lay like a seam down St. Paul's silk-stocking neighborhood. The web of social relationships and cultural values associated with that thoroughfare fascinated F. Scott Fitzgerald, who once lived beneath its Gothic elms and wrote of the human mysteries they shaded. Some of his most powerful impressions were formed during his boyhood, when the horse-drawn carriages of the city's first families traversed the eastern end of Summit along a high bluff overlooking St. Paul's commercial center. The best addresses belonged to powerful families with names like Hill and Weyerhaeuser who built huge Summit Avenue mansions on railroad and timber fortunes.

St. Paul's interplay of power, wealth, and tradition reminded Sinclair Lewis of Boston. Then the Gilded Age faded, and many of the big houses became unwanted financial burdens on later generations, which turned them over to tax-exempt religious institutions.

In reaching out for Humphrey, Macalester's administration was seeking to dilute the school's stodgy propriety by exposing students and faculty to an activist's philosophy. Humphrey by then was renowned in Minnesota as a liberal, having made his political debut during the spring of 1943. Starting as a rank novice, he lost the Minneapolis mayoral race by only 5,725 votes to an entrenched incumbent named Marvin Kline.

By the time Walter Mondale enrolled at Macalester in the fall of 1946, Humphrey had, in fact, abandoned the campus for politics. During his own Macalester tenure, Humphrey and others set out to merge the Democratic and Farmer-Labor parties. Following the success of that venture, Humphrey returned to the Minneapolis mayor's race. This time, in 1945, he chased Marvin Kline from City Hall and established himself as a statewide political force.

And so it was that Walter Mondale found himself listening raptly on that crisp night in late 1946 to the rapid-fire monologue of the oval-faced, jaunty mayor as he talked the arcane language of politicking—precinct caucuses, literature drops, envelope stuffing, voter canvassing. Humphrey was in full flight. Occasionally, his voice would swoop, as if searching for a rhetorical perch where it could pause to let the crowd applaud. Then the small, down-turned mouth, seeming to move almost mechanically, would start working again, exhorting, attacking, pleading, rejoicing.

The eager college freshman had never heard anything quite like it. He had occasionally listened to Roosevelt's clear, patrician voice on the radio, but it had seemed distant and somehow disembodied. There had also been his family's experiences in Washington when, traipsing through the Capitol like a bunch of Okies, it had descended on Shipstead. However, Mondale had been too young to remember much about that encounter, except an impression of having been overwhelmed by Shipstead's august, Olympian presence. But it was the thirty-five-year-old mayor who opened Mondale's eyes to the glories of a political dreamworld.

Orville Freeman brought him back to earth. After the speech, Mondale shook hands with Humphrey, who shunted him off to Freeman, his campaign manager and political strongman. At twenty-nine, Freeman was not given to romantic notions about politics. The son of a small merchant, Freeman had worked his way through the University of Minnesota, earned a Phi Beta Kappa key, won magna cum laude scholastic honors, and played quarterback on Bernie Bierman's single-wing football team. His views of the world were further refined by a Japanese bullet that smashed his jaw as he was leading a Marine patrol in the fall of 1943 through the Bougainville jungle in the Solomon Islands.

And so when Mondale eagerly volunteered his services, Freeman unceremoniously assigned him to the back ranks of a modest volunteer army. During the late-winter stages of the mayoral campaign, Mondale spent weeks slogging through the Minneapolis slush, passing out literature, ringing doorbells, plastering placards in store windows.

It was not the kind of work that would appeal to dilettantes, but Mondale stuck it out, even though a Humphrey landslide was virtually preordained. While his final high-school track meet demonstrated that Mondale was capable of quitting endeavors that ceased to interest him, he nonetheless was not afraid of hard work—he had done plenty as a youth. But, as he learned from his father's example in sustaining a church and a congregation, pursuing a grand commitment also meant a lot of petty, unglamorous chores. He was prepared for that aspect of politics so long as the objective was worthy.

A number of other influences were also affecting his life. He wanted to feel committed to a cause that his parents would find admirable. Moreover, as his father became more feeble, Humphrey's influence over him grew. It wasn't a father-son relationship, yet Mondale felt a great admiration for this vibrant, voluble man and wanted to be of service. There was also Jacobson, his Macalester political-science teacher, who used the classroom to advance the then-heretical notion that it was all right for educated people to dirty their hands in partisan politics. Then there was Mondale's ambition—a force that flowed with uneven intensity but that would keep him firmly fixed on an upward-leading political path for much of his life and would hold everything else in balance, including the impulses of his own strongly felt idealism.

Reinforcing all these influences was a political power struggle that began in 1944 when Humphrey, acting as part midwife, part powerbroker helped arrange a merger of the Farmer-Labor and historically moribund Democratic parties. The resulting hybrid, the Democratic Farmer-Labor party (DFL), was viewed by Humphrey and others as the instrument that would help drive the Republicans from power. But instead of battling the GOP, the DFL turned on itself in a fractious extension of the power struggle that erupted following Olson's death in 1936. In the ensuing battle, Humphrey was cast as the right-wing champion of the surviving vestiges of a state Democratic party that had historically distinguished itself by a less than ennobling commitment to patronage politics. On the other side of the DFL barricades was a raucous clique of Farmer-Laborite radicals. They included a hard-core cadre of Communists and a much larger number of fuzzy-thinking political ideologues—all united under the threadbare banner of a confused Progressive named Elmer Benson. As Olson's successor, Benson made his mark in the 1938 gubernatorial election by suffering what was then the worst trouncing in Minnesota political history, losing to an obscure Republican county attorney named Harold Stassen.

Great issues were at stake in the struggle for control of the DFL, not the least of which was Humphrey's dream of unseating Joe Ball, a former St. Paul newspaperman whose friendly reporting persuaded Stassen to pluck him from the political beat and install him in the U.S. Senate. Questions of presidential politics were also involved. Benson and his comrades had chosen Henry Wallace as their hero after Wallace had been fired as Secretary of Commerce for breaking publicly with the Truman Administration over foreign policy in September 1946. Overnight Wallace became the left wing's presidential favorite on the strength of his advocacy of a sphere-of-influence doctrine that would have left Russia unchallenged in Eastern Europe.

As a counterweight to the Wallace movement, Humphrey and other anticommunist liberals formed a new organization that became known as Americans for Democratic Action. The ADA in turn became heavily involved in helping Humphrey prepare for his showdown with the Bensonites and Wallace sympathizers in the DFL precinct caucuses scheduled for the night of April 30, 1948. That would be the moment when DFLers across the state would assemble in thousands of precinct meetings to choose local party officers and to elect delegates to county DFL conventions later in the spring. Once set in motion on that night, the delegate-selection process would determine which side—Humphrey's or Benson's—would control the state DFL convention where the final decision would be made on endorsing a candidate to run against Ball in the fall. But the crucial step was the first one. Humphrey had to make sure that more of his people showed up for the precinct caucuses than those from the other group. It was as simple as that.

The struggle soon became a kind of crucible. The heat shaped an entire generation of DFL leaders and tested their mettle, too. In addition to Humphrey, Freeman, and Mondale, the events leading up to 1948 launched the career of a lanky, erudite intellectual on the faculty of Macalester's Catholic crosstown rival, the College of St. Thomas. Eugene McCarthy, on the verge of winning his first term in the U.S. House, was to become Humphrey's enigmatic political ally before the Vietnam War turned them into rival leaders in yet another power struggle.

However, as the battle lines formed in preparation for the 1948 caucuses, there was solidarity within that wing of the party headed by Humphrey and Gene McCarthy. Mondale, a mere college underclassman at the time, was anxious for a chance to become involved. As the issues sharpened and the rhetoric escalated, campus life seemed even more pallid and tame. "We're not going to let the political philosophy of the Democratic Farmer-Labor party be dictated from the Kremlin," thundered Humphrey. "We're not going to let this left-wing Communist ideology be the prevailing force, because the people of this state won't accept it, and what's more, it's wrong."

Elmer Benson and his allies replied in kind. Benson described Truman's plan for funneling assistance to Greece and Turkey as an example of "swaggering militarism." In the same vein, he and his supporters attacked the Marshall Plan as a desperate attempt by a corrupt capitalist clique to prop up a decadent society against the purifying forces of socialism as represented by the Soviet Union.

Recognizing that the outcome of the DFL's civil war would have major implications nationally, the ADA sent field organizers into Minnesota to establish a state chapter and help Humphrey mobilize his supporters for the caucuses. By the fall of 1947, posters and handbills began appearing around Macalester advertising the formation of Students for Democratic Action, the campus arm of the ADA. The man to see was Fritz Mondale. Now a sophomore and a veteran of Humphrey's mayoral reelection campaign, Mondale eagerly took charge of the SDA's organizing efforts at Macalester, hoping to impress Humphrey and Freeman, ever the combative and demanding campaign manager, with his ability to handle a major political assignment on his own. Lounging in his shorts or slacks during dormitory bull sessions, Mondale concealed an impatience with the trivial aspects of college. What counted was the struggle. Lined with neatly stacked piles of newspapers, his room became the hub of organizing activities. From that command post, Mondale deployed SDA members on assignments to rally Humphrey's campus supporters for caucus night. Wayne Olson, an SDA coworker, remembered being struck by the incongruity of Mondale, a peach-fuzz kid, telling far older, more worldly war veterans what to do.

"We started out meeting in his room, five or six of us," Olson said. "Then we'd meet with Humphrey sometimes and Mondale would set it up. That helped the thing grow. But decisions had to be made about tactics, strategy, and so forth, and he made them. When I went to another campus to help the SDA get started there, Mondale was the one who sent me."

It was all fascinating to Mondale. Nothing in the nonpolitical world would ever seem quite so engrossing as the challenge of outmaneuvering the other side or so exciting as the thrill of winning. Lessons learned in defeat were sometimes the most valuable of all. Before Mondale arrived on the scene in 1946, the Bensonites had captured control of the DFL by launching a surprise parliamentary attack on the Humphrey forces at the state convention. That had been a perilous setback for Humphrey, threatening not only the party he had helped create but his own political future as well. Humphrey had to regain control in the 1948 caucuses.

Thereafter, Humphrey's people showed they could play the game the same way. One autumn night in 1947, the two opposing sides came together for a meeting to organize a youth group that would have official status as the Young Democratic Farmer-Labor (YDFL) organization in Ramsey County, the second most populous county in Minnesota and the one that includes St. Paul. Control of the organization was important because it would be the key to mobilizing friendly young forces for the caucuses. As Mondale walked into a barren meeting hall, he noticed that his friends were all seated in metal folding chairs on one side of the aisle, while the Bensonites were on the other side. That made it easier to keep track of the relative voting strength of the rival sides. For over an hour, late arrivals kept trickling in and taking seats with their allies. There was an almost even balance. They were like two wary street fighters, waiting for just the right opening before throwing the first punch. Neither side wanted to make a formal motion calling the meeting to order until it was certain of prevailing. Finally, one of Mondale's friends slipped out of the hall and called a supervisor at the post office a few blocks away who happened to be a Humphrey supporter. Within minutes, a half dozen patronage postal workers were in the hall. Mondale immediately leapt to his feet and convened the proceedings. By the time the evening was over, Mondale and his friends were in full control of the Ramsey County YDFL. As it turned out, the move was of major significance in the battle for control of the Ramsey County delegation to the state convention later that spring.

As a student, Mondale went heavily into debt to finance his education. There were no generous scholarship or government-loan programs available to Mondale, and it wasn't long before he had exhausted his savings from pea-lice inspecting and all the other odd jobs of his high-school years. The Mondales had approved Macalester for their two oldest sons because it had both a respectable academic reputation and a strong commitment to Christian principles. It was not a practical choice, however. Even with its relatively modest tuition and living fees, Macalester was considerably more expensive than the University of Minnesota. At first, the Mondales were able to scrape together enough to keep Pete in school. By the time it was Fritz's turn, Reverend Mondale's declining health had sharply reduced the family's resources. These economic realities forced Fritz to make pragmatic choices about how he spent his time at Macalester. When he checked out the size of the football team, he prudently decided to become interested in debate. He pleased his mother by singing in the choir and indulged his incipient political interests by joining the international-relations club and winning election as freshman-class president. When he became active in partisan politics later in his freshman year, Mondale started wearing a William O. Douglas for President button as a sign of his disenchantment with Truman and yearning for a liberal hero to pick up Roosevelt's mantle.

He was generally well prepared in class, and articulate, forceful, and clever in discussions. His interests, however, were focused on the practical applications of political science, instead of its philosophical structures, or the particular ideas that have influenced the development of specific institutions and political movements. He wanted to know how things worked. There was an element of impatience in his attitude towards intellectualized or abstract inquiries into the metaphysical nature of things, although that would change as he matured politically and personally. In later years, Mondale would grow to appreciate the complexity of political problems, whether it was preparing a tax bill or educating a disadvantaged child. Realizing the hopelessness of satisfying everyone, Mondale would find himself drawn deeply into the contemplation of fundamental problems that have no clear or simple solutions. As a student at Macalester, however, Mondale was bent on acquiring a practical knowledge of the dynamics of political and social institutions. He knew—or thought he knew—his goals; tools were what he needed.

The crucial first step of the political process was the winning of votes. Here, textbooks were not much help; the practical experience of working in the various Humphrey and DFL causes had been more educational. It had been a lesson in applied political science, and caucus night was the midterm examination. Almost a full year shy of the voting age of twenty-one, Mondale was not eligible to go to a caucus himself. And, as an obscure campus activist, he was not privy to the grand strategies being devised by Humphrey, Freeman, and others, or to the intricate guerrilla tactics of the opposing factions in key precincts across the state. The struggle was regarded as a major test of American liberalism, and politically conscious and committed labor unions, like the United Auto Workers and the CIO, lent some of their top organizers to Humphrey, who was already drawing heavily on the talent pool made available by the ADA. Despite the dramatic buildup, the climax of the caucuses did not come all at once. The results, particularly from distant points, trickled into the Humphrey headquarters slowly over the next several days. Gradually, a distinct pattern emerged. The Humphrey forces had won control of the party at the grassroots, assuring the Minneapolis mayor of a clear shot at unseating Joe Ball, the Republican senator, in the fall.

With the two-year struggle now resolved, events moved swiftly. Humphrey returned from the Democratic National Convention in Philadelphia a national figure because of a stirring speech that stiffened the party's stand on civil rights. Back in Minneapolis, Humphrey and Freeman began laying out the fall campaign, while Mondale returned to the pea fields near Elmore to earn money for his junior year at Macalester. Awaiting him on registration day would be another year of classes, reading lists, term papers, and examinations. The excitement of the fall campaign was mounting and the idea of not being part of it was intolerable. He now knew something of the animal thrill of politics and he longed to experience firsthand the color, drama, tension, and challenge of an actual campaign, when two candidates of opposite parties confront each other building to the ultimate showdown on election day. The Humphrey-Ball race would also be a chance to distinguish himself, to win recognition as a bright political prospect from professionals like Freeman and maybe even Humphrey himself.

With Jacobson's encouragement, Mondale approached Freeman with a proposal. Humphrey was strong in the Twin Cities and in the northern part of the state, but he would need a full-time field worker to organize Democrats in the Second Congressional District surrounding Mondale's hometown of Elmore. The entire district was a Republican stronghold. If Ball's strength in that area could be minimized, Humphrey's chances would be greatly improved. That was the job Mondale wanted.

Freeman was skeptical at first. His meager campaign budget was barely adequate—he had to run a central headquarters while supporting Humphrey as he raced from town to town in a 1946 Buick trying to squeeze in about seven hundred speeches over the next ninety days. Freeman finally agreed, but on one condition: Mondale would have to raise his own funds. He could expect no money from Freeman, but otherwise his efforts would be welcome.

That was all Mondale needed to hear. He immediately started hitchhiking around the district and living by his wits. Fund-raising was his first immediate problem. His idea was to open a campaign headquarters in Mankato, a growing college town and market center in the heart of the district, but he needed rent in advance. He explained his plight to Phyllis and Gordon Spielman, editors of the Tri-umph-Monterey *Progress,* a small southern Minnesota weekly. Not only were the Spielmans friends, but they were the only Democratic editors in the district. Mrs. Spielman was chairwoman of her county DFL organization, although she knew that her organization's kitty was low. She also knew where to turn when the right DFL cause presented itself.

"I know where you can get some help," she said. Ceylon was twenty-one miles away, but Reverend Mondale's stewardship there was still fondly remembered. It wasn't long before Peter C. Reding, an insurance man and the county DFL chairman, had written out a personal check for $100 and pressed it into Mondale's hand.

Mondale's enthusiasm was infectious. Lloyd Hollingsworth was a student at Mankato State Teachers College when he read in the local newspaper that the Humphrey Senate campaign would be recruiting volunteers in town. Only five people showed up, but, as Hollingsworth recalled, Mondale was "bubbling over" with optimism and enthusiasm. The first thing he did was to persuade everyone to purchase a Humphrey button for a dollar. Hollingsworth, whose education was being financed under a veteran's-assistance program, parted with his money, wondering at his own extravagance as he did so.

Another problem along with money was logistics. In area, the district was larger than Connecticut and almost the same size as New Jersey—its 318,000 citizens were spread across a slightly undulating prairie that stretched from the central heart of the state south to Iowa and west from the Mississippi River nearly to the South Dakota border. To find voters meant visiting innumerable isolated farms and scattered villages that seemed to have been flung at random across a vast countryside.

Mondale's big moment came when someone mentioned

"Crazylegs" Mondale, 1945

Fritz with his father, Reverend Mondale

Mondale and Humphrey with Macalester College President Charles D. Turck in 1947

Attorney General Mondale with JFK

that an auto dealer in Mankato, Judd Brown, was a Democrat.

"I'll never forget that—one of the most exciting days of my political career," Mondale said. "Here I was, a dead-broke kid; I'd never seen any money, been hitchhiking, couldn't get anyplace I needed, dreamed all my life of having a car. So I went there and said, 'Mr. Brown, I'm Fritz Mondale with the campaign and we've just gotta have a car.'

"My heart was in my throat. I figured he'd throw me outa there, trying to hustle him for a car. So he took me out back and there were all these cars.

"He swept his hand over the lot and said, 'Okay, kid, pick any one you want. It's yours.' "

Enterprise and persistence paid off. Mondale managed to scrape together about $5,000—in those days a respectable sum for organizing a congressional district in a state-wide race.

"You could do a lot with that," Mondale said. "You could put up signs, set up rallies, do a little radio advertising. But mostly it was trying to get the party together. You can't imagine the disarray of the party in 1948. It was practically nonexistent. We had to go out and get the older people voting again, and also bring in some younger people.

"In practically every county, we'd have to go out and almost put together a new organization. That was important. Once these organizations started clicking, it made a tremendous difference. We would swing ten, fifteen percentage points in a county just like that, with any kind of structure."

Mondale had matured quickly. Two years earlier, he had arrived at Macalester, a small-town kid with big ambitions and ideals, but what soon emerged was a cool realist who channeled his energies and enthusiasms into mastering the impersonal mechanics of organizational politics. There seemed no time for youthful dalliances with romantically idealistic movements or campus causes—that was quixotic foolishness and didn't win elections. If the world was going to be changed, it would have to be changed incrementally and in conformity with the enlightened self-interest of the electorate. He had been deeply influenced by Humphrey, because the older man seemed to fuse idealism and pragmatism in a liberal program that would inspire the voters, not outrage them as Benson had done in 1938.

The infighting against the Benson wing had taught Mondale some tricks, but they didn't always work as well as the ploy to pack the Ramsey County YDFL meeting with postal workers. The DFL candidate for the Second District's seat in the U.S. House was Milton Maxwell, a local farmer and hopeless underdog. But Mondale was anxious to harass the Republican incumbent, Joe O'Hara, keeping him too occupied to help Ball's campaign in the district. Thus, Mondale had Maxwell challenge O'Hara to a radio debate in the hopes of embarrassing the incumbent. Expecting a refusal, Mondale was horrified when O'Hara called the bluff and accepted. Since the Maxwell campaign had no funds to pay its share of the debate costs, Mondale and his candidate had to spend the next ten days hiding from O'Hara until the episode blew over.

However successful Mondale might have been at scrounging money, his was basically a one-man operation. He did get some help from Macalester classmates as he rushed through a helter-skelter fall of classes and campaigning. Mondale's longtime friend, Wayne Olson, told of driving into the Second District with five Macalester companions for a week of political field work. They were assigned blocs of counties where they were expected to help the Humphrey organizations get started, pass out literature, and talk with local opinion leaders.

As the underdog in his campaign against Republican Tom Dewey, President Truman benefited from all this activity. But many DFLers, particularly younger ones like

Mondale, were wary of linking the Humphrey campaign too closely to the president's for fear of courting a double defeat. Besides, Truman had hardly been the sentimental favorite of many Minnesota liberals. Mondale's heart had been with Douglas, and Humphrey himself had been instrumental in persuading the state convention to send an uncommitted delegation to the national convention in Philadelphia. Truman's nomination was virtually assured by the time Humphrey came out in support of the president three days before the convention's opening.

Whatever residual help Truman might have received in the Second District—or in other rural parts of Minnesota —from an active Humphrey campaign was repaid with interest by the president's own feisty stump style and his shrewd understanding of the anger stirring within the midwestern farm belt. Truman incessantly lambasted the Republican-controlled Eightieth Congress for having destroyed a commodity-storage program at a time when a bumper crop was being harvested. Unable to put surplus crops into a government reserve, farmers had no way to protect themselves from a glut that was depressing prices and bankrupting many smaller, marginal producers.

As a Republican member of that Congress, Ball's problems were compounded in rural areas by his support of tax legislation that would have adversely affected the economic strength of farmer cooperatives. Meanwhile, the labor movement had targeted Ball for defeat because of his key role in the passage of the more obnoxious provisions of the Taft-Hartley Act. To make matters worse, the hapless senator had alienated many main-line Republicans by coming out in patriotic support of Roosevelt against Dewey in the 1944 wartime election.

But Humphrey was his own biggest asset. Tireless, he crisscrossed the state several times, traveling over 31,000 miles in pursuit of the Senate seat. One of those swings brought him to Fairmont, where Mondale's father, weakened in body but firm in spirit, knew he was nearing the end of his life. A dutiful son to the end, Mondale often put aside the competing demands on his time and spent long hours with his father. Illness had done nothing to diminish Reverend Mondale's political spunkiness, and he followed Humphrey's career closely. The young mayor could be another Floyd Olson, maybe even another FDR. The very thought seemed to make something come alive within Reverend Mondale, and he would be filled with pride at the thought of his son working with such a man.

On the day of the rally, Mrs. Mondale bundled her husband into the car in hopes of getting close enough to see and hear Humphrey in person. A large crowd had already gathered, however, and they had to park several blocks away. The once-hardy preacher was too feeble to leave the car. Humphrey was characteristically hours behind schedule already, but as soon as the event was over he set off to find Reverend Mondale. There seemed to be an instant bond of affection and respect between the two men. Reverend Mondale was obviously moved by Humphrey's praise of Fritz. And when he wished Humphrey luck as they parted, it was like a benediction.

Fritz Mondale watched as the two generations met—both representing an evangelical populism and a profound concern for the human condition. While one spread his message from the pulpit and the other from the political stage, young Mondale could not help but feel that Humphrey, half the age of his father, represented an essential continuity in the traditions and values that had shaped his own life. Reverend Mondale died of a stroke about six weeks after Humphrey carried the Second District by 8,500 votes on his way to a landslide statewide victory over Joe Ball.

4

Politics, the Law— and Independence

Walter Mondale was tense and distracted in the aftermath of the 1948 election. Hubert Humphrey's race for the Senate had built to a climax with an incredible and exhilarating intensity, but the postelection letdown had been sharp and immediate. After frenetic days and nights filled with feverish and last-minute maneuvers, Mondale found himself facing a void. The campaign had vanished. Mondale's friends noticed that Fritz had become moody. The outbursts of laughter, of exuberance, were less frequent. Once a blithe spirit, now he was having to bear the anxieties of early adulthood. There was no more politicking to blot from his mind the two central facts of his life. His father was dying. He was broke.

Having wise and sympathetic advisers like Jacobson and another political-science professor at Macalester, G. Theodore Mitau, helped. At first, Mitau thought Mondale's only problem was money. At a school as small and intimate as Macalester, there should be an easy solution. Mitau went to his friend and boss, Charlie Turck, the college president. Turck impulsively wrote a personal check for $100. Though touched by the gesture, Mondale refused the money. The lack of funds—certainly a major concern— only ratified a decision that had slowly been taking shape in his mind for some time, but that solidified quickly during the anticlimactic days following election night. The campaign had been a crash course in applied political science, and the results of the final examination demonstrated that he possessed talents that could not be improved by classwork. While other factors clearly helped, Mondale could legitimately claim partial credit for the fact that both Humphrey and Truman polled more votes in the Second District than their opponents. Not even Humphrey at his most optimistic expected such success at raiding the Republican citadel in southern Minnesota. With that experience behind him, college life seemed dry and sterile.

His father's death in December severed lifelong bonds. Mondale had mentally steeled himself for this moment but it was still devastating. Theodore Mondale had dominated Fritz's life—as a symbol of authority, as a teacher, as a friend, and finally as a man whom he loved and admired. His father had once told him, "You're either going to wind up at the top or at the bottom. You're not going to be in between somewhere." As he grew older, Fritz was determined to prove that he belonged at the top. Years later, he still would measure his accomplishments against his father's expectations.

Watching Reverend Mondale die had also been a painful family experience and everyone rallied around Claribel. She was a strong woman, and once her husband's personal affairs had been sorted out, she was ready to start anew. The children were mostly grown—Fritz's younger brother, Mort, was in high school now—and everyone was confident of her ability to negotiate the years ahead.

The developments of that year, culminating in his father's death, left Mondale only briefly confused and uncertain about his next move. As was to happen at other critical junctures in his life, Mondale was soon presented with a clear-cut opportunity. Bill Shore, an ally in the struggle with the Benson wing and newly elected president of Students for Democratic Action, offered Mondale the chance to work as the SDA's salaried executive secretary in Washington. That was where Shore was headed as Humphrey's research director. After talking it over with Jacobson and Mitau—and winning their support—Mondale gratefully accepted.

Several weeks later, in early 1949, Mondale and Shore moved into an old crumbling rowhouse on Washington Circle, a few blocks from the White House. Their basement apartment was infested with cockroaches and mice, and the morning sunlight was often blocked by sleeping drunks slumped against the apartment's sidewalk-level windows. But the $50-a-month rent was hard for Mondale to pass up on his $250 monthly salary. It was only when Shore and Mondale woke up one morning to find that a mouse had been electrocuted by an exposed wire that they decided to move.

Their next address was the third floor of a Georgetown house that had been purchased and rehabilitated by an architect who lived on the first two floors. By this time, Shore and Mondale had acquired several additional roommates—most of them drawn by politics to Washington. Even within this group Mondale's intensity was unique. As the year passed, Shore and others of their friends found themselves beginning to drift away from politics into marriage and graduate studies. "I realized I just couldn't be totally absorbed by politics from morning till night—totally committed to it. That was the big difference between Fritz and the rest of us," Shore said.

As executive secretary, Mondale's duties were both organizational and political. The excitement of the 1948 election had helped establish a number of SDA chapters on campuses across the country, but the volatility of student interests and the normal turnover in enrollments required Mondale to divide his attention between reviving old chapters and establishing new ones. By this time, the ADA and SDA were in fundamental harmony with Truman. With a staff of two field men and a limited travel budget, Mondale's resources were not impressive. Even so, he worked enthusiastically to establish the SDA as a source of strong support for administration policies. Certain campuses, like Harvard, Michigan, and the University of Chicago, became SDA strongholds. Elsewhere, student apathy was often overwhelming. But where activism flourished, Mondale often would find himself vying with Henry Wallace progressives and Communist-front organizations. Meanwhile, Soviet sympathizers were working actively within international student groups as a part of a scheme to influence opinion and embarrass the United States. To counter these trends, Mondale joined forces with another young student organizer, Allard Lowenstein, in building the National Students Association as an anticommunist campus voice on world affairs. Nearly twenty years later, Mondale and Lowenstein would be deeply divided over the Vietnam War, with Lowenstein emerging as a prime architect of the peace movement's effort to drive another Democrat, Lyndon Johnson, from the White House. Compounding the irony was the fact that Lowenstein's candidate in 1968 was Mondale's onetime ally in St. Paul politics, Gene McCarthy.

But the world seemed like a less complicated place in 1949. Anticommunist liberals could happily join the national consensus supporting the Marshall Plan because that was obviously the right policy at the right time. Similarly with domestic affairs. As he became old enough to absorb his father's commitments, Mondale embraced the standard liberal notion that the federal government has an affirmative duty to use its might to improve the lot of the disadvantaged. His leadership of the SDA thus was nourished by a devotion to the principles of Truman's Fair Deal program and its premise that FDR's presidency was only the beginning of a far-reaching effort to uplift the nation's social and economic life. While Mondale remained true to that premise in later years, he also discovered that government programs—no matter how generous their pricetags—were often not the answer.

The post–World War II era also marked the dawn of the modern civil-rights movement. Increasingly, liberalism's commitment to broad goals of economic justice and social welfare was being expanded by a sharpened sense of the public and private wrongs that historically had been inflicted on American minorities, particularly blacks. Growing up in Elmore, Mondale could have seen civil rights as little more than an abstraction, articulated by his parents and occasionally dramatized by black college singing groups. By contrast, the economic breakdown, represented by the Great Depression, was all around him. He may well have been unaware of his family's relative poverty because everyone else was in the same straits. However, adult anger over seemingly malevolent market forces permeated the social climate in which he grew up. At one point, a young Walter Mondale had watched as a group of desperate farmer-neighbors blockaded roads and attacked truckers in an attempt to enforce a strike aimed at raising prices by keeping crops off the market. The radio, newspapers, and grownup conversation in 1934 had been filled with accounts of open warfare on the streets of Minneapolis between striking teamsters and employer goon squads, aided by the local police. One clash had left two strikers dead. Mondale's hostility in later years to what he felt were the abuses of corporate power and the arrogance of wealth had a visceral quality derived from those earlier experiences. Mondale's devotion to civil rights was steadfast throughout his public life, but it lacked the emotional intensity of his focus on economic issues. Running for president in 1974, he did not advertise earlier roles in the Senate as a fighter for open housing and school desegregation. On the other hand, he did not miss an opportunity to flay the major oil companies for what he regarded as wanton profiteering at the expense of an energy-hungry nation. Similarly, economic dislocations were a major theme of Mondale's vice-presidential race. Civil rights was not.

On the other hand, no one could articulate the compelling nature of that issue more effectively than Hubert Humphrey, who was chosen national chairman of the ADA in 1949. In large part, Humphrey owed his rapid rise as a national liberal spokesman to his dramatic speech a year earlier on the civil-rights plank at the Democratic Convention in Philadelphia.

Despite the remoteness of civil rights from his own personal experience, Mondale found himself in a similar situation in late 1949 at a national convention of young Democrats in Chattanooga. Chosen to lead a Fair Deal caucus, Mondale discovered that his Southern opponents were cleverly deployed to control all the key convention posts, including the critical Resolutions Committee. Still embittered by Humphrey's success eighteen months earlier but outnumbered on the convention floor, the Dixiecrat strategy now was to bottle up civil rights. "We're not going to have civil rights jammed down our throats," shouted the national chairman of the young Democrats, a Texan. Also helping steel the will of the Southern delegates was a rousing speech on states' rights by Herman Talmadge, then governor of Georgia.

But Mondale was anxious for a victory. Defeat on a key issue like civil rights would embarrass Truman, who was already on the defensive from conservatives—Southern Democrats as well as Republicans—in Congress. Beyond that, Mondale was already thinking ahead to his return to Minnesota and the political opportunities awaiting him. Freeman was now state DFL chairman and soon the 1950 statewide campaign would be starting. The best jobs would go to those with the best records. Politics, as Mondale had discovered by now, was a constant process of proving yourself.

Overcoming the entrenched power of the Southern dele-

gates entailed rallying the scattered and unorganized liberal forces and molding them into a power bloc to pressure
wavering members of the Resolutions Committee into
signing a minority report on civil rights. With enough sig-
natures challenging the committee's pro-Southern bias, the
issue could be brought to the convention floor. That had
been Humphrey's tactic in Philadelphia.

Mondale's caucus worked around the clock for several
days, churning out leaflets on a borrowed hotel mimeo-
graph machine. Like a professional political operator,
Mondale haunted hotel corridors and coffee shops, hus-
tling delegates and building support. Confident finally of
having isolated its adversaries, the caucus drafted a civil-
rights proposal calling for an end to segregation in the
military and in interstate travel, the abolition of the poll tax,
and passage of antilynching laws. When the minority report
reached the floor of the full convention, Mondale made a
brief but impassioned plea for its adoption and then
watched with satisfaction as it carried by nearly a two-
to-one margin. Adding spice to the victory was the bitter,
unreconciled commentary of the Chattanooga *News-Free
Press,* which likened the liberal bloc to "the shadow of
Thaddeus Stevens walking again."

It was a performance worthy of Humphrey himself. But
despite their political kinship and kindred experiences,
Mondale discovered that he and Humphrey inhabited two
different worlds once they arrived in Washington. As a
twenty-one-year-old organizer still a year shy of a college
degree, Mondale had little to offer Humphrey, who was
having his own troubles getting started after storming into
the Senate like a latter-day Carrie Nation raiding a sherry
party at the Harvard Faculty Club. Years later, Mondale
would grow to appreciate the importance of relying on
people whose experiences and talent would be appropriate
for the moment. Occasionally that would mean shedding
associations that were no longer useful. He was still green,

though, when he took the SDA job and had not yet learned that lesson. Mondale was humiliated one day when he tried to telephone Humphrey shortly after arriving in Washington. He was intercepted by an aide, who upbraided him: In the future, he should deliver messages to junior staff members who would relay them to the proper person. Humphrey himself seemed as friendly and appreciative as ever when they met—which was infrequently. But the incident rankled. In a letter to a friend in Minnesota in March, 1949, Mondale complained bitterly of insiders who were insulating Humphrey from other points of view.

"That hurt me," Mondale recalled years later. "I worked my damn heart out for the guy. I can see now that I'm older that it was a minor matter, but as a young person you give it significance."

But in virtually every other respect the year was enormously valuable and encouraging to Mondale. He met many leading liberals on the national scene, and had a chance to measure himself against some of the emerging leaders of his generation. He felt in all honesty that he had fared pretty well.

The experience was broadening as well. During the summer of 1949, Mondale led an SDA-sponsored tour to England. The idea was to expose about forty young liberal American activists to the traditions, theories, and practices of the British Labor party and its allies in the trade-union movement. For about six weeks, the group toured the country, living in private homes and attending summer schools and conferences sponsored by the party and the unions. During a visit to Parliament, Mondale and his companions met Clement R. Attlee, the Labor prime minister, and members of his cabinet.

The daytime schedule involved seminars and lectures. At night, they drank beer with young Labor party friends, arguing the merits of British socialism versus American liberalism until the debate would dissolve into boozy choruses of "It's the Same the Wide World Over" and other worker songs.

Mondale returned to the United States that fall not much impressed by what he had seen and heard, other than the songs. England was in the midst of a political transformation under Labor party leadership. The nature of that change was epitomized by the establishment of the National Health Service, which revolutionized medicine by offering free medical care as a matter of right to all within the country. Although many American liberals admired— or at least were fascinated by—the Labor party program, the experience seemed not to excite Mondale; he was unable to see how the British experience could have a practical application to American politics in 1949. Even the British Fabians—a particularly pragmatic and nondoctrinaire element of the left wing—struck him as theoretical and unrealistic.

"One of the most important nights of my life in politics, I think, was the night I spent with the head of the coalminers' union," Mondale said. "He told me that nationalization wasn't worth a damn. He wished the old bosses were back. He said you can't negotiate with the government. You can't win a strike with them. He said that it doesn't work. I never was a socialist, but that's where I really began to think about whether the system worked."

He had matured emotionally. The year had snapped him out of the depression that had gripped him after Humphrey's election and his father's death. Enrolling at the University of Minnesota in the winter of 1950 to continue college, Mondale had a clearer idea of where he was headed. When he had first gone to Washington, he had aspired to become a political professional—perhaps a bigtime campaign manager or a top staff assistant to an important senator. But the chastening rebuff from Humphrey's staff and the experience of executing directives from the ADA board stripped the idea of its romance. He returned to Minnesota, resolved to be the politician—someone else could be his staff aide. Independence was the key—the freedom to draw up his own agenda, choose his own issues, subject only to the will of the voters. Independence also meant something more mundane. It meant being able to earn a living without becoming a party hack. For Walter Mondale, it meant going to law school.

Mondale's final months as an undergraduate at the University of Minnesota were different from his earlier experience at Macalester. For one thing, he sharply reduced the amount of time he spent away from classes working on politics. Now he buckled down, partly to get into law school, but partly also because of deepening academic interests. He became fascinated by a couple of courses in social psychology and intergroup relations.

However, studiousness did not preclude politicking in his spare time. When Orville Freeman was drafted by the DFL to run for attorney general, he asked Mondale to manage his campaign. Mondale readily accepted the offer, even though Freeman's opponent was a popular Republican wheelhorse whose career had included six years as governor during the World War I era. No one—least of all Freeman himself—was under any illusions. Freeman was going to lose, but he wanted to use the campaign as an opportunity to build the party, as well as his own personal political base. With Humphrey in Washington, Freeman seemed certain to be the DFL's next rising star. Mondale was not only eager for the experience of marshaling a statewide campaign but also for a chance to join up with a politician on the rise.

As expected, Freeman lost, but the experience exposed Mondale to a broader range of problems and personalities than he had ever known. It also marked his emergence as one of the best and brightest of the young guard clustered around Humphrey and Freeman. He had become an equal among such party leaders as Karl Rolvaag, the party chairman and a future governor; Ray Hemenway, a key liberal activist who would later serve as state chairman and national committeeman; and Gerald Heaney, also a future party officer who eventually became a judge on the U.S. Circuit Court of Appeals.

One member of that inner circle recalled his initial impressions of Mondale in the early 1950s. "He struck me as a very organized, very well disciplined person—very cool, not as emotionally involved, at least on the surface, as the rest of us. He really seemed to have Orv's sense of discipline and Humphrey's sense of PR—knowing what to do and when to do it."

He also had the gift of humor. The most notable feature of Mondale's wit lay in his ability to avoid taking himself too seriously. Used in this fashion, it helped shape an appealing image of a politician able to view himself with a bemused and healthy detachment. Emerging on the national stage in the post-Watergate era, Mondale, with his perspective, was reassuring and unthreatening. About two weeks after starting his vice-presidential campaign, Mondale arrived at a posh resort at Hilton Head, South Carolina, for a strategy session with high-ranking members of Jimmy Carter's staff. As Mondale alighted from the car, a dozen microphones were thrust into his face. Reporters were shouting questions at him from all sides. Ignoring the tumult, Mondale gazed around at the elegant condominiums and expensive boutiques. Then, staring gravely into a television camera, he said, "You know, this low-income housing doesn't look half bad once you get it built."

Once installed in the vice presidency, Mondale liked to recount a conversation in which Carter compared the presidency with the governorship of Georgia. The punchline had Carter saying, "The Congress reminds me of the Georgia Legislature, and you remind me of Lester Maddox." On many occasions during his travels campaigning for causes or candidates favored by the Carter White

House, Mondale would say that the vice presidency really
is like being a national rent-a-car: "You just get in and drive
'er around."

Other times, Mondale would use his wit not to amuse but
to defend. As he grew older and more involved in politics,
he became wary of people and their motives. Except when
he was among close, longtime friends—particularly a
group of hunting and fishing companions—Mondale's political guard was always up. He would use his wit the way
a prizefighter uses a jab or a counterpunch—to keep an
opponent at bay. Only in Mondale's case it could be anybody, including a member of the public whom he was meeting for the first time.

Early in his own vice-presidential campaign, Mondale
was working his way clear of a crowd after having spoken
to the New York Society of Security Analysts. One beet-
faced investment banker, incensed by Mondale's financial
views, confronted the then senator from Minnesota.

"You just lost my vote," he announced.

"You know what?" interrupted Mondale coldly. "I'll bet
we never had it."

Before the banker could reply, Mondale had swept past.

Mondale's humor sometimes irritated even members of
his family. When a stranger confronted Mondale in the
Capitol basement and introduced himself as a friend of a
relative, Mondale replied, "Oh, yeah, he's the one who
likes to tell me how to be a senator."

In his younger days, Mondale's prankishness was irrepressible. During the losing Freeman campaign of 1950,
Mondale's close friend and roommate, Tom Hughes,
worked in the DFL headquarters, a few blocks from the
Freeman office. Both locations were near Minneapolis's
skid row.

"Over at our place, we'd get a lot of people who would
come in off the street," Hughes recalled. "These people
kept coming over and we couldn't figure out how in the

world these people knew where the DFL headquarters was on the third floor.

"And that damn Fritz was telling people, well, all he was doing was working for one guy in the campaign. If they wanted a job, you know, or money or a package of cigarettes, he'd tell 'em, 'I know where you can get it.' And he'd send 'em over to our place."

Hughes later turned the tables on Mondale, however. Mondale graduated with honors from the university in 1951. He went almost immediately into the Army and wound up at Fort Knox—where he encountered Hughes, an earlier inductee. When Hughes returned from a leave in Minnesota, he showed Mondale a copy of a letter addressed to the then chairman of the Democratic National Committee and signed by Karl Rolvaag, the state chairman. The letter, ghostwritten by Hughes, thanked the national chairman for having secured preferential treatment for Private Mondale. Mondale, envisioning the letter winding up in the hands of some future political foe, was in a panic until Hughes confessed. The letter was never sent.

Mondale's army career was otherwise undistinguished. He went through a leadership-training course, but was never sent overseas, even though the Korean War was then far from settled. The day after his discharge in 1953 as a corporal, he enrolled at the University of Minnesota's law school.

Now started a real grind, as well as a challenge. "I went in there wondering whether I could do it," Mondale recalled. "The thought of trying to be a lawyer looked pretty rough to me at the time."

"He wasn't sure of his ability," Pete Mondale recalled. "And so law school was a test, and he didn't want to be fooled. He wanted to know how good he was and what he could expect. And he was prepared to accept a negative as well as a positive result. The only requirement was that he work his rear off and do his very best, and whatever happened, happened."

Mondale did indeed work hard. To save money and avoid distractions, he moved in with his mother, by now sixty-one and living in St. Paul. She had taken a job as a Sunday-school superintendent at Hamline Methodist Church, having bounced back from Reverend Mondale's death five years earlier with a resiliency that would have been remarkable even in a far younger woman. Without any formal training in the field, Mrs. Mondale had become an acknowledged expert in religious education.

Now Mondale really cut back on politics, although he did allow himself a modest role in helping elect Freeman to his first term as governor in 1954. Mondale responded well to the competitiveness of law school, finishing near the top of a distinguished class whose graduates were to become leaders of the Minnesota bench and bar. He shared the traditional honor of top students by being chosen to the law review and won a coveted clerkship during his senior year to a respected state supreme court judge, Thomas Gallagher.

But, as had been the case during his undergraduate years, no one was likely to mistake the direction of Mondale's interests. When he wrote a major law review article on campaign financing—a subject he would hold dear as a political issue later on—it was judged to be acceptable but not distinguished. Mondale accepted the verdict pragmatically. It told him what he already knew—that his talents did not lie in deep intellectual analysis or strict scholarship.

During his first year or so, Mondale met regularly in a study group with three other law students to discuss cases and course work. As it turned out, his three companions were Republicans, although one, Harry MacLaughlin, later became Mondale's law partner, a born-again Democrat and judge on the U.S. District Court. Another member of the group was Douglas Head, who entered politics as a Republican and eventually won election as attorney general.

"Law review was never particularly attractive to Mondale," Head said. "I think that was a little too scholastic in the intellectual sense—too many people playing Aquinas and splitting legal hairs about how many angels could stand on the head of a pin. He was more practical. None of us had the feeling Fritz was going to become a legal scholar or a courtroom giant. That just did not seem to be his bent. He was going to be in politics."

While Mondale disciplined himself to do well in courses he found boring—like property law—he sparkled when it came to public policy or political issues. Classes on constitutional, administrative, and criminal law delighted him because the assignments involved issues of deep significance to him politically. On the spur of the moment he would be on his feet arguing that human rights were more important than property rights. The next class might find him heatedly denouncing the class's reactionaries, who would dismantle the federal government to enhance states' rights. Those classroom discussions enabled him to define and defend values that would guide him consistently once he became a real politician responsible to real constituents with real problems.

As a law student, for example, Mondale was required to come to grips with the constitutional problem of balancing the rights of a criminal defendant against the interests of society in order to assure a fair trial. Although the landmark rulings of the U.S. Supreme Court were still years away, Mondale embraced the spirit and philosophy of those opinions that were to force the courts and police to pay greater respect to the rights of the accused. When the Warren Court was deliberating in 1962 over Clarence Earl Gideon's claim that he had a right to free legal counsel, Mondale injected himself into the case as Minnesota's attorney general and marshaled support from other attorneys general for the penniless defendant. The court sided with Gideon in a landmark ruling that laid down the right of future indigents to free legal counsel in defending themselves against criminal charges.

Mondale's values and beliefs were also foreshadowed by late-night arguments with his Republican study partners—particularly Head. Listening to the disputes, Clay Moore, another member of the group and frequent Mondale adversary on ideological questions, came to sense a powerful and instinctive distrust within Mondale "for the possession of power gained by wealth."

"There was a core of belief," Moore said. "You could strip away some of his peripheral beliefs and he might even agree with you. Reasonable minds can agree on a lot of things, but when you got down to the core, I felt he was immovable."

5

Getting into Position

Walter Mondale met Joan Adams on a blind date early in the summer of 1955. Until that moment they might as well have lived on different planets. It is doubtful she had ever heard of a precinct caucus before the evening of June 21, when she appeared for dinner at the small apartment in St. Paul where her younger sister, Jane, lived with her law-student husband, Bill Canby. By the same token, Mondale was blissfully ignorant of the art world, ancient or modern, and had lived his life unmoved by French Impressionists, Cubists, or Abstract Expressionists. At twenty-four, Joan was an attractive, dark-haired, vivacious, and extremely bright product of a genteel family lineage that dated to colonial days and that included scholars, doctors, editors, and ministers. Figuratively, she had grown up on the other side of the tracks from the tough Norwegian immigrants who had had to struggle to establish themselves in the narrow, parochial society of southern Minnesota. Joan, the eldest child in her immediate family, and her two sisters, Jane and Joyce, had all graduated from St. Paul's most exclusive girls' college-preparatory school, Summit School. Until she met Fritz, most of her beaux had graduated from Summit's male counterpart, SPA, short for St. Paul Academy. The two schools were mainly in the business of educating the offspring of moneyed families living in large Victorian houses on Crocus Hill, the city's self-conscious equivalent of Beacon Hill. Their paths then led east to Ivy League colleges. Those who returned—at least among the SPA graduates—did so to follow their fathers' footsteps in business or the professions. Mostly they were very Republican.

Joan Adams, however, did not fully fit the mold. First, she was a Democrat, having come from a family of Democrats. When it became time to pick a college, she chose not to go east but enrolled instead at Macalester, where her father, the Rev. John Maxwell Adams, was chaplain. There, she majored in history and minored in art and French. But it was art that captivated her after she spent a spring vacation with her uncle, Phillip Adams, then director of the Cincinnati Art Museum. Returning to Macalester, she became a volunteer at the Minneapolis Institute of Art, teaching children's classes on Saturday mornings and cataloguing prints on Thursday afternoons. After graduation, she took a job in the slide library of the Boston Museum of Fine Arts. That lasted for a year, until the Minneapolis Institute hired her back to work in its education office.

Mondale became one of her willing students after the evening at the Canbys', or at least a tolerant suitor. If his political education had not included art appreciation until that moment, at least he was willing to keep an open mind. When Joan suggested on one of their early dates that they visit Steichen's Family of Man exhibit at the Walker Art Center in Minneapolis, Fritz readily agreed. But that was a fairly minor concession compared to the patience and forbearance their rapidly blossoming courtship required of Joan. It was summer break before his final year of law school, and the DFL had hired him to travel the state, recruiting state legislative candidates.

"He was home one night a week—Saturday night—courting me," Joan Mondale recalled. "We had a date a week. Now, what's seven into fifty-three? We were engaged fifty-three days after we met. We had, like, eight dates. I mean, I never saw him. He'd call up Friday night: Do you wanna go out Saturday night? I'd say yes. And that was it. And the first time he called, I already had a date; that was very b-a-a-a-d.

"So he asked me out for Sunday, which was fine. The first date we had, we went to hear Dixieland jazz, Doc Evans . . ."

Mondale's appearances on her doorstep were made even more unpredictable by the ancient Hudson that he used for his pursuit of likely legislative candidates in remote corners of the state. The jalopy would boil over every hundred miles or so. The malfunctions could most reliably be counted on to occur on Saturdays when he was headed back to the Twin Cities to pick up Joan. Yet his absences underscored the very qualities that made him so excitingly different and so appealing to Joan. Compared to the SPA-Summit set, Mondale seemed a free spirit—unconventional, irreverent, unpretentious, on the move, committed to liberal causes that would be fiercely resisted on Crocus Hill.

Mondale appreciated the irony of the situation. By August, he and Joan were engaged. He was now linked, however loosely, to the vested interests of the upper crust, even though the Adamses were different from most of their social peers. A Presbyterian churchman, Reverend Adams called himself a Democrat but in fact had voted for Norman Thomas. To the horror of her Republican neighbors, Mrs. Adams had worked the precincts for the Democratic party. For all the differences in family heritages, the Adamses stood for the same basic human values as Mondale's parents. Both families shared the conviction that politics and religion alike must ultimately serve man's needs, temporally and spiritually. Both were humanists and reformers.

However, the Adamses did enjoy a different lifestyle. Joan was born in 1930 on the University of Oregon campus, where Reverend Adams was then the chaplain. After an assignment in Columbus, Ohio, the family moved in 1936 to Philadelphia, where Reverend Adams took a position with the Presbyterian Church's Board of Christian Education. The Adamses built a house in the lovely suburb of Wallingford, and Mrs. Adams became especially active in Democratic causes. In 1947, Reverend Adams was named chaplain of Macalester. They bought a rustic old farmhouse in Highland Park, an almost rural neighborhood that in time would rival Crocus Hill in elegance and respectability. Unquestionably upper-middle-class, the Adamses were members of an even more refined elite—a campus gentry that valued good taste and serious intellectual pursuits. For Joan, the arts had been such a pursuit. Now politics became another. She perceived a common humanistic bond between art and politics—a shared concern, felt at least by some artists and some politicians, for the human condition.

On December 27, 1955, Reverend Adams married the couple in a candlelight service in the Macalester Chapel. The day before, Mondale and his friends lined the chapel with Christmas trees collected from the open lots where they had been on sale. Both Humphrey and Freeman were on hand for the ceremony. Their presence apparently disturbed some of the other guests. At the reception afterwards, several of the Adamses' white-gloved Republican friends came through the receiving line to whisper disapprovingly, "Those men are here."

By now, Mondale was nearing the end of law school. Soon he could reenter politics on his own terms, having guaranteed his independence by an excellent law-school record. The opportunities for DFLers had improved enormously since the 1950 campaign. The party had scored a major breakthrough in 1954, electing not only Freeman as governor, but Karl Rolvaag as lieutenant governor, and a colorful, energetic young lawyer named Miles Lord as attorney general. The DFL's unprecedented success was a tribute to Humphrey's popularity and Freeman's tireless

efforts at building a progressive, grassroots political movement. The vote was also a sign that Minnesota's Republican
party, after decades of dominance, had seriously atrophied.
With the Stassen era at an end, the GOP well of talent had
run dry. What remained was a party organization that had
forgotten how to hustle for votes and an array of unexciting
party hacks.

Freeman used his opportunity well. Soon after taking
office, he launched a well-publicized effort to reorganize
the state government and reform its archaic administrative
procedures. In the process, Freeman's reorganization men
uncovered such extraordinary examples of waste and ineffi-
ciency that even some of the most partisan supporters of
his lackluster Republican predecessor were horrified. In
addition to revamping the executive branch, Freeman also
challenged the Republican-controlled Legislature with a
series of progressive initiatives for revising the tax laws,
conserving natural resources, and reforming the state's
corrections and mental-health facilities. That agenda, for
the most part spurned by the Legislature, provided a strong
basis for his reelection campaign in 1956.

Winning a second term was far from a sure thing for
Freeman. Earlier that year, the DFL had endured another
bitter internal fight, when Sen. Estes Kefauver of Tennessee whipped Adlai Stevenson in Minnesota's presidential
primary. Since Stevenson had the backing of Freeman,
Humphrey, and the rest of the state party leadership, the
outcome demonstrated again the volatile and unpredictable nature of the DFL coalition. Minnesota Republicans,
moreover, had regrouped by nominating a strong candidate, Ancher Nelsen, to oppose Freeman. In addition to his
Scandinavian name, rural background, and folksy manner,
Nelsen had another advantage: He could clutch the long
coattails of highly popular President Eisenhower.

With law school behind him, Mondale joined Freeman's
1956 reelection campaign that summer on a full-time basis.

Preoccupied with governing, Freeman had allowed the campaign to drift dangerously, with no sense of purpose or common theme. While he did not have the title of campaign manager, Mondale took charge, nevertheless, at Freeman's request. He soon had Freeman and Humphrey moving around the state and lambasting the Republicans. Freeman narrowly won reelection with 51.4 percent of the vote.

In 1958, Mondale was again at Freeman's side, this time with the official designation of campaign manager and the unofficial reputation of being the state's top political strategist. He was also well established in private law practice. After the 1956 campaign, Mondale's first move had been to take a job with Freeman's former law firm. Freeman's name had been dropped from the title by the time Mondale and his closest friend from law-school days, Harry MacLaughlin, joined the firm's roster of eight lawyers. But it seemed an ideal spot for Mondale, since the senior partners had a policy of encouraging, or at least tolerating, extracurricular political activities by their associates. While that permissive policy was nearly unique among Twin City law firms, Mondale still found the atmosphere confining. "It was clear to me that the firm had had enough politicians and there was a lot of resentment at the junior level toward the reputation that the firm had gotten of being primarily political," Mondale recalled. "When I came in they had just about had enough of it and didn't want any more, and I could sense that: They didn't want another politician in that shop."

Three years of law school had not dulled the edge of Mondale's ambition. The lessons of his earlier years in politics remained valid. He needed to be his own man— free professionally as well as financially—in order to make his way in politics. There was no telling when the opportunity would appear, but it was important to be in a position to grasp it. It was time to begin moving. After eighteen months of routine work as freshman attorneys, Mondale

and MacLaughlin announced they were leaving to set up
their own practice. The news distressed several colleagues
who felt the pair owed more service in return for their
apprenticeship. Though there was nothing improper about
their departure, and though they left with the blessings of
the two most senior partners, it did seem a bit abrupt. That,
of course, was all part of the impersonal nature of politics.
Mondale realized that he could jeopardize his political career if he allowed other professional commitments to distract him from the task of strengthening his position within
the party.

Professional independence also brought incredibly long
hours. Mondale and MacLaughlin had to work harder than
ever to build a practice and achieve a tolerable income
during the early months. Still, they had a mutual understanding: Mondale would have the freedom he felt he
needed. "I said we'd do our best to make it good, but I
never abandoned the political life," Mondale said. And so,
when Freeman asked Mondale to run his 1958 campaign,
the young lawyer said yes without hesitating.

"I had confidence in Mondale," Freeman said. "I was out
most of the time, meetin', greetin', speakin', and handsha-
kin'—and being governor. Doing that and campaigning
was one helluva burden, so I let Mondale run things with
a free hand."

By now, Mondale's maturity as a political operative was
impressive. Freeman's opponent, George MacKinnon, was
a Stassen Republican who had served in the Congress and
as U.S. district attorney immediately before running for
governor. He pursued a wild, mud-slinging campaign, linking Freeman and the Democrats to some of the more notorious mob elements in Minnesota. It was a campaign of
desperation. MacKinnon, the underdog, wanted to goad
the hot-tempered governor into overreacting, but Mondale's cool head prevailed. Angered, anxious to retaliate,
Freeman nonetheless bowed to the judgment of the man he

had trained in the art of politics. Other than a few measured responses, Freeman held his fire and campaigned on his four-year record as governor.

That was also the year that Eugene McCarthy, the scholarly congressman from St. Paul, was attempting to become the first Catholic to get elected to the U.S. Senate from a state where Scandinavian Lutherans significantly outnumbered all other voting blocs. McCarthy's opponent was a taciturn Norwegian farmer named Ed Thye, a Stassen Republican, who had been elected governor in 1944 by the largest margin ever recorded up to that point. He had also been elected and reelected to the Senate with solid majorities. Under the circumstances, McCarthy chose to mesh his campaign with the governor's. Mondale played a key role in orchestrating both efforts.

"That McCarthy-Freeman campaign was about as smooth a joint effort as you'll find in politics," said Bob Hess, then vice president of the Minnesota AFL-CIO and one of the most respected figures in DFL politics. "Thye looked like a tough guy to beat and he was, but everything clicked.

"I remember this Catholic group put out a history of the original Catholic settlements in the state and something about each of them, and Mondale said, 'Now we'll know where to go with McCarthy.' He just did a helluva job."

Freeman won with 56.8 percent of the vote. McCarthy's share was 52.9.

Now thirty, Mondale had proven himself a master at helping someone else get elected. He knew how to raise funds, assail an opponent, defend an issue, evade a question, and fudge an answer. But somehow it was all bloodless. Compared to Freeman, he had nothing personally at stake. Campaign managers do not see their names in banner headlines the morning after an election. It was the same way with his modestly flourishing law practice. Winning a case was professionally important to him but it was the client who invested the emotional expense and who would have to live with the reckoning-up afterwards. Missing from Walter Mondale's life was the challenge of putting himself on the line, of running for office in his own right and letting the voters judge his worth as a person, as a politician, as an embodiment of a set of principles.

The situation confronting Mondale was not unlike that moment ten years earlier when the end of Humphrey's 1948 Senate campaign had left Mondale emotionally adrift and deeply unsettled about the direction of his life, the true thrust of his interests. There was an important difference, however. In the decade between the two elections, Mondale's focus had become precise, while his interests had broadened. He now knew his ultimate goal; the question was the next step. He also now had a family—Joan had given birth earlier in 1958 to their first child, Teddy. And there was a law practice that guaranteed him the financial freedom to be picky about what he might do next in politics. His stature within the party was steadily growing. Late in 1958, Ray Hemenway, the state DFL chairman, named Mondale the party's state finance director—enabling Mondale to expand his influence and build up contacts at all levels of the DFL.

The next year brought another significant change in Mondale's life. That fall, he moved his family from St. Paul to a small house in a comfortable middle-class neighborhood in south Minneapolis. The ostensible reason for the move was to be closer to his law office in downtown Minneapolis. Few took that at face value, however. John McDonald, the political reporter for the Minneapolis *Tribune,* was not alone in wondering at the apparent coincidence of Mondale's moving into the middle of a newly created state legislative district. McDonald pointed out that the voters in the district, which was created by the state Legislature as part of a reapportionment plan, would be choosing two new state representatives and a state senator in 1962. All candidates would have a clean shot at the three seats; there would be no incumbents. Others noted that Mondale had moved from a U.S. congressional district in St. Paul that had a DFL congressman to one that had a Republican incumbent. Another possibility opened up by the move was the Minneapolis city council. Mondale had greatly expanded his field of opportunity in a way that surprised no one who knew how ambitious he was.

Increasingly, friendly DFLers were urging Mondale to emerge from the anonymity of the campaign manager's role and to run for political office in his own right. Over coffee one morning in early April, 1960, York Langton, then vice chairman of the Hennepin County DFL organization, raised that question with Mondale. Sitting in a drugstore across from the City County Courthouse in Minneapolis, Langton said, "Fritz, one of these days we'll have to run you for something."

Mondale was not coy in his reply.

"Yeah, I just want to get a couple hundred dollars in the bank, build up my practice a bit, and then run for the State Senate," he said.

Mondale was still plotting his course with great caution when, on a quiet Tuesday morning later that month, he received a telephone call from Freeman's office. The caller was Tom Hughes, the former Army buddy who had cooked up the gag letter. Hughes was now Freeman's executive assistant, and this message was no joke.

Miles Lord, the state's mercurial and combative attorney general, had just stormed out of Freeman's office. Angered over the governor's refusal to appoint him to a vacancy on the state supreme court, Lord had huffily announced he was going to quit government after having run and won three times as a member of Freeman's team. His departure would open up one of the prizes of state politics—an office second only to the governorship in terms of influence, prestige, and sheer power. That Lord would give up such an office was incredible. An unknown six years earlier, Lord was a swashbuckling crusader who hounded mobsters, smote down vested interests, and harangued the state supreme court for being the lackey of big business. But ever since his roisterous days as a youth in a logging and iron-mining town in northern Minnesota, Lord had dreamt of becoming a people's judge, evening the scales of justice and maybe even tipping them a little in favor of the down-trodden and oppressed. From the outset, Lord's showmanship had strained relations with Freeman, whose approach to politics was disciplined, puritanical, and humorless. The latest blowup was ignited when Lord went to inordinate lengths to plant a story in the Minneapolis *Star,* speculating on the likelihood that Freeman would appoint him to the court vacancy. The transparent ploy only infuriated Freeman, who named a former law partner instead.

While Freeman's confidants knew of the developing friction between the two men, Hughes's call still caught Mondale by surprise. Having delivered the news, Hughes swore Mondale to secrecy. Lord had not indicated when he might resign, and a premature leak could well produce the opposite result. Hughes was also careful not to commit his boss's hand in advance, but he promised his own personal support if Mondale were to seek an interim appointment until that fall's general election.

In all his calculations, the thought of winning such a plum had occurred to Mondale only as a remote, future possibility. And the prospect of being handed the job of attorney general—without having to struggle for it—left Mondale exhilarated and breathless. With its powers to act in the public interest, the post's potential was limitless, or nearly so. Mondale had firsthand knowledge of what an opportunity this was. Lord had hired Mondale in 1958 as a special-assistant attorney general to work part-time on particular problems like bringing court actions to knock down trade barriers to the interstate marketing of Minnesota's dairy products. Those two years had given Mondale a glimpse of what could be at his fingertips if Lord were really to step down. The next step could be the governorship itself, and after that . . . Mondale's imagination was awash with all the possible scenarios. And yet the politician's brain also flashed a warning. As Mondale broke the news to Joan later that day, he also began to imagine how the appointment might be perceived. His mind conjured up the headline: "Freeman Rewards Campaign Manager with AG Post." And then the story: "Gov. Freeman today handed the state's top law enforcement job to his former campaign manager, a thirty-two-year-old DFL activist with only four years' experience as a practicing attorney. . . ." That, at least, would be how the Republicans would play it.

Later that week, the Mondales got together for a quiet evening with the Freemans at Tom Hughes's apartment. Karl Rolvaag, the lieutenant governor, was also there. All old friends, they were able to discuss the possible appointment frankly. By the time the guests left, two things were clear. Mondale wanted the job, risks and all, and Freeman was inclined to bestow it on him.

However, the possibility at that point was still academic. It did not remain so for long. That Saturday—April 30— Lord publicly announced his intention to resign the following week. Once again, he caught everyone by surprise— including Freeman, who was in West Virginia campaigning on behalf of Hubert Humphrey in his ill-fated attempt to wrest the presidential nomination from John F. Kennedy. Freeman hurried home, determined to make a quick appointment before factions could coalesce around rival candidates. By Monday, however, that process had already started, although support for Mondale materialized spontaneously. Backing him from the beginning were many of the party heavyweights—Hemenway, the state chairman; Hess, the vice president of the state AFL-CIO; and Hess's boss, Bob Olson, who had been impressed by Mondale's cool style as Freeman's 1958 campaign manager.

Mondale soon had a formidable foe. He was Hennepin County Attorney George Scott, a colorless but decent man of ordinary intellect who would be broadly acceptable to almost everyone in the party except a few Minneapolis liberals who had their hearts set on Mondale. Scott's principal asset was his ability to command the unswerving loyalty of organized labor in Minneapolis. That provided Scott with an alluring dowry, but, for Freeman, whose ties with Minneapolis's labor bosses were weak, it would be a marriage of convenience, not love.

The arguments swirled around Freeman for the next couple of days. Then, late on the afternoon of May 2, Freeman summoned the DFL's executive committee to his rococo reception room in the state capitol. The arguing started as soon as the doors closed. Seated around the massive oaken table were about thirty party leaders from around the state, whose support for Freeman ranged from intense to cool. Slowly the governor went around the table, seeking the views of each in turn. Mostly the discussion turned on the advantages and disadvantages of a Mondale appointment. The tone was low-keyed, restrained, amiable, although Mondale's friends would visibly bristle at disparaging references to their candidate as a "young party hack" or a member of a self-appointed palace guard. Mondale's liabilities were his youth and identification as a Freeman loyalist. Some older Democrats were never reconciled to Freeman and his supporters from university circles. To top it off, Mondale did not represent an important constituency whose votes might otherwise be in doubt.

At one point, a committee member named Arvonne Fraser lashed out at Mondale's critics for their parochial unwillingness to recognize what she insisted were his superior qualities. Echoing Freeman's own views, she conceded the short-run political advantages of naming somebody like Scott, but argued passionately that the party's long-term interests would be better served by going with a bright young talent like Mondale. She was answered by one of the party's most influential figures, Gerald Heaney, then a Democratic national committeeman. Heaney's authority flowed from his key role in building the DFL into a powerhouse in the iron-mining and timber-cutting country of northeastern Minnesota, an ethnically diverse enclave of Finns, Bulgarians, Poles, Ukrainians, Serbians, Croatians, Italians, Hungarians. Heaney was also one of Freeman's closest friends. They had been in the same law-school class and remained loyal to one another over the years. When it came to statewide political questions, Heaney tended to think in terms of Freeman's best interests.

That was Heaney's concern as he attempted to rebut Fraser, whose husband, Donald, was a highly regarded state senator and also an old friend of Freeman's. The issue, Heaney argued, was Freeman's attempt to win reelection that fall to a fourth term—a feat no other governor had ever attempted in Minnesota. As everyone in the room understood, Freeman's prospects for pulling it off did not look particularly promising. He had been a good governor but also a combative one who had not minced words with his opponents in the Legislature or with interest groups around the state. As a result, Heaney warned, Freeman did not lack enemies. A particular sore point was Freeman's relationship with Minneapolis labor leaders, who practiced politics with all the intrigue of the Medici. Freeman never tried to hide his disdain for their methods. Characteristically stubborn, he openly antagonized them by ignoring their views on party affairs and refusing to honor their patronage requests. Instead—and here Heaney was particularly blunt—Freeman deliberately drew his closest associates from an educated elite that moved into politics from the campus rather than the union hall—people like Tom Hughes, Dorothy Jacobson (who had left Macalester to work on Freeman's staff), the Frasers (Don Fraser's father had been the widely respected dean of the university's law school), and Mondale himself. In appealing to Freeman's instinct for self-preservation, Heaney argued that Mondale was too young and inexperienced, and that labor's unappeased hostility in Minneapolis would be damaging. It could cost him the election. As Freeman conceded in an interview years later, a Mondale appointment "had no moxie behind it."

Two days later, Walter Mondale was sworn in as attorney general.

6

In the Public Eye

Walter Mondale started scared. Who would have thought that someday Reverend Mondale's kid from Faribault County would be sitting at the age of thirty-two behind a big door with a sign pointing the way to his office—the office of the attorney general of the state of Minnesota? It was heady stuff, but even as he was pinching himself, Mondale never let himself forget that he was on political probation. He had only six months to win the approval of Minnesota's million and a half voters. The Republicans were having a field day with the appointment, saying all the things he knew they'd say. In his heart, of course, Mondale knew he was right. It *had* been a meritorious appointment. He *was* the most qualified candidate for the job. It was *not* a sleazy payoff but an investment—he didn't mind saying it —that would bear future dividends for the DFL and the state. He was sure of all this. It was one thing, however, to sit in a campaign office and mastermind the candidacies of others. Putting yourself on the line was quite a different matter. The stakes were high. A young politician could lose a race for an obscure job, like city council, and no one would really notice or remember. But he was right up there at the top with no place to hide. Defeat was unthinkable. That was why it was so important for him to bear in mind the reasons why Heaney and others in the party had opposed his appointment.

"You just watch," he told a friend shortly after being sworn in. "I'm not going to smile for a year."

Sober, serious, restrained, cautious—that was the image Mondale wanted to project. He would be the "people's lawyer," the very antithesis of a "young party hack." He was also anxious to strike a sharp contrast with Miles Lord, whose six years in office had been marked by a series of highly publicized exploits that had stamped him as the state's most controversial politician. As a candidate in 1954, Lord demonstrated his flair for showboating when he arranged to accept the surrender of an escaped convict in his campaign headquarters. Later, he led a gambling raid on a resort less than two miles from the home of a former Republican governor—but only after alerting the editors of the Minneapolis newspapers to what was afoot. Then there was his feud with the Minnesota supreme court, which finally resulted in a severe reprimand from the justices for his defiant behavior in a dispute over daylight saving time. Lord's tenure was not an act Mondale cared to emulate. Having worked for Lord earlier, Mondale retained a warm affection for his feisty predecessor. But Mondale also told his aides that Minnesota was ready for something different.

What that might be was unclear at first. Mondale's initial efforts at campaigning on his own behalf were alarmingly amateurish, considering his long experience as a political operative. About the only thing he did well was work hard. And that he did. Six weeks after being appointed, Mondale took off on a three-day swing around the state. His staff billed it as a "grassroots tour." After campaigning all day in Duluth, Mondale left at midnight for Olivia, a small market center in southern Minnesota. It was a four-hour drive and Mondale slept on a mattress in the back of an aide's station wagon. Olivia's big attraction for Mondale was a festival—then in its eighty-sixth year—known as the

Olivia Gopher Count. The idea was to encourage local farmers to catch gophers and present their paws to a festival official for a twenty-five-cent bounty. Skunks would bring two dollars. People from all over the county flocked to the event, and about 125 gathered at 11:00 A.M. in the town's knotty-pine hall to hear the new attorney general. Mondale rewarded their curiosity with a speech filled with pious platitudes and sober declarations of humility.

"The task of becoming attorney general is a difficult one," Mondale asserted with great earnestness. "I am a young man. I have an awful lot to learn."

Later that day, Mondale had his first television interview. Again his style was stiff and mawkish. While his aides cringed, Mondale told the reporter with heavy sincerity that his first six weeks in office had been "the most indescribable experience in my life."

He added: "Frankly, I was a little afraid of public life, but Democrats and Republicans alike are so nice to me that they just warm your soul."

Those who observed Mondale at such moments could not doubt the unvarnished genuineness of his sentiments. Although his shrewd instincts warned him of the dangers inherent in the appointment, his earliest efforts as a campaigner were remarkably uncontrived and innocent. Even though he fretted about his youthful appearance, Mondale's style on the stump was that of a small-town preacher's son, eager for the affection and tolerant understanding of his good-hearted neighbors. The example of his parents' lives, which had been filled with Christian warmth and charity, had left a deep imprint.

Mondale recognized his own ineptitude as a campaigner. "I'm finding I'm a little stiff in meeting people," he told an interviewer. "And in speaking, I'm a bit too factual. I don't have a fund of stories for a change of pace, for instance."

Nonetheless, there were important state issues to be addressed as attorney general. During his first days in office,

Mondale began an intensive and solitary review of his powers and duties. As an activist and a liberal, Mondale wanted to use his public office in an affirmative way that would not only establish him as a politician but would also benefit the public. It was not long before even Lord's loyalists on the staff were expressing admiration for Mondale's political and legal abilities.

The townsfolk of Olivia might also have been interested in how Mondale was spending his time, but he did not enlighten them on this point. Besides his painfully apparent earnestness, Mondale had yet to get the hang of touting himself. After he had finished his speech that morning, an elderly citizen walked out into the sunlight to inquire of her neighbor, "Is that young man really the attorney general?"

She probably would not have asked that question two weeks later. Indirectly, Miles Lord had not only put Mondale into high public office but had also supplied the issue that virtually guaranteed his successor's election. The bombshell was contained in a voluminous file—enigmatically labeled "Sister Kenny"—that Mondale found awaiting him his first day on the job. If Mondale had any doubts about whether he had stumbled into a political goldmine, they were dispelled by the blazing headlines heralded by his disclosure June 27 of one of the most shocking frauds in Minnesota history. In its afternoon editions that day, the Minneapolis *Star* tersely recounted the results of a four-month investigation into the financial dealings of the Sister Elizabeth Kenny Foundation. The newspaper told its readers of "evidence of widespread irregularities, deceptions, fee splits and possible fraud amounting to millions of dollars" in the foundation's fund-raising activities. Huge sums raised from generous and compassionate contributors for rehabilitating the physically handicapped had been cynically pocketed for personal profit, Mondale told a press conference.

He looked grim. Crooks had been bilking the charity

dedicated to carrying on the good works of Elizabeth
Kenny, the Australian nurse who pioneered in treating kids
crippled by polio. The central figure in the nefarious plot
was Marvin Kline, who had been driven from the Minneapolis mayor's office by Hubert Humphrey in 1945.
Mondale accused Kline of using his $48,000-a-year posi-
tion as the foundation's executive director for what Mondale described as "unconscionable personal profit." Mondale also started educating the public about the arcane and
shady dealings of the Koolishes, a father-son team in Chicago who ran a string of direct-mail fund-raising companies. Both were awaiting trial elsewhere for unrelated mail-
fraud charges involving other charities. It was the best news
story in Minnesota that year. Lord had started the investigation, but his name was buried in the initial accounts of
the scandal. After a few days, it disappeared from the newspapers altogether. Mondale's dominated the headlines.

For the newly installed attorney general, the scandal was
as fortuitous as Lord's resignation. What Mondale supplied
was the skilled touch that transformed raw opportunity into
a nearly insurmountable political advantage. The conspir-
acy to plunder the Sister Kenny Foundation was concealed
within thousands of pages of financial reports, minutes,
vouchers, canceled checks, bank records, and other docu-
ments used by Kline and his cohorts to befuddle the charity's directors and auditors. As Mondale leafed through the
Kenny books and records bequeathed him by Lord, the
outline of the plot was far from clear. The legal case had
to be coaxed from the densely packed facts and figures
assiduously gathered by Lord's investigators. As Mondale
and his assistants bored closer to the heart of the scandal,
there emerged a pattern of phony bookkeeping transac-
tions that funneled huge sums into the hands of the conspirators. Personally, Mondale was outraged. The plunder-
ing of Sister Kenny violated his deepest notions of
compassion, charity, and justice.

And as a political issue, it couldn't be beat.

Mondale was careful not to make extravagent claims about his role in the investigation. He didn't need to. The issue quickly assumed a life of its own, carrying Mondale along with it. Across the state, local officials took careful and well-publicized looks at local regulations on charitable fund-raising. A federal investigation was launched on the strength of Mondale's initial report. Mondale himself received wide coverage when he proposed legislation—later adopted—to forestall future charity frauds. The Kenny board was reorganized. The State Board of Accountancy moved against the foundation's bookkeepers. Mondale and the Kenny Foundation jointly sued to recover $3.3 million from Kline and an associate and $2.3 million from the Koolishes and their Chicago operation. (Kline and the Koolishes were convicted on criminal charges about six months after the 1960 election.) Mondale and the foundation also teamed up in a second legal action to conserve the foundation's remaining assets.

And so it went throughout the autumn. "It was a major source of strength to me," Mondale agreed years later. "You know, it was my first big public issue and I was scared to death, because even though I was trained as a lawyer and had been in politics for some time, it was sort of awesome to take this on. And so I was very apprehensive. But, in fact, what happened was that I went into office in May unknown, untested, and very young and inexperienced, and within a month or two I was a very well-known state figure. There was a tremendously good public reaction to . . . what we did there."

Still, Mondale took nothing for granted. From the moment of his appointment until election day, he pushed himself and his staff to near exhaustion. "He was very intense about it and would get jumpy in the office," said one aide, Bill Mullin. "His intensity made people uncomfortable. It was a high-keyed deal. I was keyed up. So was everyone else. I don't think he liked people who were relaxed. We all worked like slaves."

That included Joan Mondale, who gave birth to their second child, Eleanor, shortly after their move from St. Paul to Minneapolis. Their new neighbors soon came to know her as a committed DFL worker who was, if anything, even more active than her husband in the local ward club. Soon she was busy arranging DFL fund-raisers, working on voter-registration drives, canvassing the ward to identify potential DFL voters and workers, and getting elected chairwoman of the club. She and Fritz had solid reasons for optimism about winning Lord's job once it became vacant, but, even so, Freeman's announcement threw the household into turmoil.

"It was just awful," Joan recalled. "The day Fritz was announced, the phone rang incessantly. Eleanor was a baby. She was four months old and I was changing her in the bassinet and the phone rang, rang, rang, and she rolled off and fractured her skull on the bathroom floor . . . a hairline fracture.

"I also got a call from the bank and I was overdrawn forty dollars, which knocked me out. It had never happened before. It was just insane."

Life would not soon return to normal. For the young couple, politics was no longer an avocation pursued after the children went to sleep; it was a preoccupation, an almost all-consuming challenge that required sacrifice of everybody in the family. Fritz would be gone for days at a time during the summer and fall of 1960. Joan not only accepted temporary widowhood but willingly contributed her time to the campaign, touring the state with other political wives, working in the campaign headquarters, raising money. The young couple did not then question the necessity of submitting to the impersonal rhythms of public life; it was simply a matter of adapting to politics' distracting demands. Those pressures, never wholly absent from their lives in years to come, would peak with every campaign. All this seemed part of the natural order of things, but at some point a seed of doubt began to sprout. Years later, Mondale would finally rebel and renounce a chance at the presidency itself when the requirements of campaigning became too insane. But in 1960 there was the challenge of winning that first election.

Actually, the contest was never in doubt. Mondale's Republican opponent, Gaylord Saetre, tried to make some headway by exploiting the obvious issues of youth and legal inexperience in office. Some of Mondale's young assistants were making what Saetre thought were inappropriate salaries, ranging from $9,000 to $12,500 a year. Mondale's own salary was set by the Legislature at $16,000. His appointment, Saetre charged, was patronage, profiteering, and cronyism at their worst.

The voters were unimpressed by the Republican charges. Mondale won election in his own right by a margin of 246,000 votes. Karl Rolvaag, running for reelection as lieutenant governor, also won, as did Humphrey, campaigning for reelection to the Senate. Nonetheless, the mood among Minnesota Democrats was muted, despite the whisker-thin victory of John F. Kennedy over Richard Nixon in the presidential race. Gov. Orville Freeman, the DFL's drill sergeant, lost by a narrow margin to a St. Paul businessman and state senator named Elmer L. Andersen. Having appointed Mondale to political office, Freeman had to entrust the running of his campaign to less experienced and capable hands at a time when he was bearing the accumulated burdens of six years in office. Freeman fell short by less than 23,000 votes, or 1.5 percent of all votes cast in the gubernatorial race.

Victory at the polls legitimized Mondale's claim to the attorney general's office and established him as a statewide political figure with a broad base and considerable popularity. Freeman's defeat and subsequent departure to join

Kennedy's cabinet as Secretary of Agriculture also left Mondale as the most powerful DFL officeholder outside of the state's Washington delegation, and the party's most exciting resident politician. All this had come to pass in just six months. He achieved this plateau by skipping one of the toughest tests a politician faces—the challenge of earning public office by fighting for it in the public arena as an outsider or lower-ranking politician. When the time came to prove himself, he was armed with the derivative power of the incumbency. But he wielded the power well, taking advantage of every opportunity to use the office in a creative and affirmative way.

With the election behind him, Mondale continued to build himself politically. At the height of the campaign, he had established a consumer-protection unit in his office, headed by Bill Mullin, one of a number of bright young law-school graduates drawn by Mondale's rising political star. Many of them had graduated at or near the top of their classes at Harvard, the University of Michigan, Notre Dame, and the University of Minnesota. They were all partisan and aggressive, and some were politically ambitious. As a team, the recruits were evidence of Mondale's ability to attract young talent to government, inviting comparison with Kennedy's efforts to put together an administration in Washington. Like Kennedy, Mondale was trying to instill a new spirit in an inherited bureaucracy. Undaunted by his own inexperience as a lawyer, Mondale was determined to get control of a legal operation that, with a staff of about eighty full- and part-time attorneys, rivaled the state's largest law firm in sheer size. Many of those lawyers had served under more than one administration; some were incurably infected with the inertia and cynicism of long service in a government that could be reliably expected to do little else except grow. Mondale's recruiting reflected an awareness that he needed intelligent newcomers to help him redeem his campaign promise to serve as the "people's lawyer."

In addition to the consumer unit, he formed a small antitrust team that won several legal victories to protect Minnesota taxpayers from various price-fixing and bid-rigging schemes by suppliers doing business with the state government, local jurisdictions, and school districts. Both in style and substance, Mondale demonstrated a genuinely creative political touch. Although Lord had started to bust loose from the job's moorings, his predecessors had tended to adopt a narrow view of their responsibilities and powers. As a result, they undertook only the most obvious of legal chores—handling condemnation cases for highway right-of-ways, issuing advisory opinions to state and local officials, representing the state in legal and administrative proceedings. It was hardly the stuff of which exciting political careers are made.

In addition to Lord's aggressive example, Mondale was also able to profit from the work of his fellow attorneys general in New York and California, where the embryonic consumer-protection movement had already started to take hold.

"I think I'm inherently an activist," Mondale said. "I was looking for ways of using the office not in the old traditional passive way, but in an affirmative public protection role. But there was not the structure for it. I sat down when I was a brand new attorney general . . . spending about a week, night and day, going all over the lawbooks and the case law on the attorney general's office to find out what our powers were."

When the attorney general's office began receiving complaints about a furnace-repair hoax, Mondale moved quickly to protect potential victims, even though his legal authority was far from clear. Some Minnesotans had already been bilked by salesmen for the Holland Furnace Company, who seemed to thrive by preying on widows and the elderly. The scam's object was to terrorize customers into believing that their lives were in danger unless they let

Holland repair their furnaces immediately. They would wind up paying outrageous sums for unneeded or minor repairs. Sometimes, the salesman would actually crack the furnace wall with a hammer when the homeowner wasn't looking.

In the absence of a clear-cut consumer fraud statute, Mondale's consumer-protection unit invoked a public-nuisance law written to protect the citizenry from barking dogs rather than from swindlers. Indeed, Mondale adopted the theory that the company was like a barking dog. Innocent citizens were having their peace of mind disturbed by a pattern of actions beyond their control. They were being victimized, and the state had an obligation to protect them.

"It looked like a loser," remembered Bill Kennedy, one of the young lawyers on the case. Mondale and his assistants may have been philosophical activists but they were worried about how far they could stretch the law. Reviewing the prospects during a gloomy staff conference, Mondale finally exploded: "You mean we can shut up barking dogs but we can't put these crooks out of business? To hell with it! Let's go to court and find out."

The filing of the lawsuit—and the publicity it engendered—flushed out about thirty other complaints against Holland. After an intermittent trial of about four months, the judge agreed there was a pattern of exploitative behavior and that Holland was the central instigator. Soon thereafter, the company went out of business in Minnesota.

In addition to his court successes, Mondale worked quietly behind the scenes to settle other citizen grievances, persuaded the Legislature to pass several bills cracking down on consumer and charity frauds, and issued a lot of press releases. In fact, to make sure that his consumer-protection unit received adequate attention, he hired Bill Brooks, a former Minneapolis newspaper reporter turned lawyer. Brooks's duties included helping to write a column

—"Protecting Your Dollar"—that was regularly published by most of Minnesota's weeklies.

Mondale's relationships with his top policy-making aides were for the most part professional and impersonal. Some younger staff members, even those with brilliant law-school records, were dazzled and often intimidated by Mondale's ability to grasp complicated legal issues with ease and rapidity, and then to ask penetrating questions that would quickly reveal the limitations of their preparation and knowledge. He soon came to be regarded as the best lawyer in the office. Besides establishing the broad political and policy goals of the office, Mondale reviewed all important legal questions and occasionally overruled recommendations from his staff.

Though accessible to his top aides, Mondale remained remote and secluded from others in the office, including the clerical help and secretarial pool. Small talk made him impatient and uncomfortable. Even at office parties, Mondale would invariably be one of the first to arrive—and the first to leave. His guard would always be up; he would never let himself be photographed with a drink in his hand or be seen talking to an unattached woman.

Finally, one of the secretaries complained about Mondale's aloofness. The senior staff, in turn, persuaded him to stop ducking into his private office through a side door in the morning and instead to spend a few minutes campaigning for the goodwill and affection of the office help. Several years later, a different staff would feel obligated to make an identical suggestion to Mondale.

Also in the interests of breathing a little warm informality into office relationships, Mondale was persuaded one Saturday to ask about a dozen members of his staff to drop over for beer and hamburgers in his backyard. The guests thought it odd when they arrived to discover that only ten bottles of beer were on ice.

People who dealt with Mondale on a more or less equal

basis on political or legal matters were charmed by his wit and easy irreverence. But behind the bantering was a core of privacy that Mondale jealously guarded. Public life thrust him into an unending series of political relationships. It was important for him to deal with each calmly and dispassionately. In a way never before noticed by friends, Mondale seemed to keep the world at arm's length, while preserving the strength of his deep convictions about social justice, Christian compassion, and fair play. Aides driving him to appearances in remote parts of the state found conversation difficult during the long hours alone. They would discuss politics, go over his speech, and then drive in silence, while Mondale dozed or read.

The attorney general also seemed anxious to avoid direct personal confrontations. On one occasion, a staff member reported for work one morning to discover his desk occupied by someone else. That was Mondale's way of telling him that his job was in jeopardy. On another occasion, an aide returned from a meeting with a civic group to report renewed criticism of the office's salary structure. Somewhat later, the aide was surprised to discover that a promised pay raise had been sharply reduced. After the matter festered in his mind, the aide brought it up. Mondale, his face somewhat reddened, listened to the aide's heated protests but offered neither an explanation nor a more generous pay raise. The aide was baffled. Finally, he concluded that Mondale was sensitive to the criticism but unwilling to discuss the matter in a frank and personal way.

A political personality was emerging. To many longstanding friends, the guarded, edgy young man in the attorney general's office was a stranger. He certainly seemed to bear little resemblance to the carefree political hustler who had cheerfully set out to hitchhike across the Second District in search of votes for Humphrey or who had drunk beer in college taverns with other young political activists as they regaled each other with tall political tales or plotted byzantine strategies for taking over the DFL Central Committee. Once in office, he saw the world as a different place. The deeply felt idealism of his parents had pushed him toward politics and a career devoted to reforming and improving the lives of fellow citizens. Those impulses turned out to be incredibly naïve once Mondale became involved in the pursuit of power. There is nothing particularly high-minded about the politician's art of reconciling competing interests. However, a failure to master that skill, and to exploit it daily, will doom even the most principled officeholder. Mondale thus confronted the fundamental conflict between the roles of the minister and politician. The one deals in moral absolutes which the other must meld and manipulate to satisfy political needs and ambitions.

Sometimes Mondale was uncertain and defensive in the way he handled the inevitable conflict. Other times, there was a graceful decency in his approach to the problems of others. One episode during his tenure as attorney general demonstrated that he was a deeply compassionate and kind man, willing to go to great lengths to help others in personal distress. One of his lawyers had such a serious alcohol problem that he was caught drinking in a courtroom. For Mondale, it was a potential embarrassment, politically and professionally. Rather than fire the luckless lawyer, Mondale patiently tried one approach after another in hopes of helping him cope with the problem. Mondale finally put the man under the supervision of two sympathetic attorneys. When that didn't work either, Mondale let him go—but only after steering him into an alcohol-treatment program.

Mondale's compassion for those in trouble was matched by his commitment to using his political office on behalf of the underprivileged, the poor, and the oppressed. That commitment—a powerfully felt legacy from childhood—affected his response to a letter in the early summer of 1962 from Richard W. Ervin, attorney general of Florida. Ervin was asking his colleagues in the other forty-nine states to

support Florida's side against a petty thief named Clarence
Earl Gideon in a case then before the U.S. Supreme Court.

It seemed a routine criminal matter when the Supreme
Court received Gideon's petition on January 8, 1962, asking that it review his conviction for burglary. Writing from
his prison cell, Gideon argued simply and directly that even
the poor are entitled to a lawyer and that the lower courts
had deprived him of his constitutional rights at the trial by
refusing his request as an indigent defendant for court-
appointed counsel.

On June 4, however, a terse communication announcing
that the court would consider Gideon's petition signaled to
court observers that the humble case might be the occasion
for a landmark ruling.

With that in mind, Ervin wrote other attorneys general,
asking for briefs in support of his contention that Gideon's
petition threatened "the right of the states to determine
their own rules of criminal procedure." Mondale's reply
two months later was not exactly what Ervin had in mind.

"I believe in federalism and states' rights, too," Mondale
wrote. "But I also believe in the Bill of Rights. Nobody
knows better than an attorney general or a prosecuting
attorney that in this day and age furnishing an attorney to
those felony defendants who can't afford to hire one is 'fair
and feasible.' Nobody knows better than we do that rules
of criminal law and procedure which baffle trained professionals can only overwhelm the uninitiated . . . As chief law
enforcement officer of one of the 35 states which provide
for the appointment of counsel for indigents in all felony
cases, I am convinced that it is cheap—very cheap—at the
price.

"I can assure you that such a requirement does not dis-
rupt or otherwise adversely affect our work. . . . Since I
firmly believe that any person charged with a felony should
be accorded a right to be represented by counsel regardless
of his financial condition, I would welcome the court's im-

position of a requirement of appointment of counsel in all state felony prosecutions."

Mondale sent a copy of his letter to several friends and colleagues whom he knew would be interested in the issue. One of them was the Massachusetts attorney general, Edward J. McCormack, Jr., who in turn showed the correspondence to an aide handling civil-rights and civil-liberties matters. As Mondale's letter was passed around, an idea emerged for a brief, taking not Ervin's side of the argument but Gideon's. Mondale readily assented and went to work lining up other states to join the case in opposition to Florida.

The McCormack-Mondale brief set forth the views expressed in Mondale's letter. It eventually was signed by twenty-two states and it figured in the Supreme Court's decision to reverse Gideon's conviction.

7

"I Just Heard a Train Pass . . ."

Republican Elmer Andersen's election in 1960 to the governorship was a severe blow to Orville Freeman and the DFL. It was also a golden opportunity for ambitious DFL aspirants like Walter Mondale. For six years, the DFL had gobbled up the major political plums—Freeman as governor, Lord as attorney general, Humphrey and McCarthy as senators. Now there was a Republican governor to knock off. A chance like that might not occur again in Mondale's political lifetime. No one was better positioned. A proven vote-getter, popular as attorney general, young, energetic, Mondale at thirty-four seemed on the verge of great things as DFLers geared up for the 1962 general election.

There was only one problem—Karl Rolvaag, the lieutenant governor elected with Mondale in 1960 while Freeman was losing to Andersen. To get at Andersen would first mean a bare-knuckle fight with Rolvaag, an older man, a friend, and an admirably battle-scarred political warrior. In the euphoria of his victory in 1960, Mondale had promised Rolvaag his backing for the governorship in the next election. It had not exactly been a blood oath, but nonetheless the words had been spoken. There was also Rolvaag's long record of service to the DFL to consider. It dated back to 1946, when Rolvaag, a wounded tank commander, returned from Europe to run for Congress against an entrenched incumbent in the solidly Republican First District. Although Rolvaag lost badly, that campaign only marked the beginning of a long and stormy career that was to have a profound impact on the DFL's future.

The Rolvaag name itself was identified with a heroic pioneer tradition underlying the political, cultural, and economic development of Minnesota and the Dakotas. Karl's father, Ole Rölvaag, was one of the Norwegian immigrants who settled South Dakota. Later, as chairman of the Norwegian Department at St. Olaf College in Northfield, Minnesota, he wrote *Giants in the Earth,* a classic in the 1920s, recounting the heroism of the prairie pioneers and their struggles to establish homesteads despite locusts and loneliness, drought and dreariness.

In 1954, Karl Rolvaag wound up as the DFL's candidate for lieutenant governor on the same ticket as Orville Freeman. In a general housecleaning, the voters swept out the Republicans from the top posts in state government and elected Freeman, Rolvaag, and Lord. For the next two elections, the trio ran and won, until the pattern was broken in 1960 by Lord's resignation, Mondale's appointment, and Freeman's loss. That year's results left Rolvaag as the senior state officeholder in the DFL and the one next in line of succession to the governorship.

That was one way of looking at it. However, there was another, more hard-boiled, school of thought. Andersen was an attractive politician, an adjective not easily applied to Rolvaag, whose speeches were wooden and inarticulate. As a personality, he was less than captivating, and his appearance was hardly prepossessing. Those deficiencies became all the more glaring since the Kennedy mystique was then in full flower, and style was at least as important as substance to many younger DFLers. Appalled by Rolvaag's lack of charisma, a group of DFLers—centered mainly in Minneapolis—began working to build up support for Mondale as the strongest available DFL candidate for governor.

The chief leaders were a young state senator with excellent Ivy League credentials named Sandy Keith and a bald university professor, Forrest Harris. They typified an emerging generation of DFL activists—well-educated, young, financially secure, imbued with the spirit of the New Frontiersmen then running the country from the White House.

Many were relative newcomers to Minnesota—or at least to Minnesota politics—and did not feel bound by the same ties of party loyalty that would cause others to hesitate about abandoning Rolvaag.

Outwardly, Mondale maintained a posture of calculated ambiguity towards what Keith and Harris were doing. He protested that he was not interested—but not so strenuously as to cause them to discontinue their efforts. Inwardly, he was in a quandary. Rolvaag, after all, was not the incumbent. Until the party acted, the gubernatorial endorsement was fair game. And, with the polls showing Mondale as the DFL's strongest candidate against Andersen, wasn't he obliged to come to the aid of his party? Moreover, there was his career to consider. Was it fair to himself to pass up such an opportunity? Besides, Fritz Mondale was no party interloper, no crass opportunist. His party resumé—dating from 1947—covered nearly as many years as Rolvaag's, although his service was not at the same levels and had been interrupted by college, army, and law school.

Almost without his doing anything to encourage it, momentum was starting to build behind what newspapers were calling a draft-Mondale campaign. It was a dazzling prospect. There had been younger governors—Stassen was thirty-one when elected in 1938—but not many, and a victory over a Republican as impressive as Andersen would endow Mondale with national stature. It would certainly put him near the top of his political generation. Two of his more politically ambitious aides, Bill Kennedy and Bill Brooks, persuaded Mondale to assess the situation by discreetly sounding out different party leaders. The response was generally promising, but some warned of the possibility of damaging party infighting if he contested Rolvaag for the endorsement.

Those cautionary signs flashed with high-voltage intensity when the Minnesota AFL-CIO convened in Duluth. At one point during the convention preliminaries, Rolvaag and Mondale were called before the executive committee of the state Culinary Council, the AFL-CIO bargaining agent for bartenders, waiters, cooks, and other restaurant employees. Looking hard at Mondale, the head of the council said, "We've got a $3,000 contribution to make and, goddamn you, Mondale, if you run, there ain't gonna be a goddamn dime."

Later, during the convention itself, Rolvaag made a strong speech extolling labor and touting its issues. The delegates, stirred by the lieutenant governor's uncharacteristically strong oratory, shouted their approval of a resolution endorsing Rolvaag for governor. When it was Mondale's turn to speak, he remarked dryly, "I think I just heard a train pass me by."

The message was clear. The AFL-CIO spoke for an important segment of the DFL's rank and file. If Mondale wanted party support for governor, he would have to fight for it at the risk of damaging his career and fracturing party unity. The question was whether he would take that risk.

"I know there was some confusion within the party," Mondale said in an interview recalling the moment. "I'm not saying there wasn't some confusion in my own mind, because there probably was—I think there was. I was torn between what I thought my commitment was to Karl and the reaction I was getting around the state and those polls. But I think I was strongly inclined not to run, since I had given my word, and also deep down, I didn't feel I was ready.

"I just wasn't sure I was ready to run for governor."

That seemed to be Mondale's state of mind when he told DFLers at a party function in early March 1962 that he was supporting Rolvaag for governor. Mondale's words were unequivocal and reassuring to those who worried either about party harmony or Rolvaag's political fortunes. The surprise announcement came a day after the Minneapolis *Tribune* published a poll showing that both Rolvaag and Mondale would edge Andersen. However, Mondale's margin was eight points; Rolvaag's was only two.

Yet, despite Mondale's unqualified denial of any interest in the 1962 governor's race, there were still efforts to drum up support for inserting his name at the top of the DFL's state ticket that fall. Curiously, Mondale did not step forward and unequivocally repudiate the continuing machinations of Keith and Harris. Instead, Mondale held back, watching their efforts take shape and wondering whether real momentum might begin to build, even though the Minneapolis newspapers—the state's main conduit for political news—were on strike. Other reporters, attempting to resolve the discrepancy between Mondale's earlier declaration of support for Rolvaag and his subsequent actions, found the attorney general either inaccessible or unwilling to say anything beyond a terse "no comment." This ambiguous state of affairs continued until Ray Hemenway, the DFL's national committeeman, stepped in. Like Mondale, Hemenway came from southern Minnesota, where times were always tough politically for DFLers. A fighting, outspoken liberal, Hemenway called Mondale and told him bluntly that the lingering uncertainty about his intentions would wind up hurting the party and that he should make it clear he was stepping aside for Rolvaag.

Now things started to happen. There was a flurry of public statements, one by Hemenway and others by Harris and Mondale. They all boiled down to the same thing. There was but one DFL candidate for governor and his name was Karl Rolvaag and not Walter Mondale.

"I have stated my position several times in the past—that I support Rolvaag for governor and that I am a candidate for reelection, and that position never changed," Mondale told the St. Paul *Dispatch*. "There were some who were hoping they could change my mind. I have simply called them and restated my position."

Mondale's statement revealed little of what had actually gone on. It was true that his public position was unchanged. He had never publicly acknowledged a serious interest in running for governor, although his private actions left no doubt on that score in the minds of intimates. A number of factors dissuaded Mondale—loyalty and affection for Rolvaag, concern for party unity, self-doubts about his political maturity, uncertainty of the outcome. Solidifying Mondale's decision was Hemenway's forceful and blunt intercession. Hemenway had enthusiastically backed Mondale's appointment as attorney general two years earlier. He also held no brief for Rolvaag, other than a strong conviction that neither Mondale nor the party was ready for a stop-Rolvaag struggle. The opposition of Hemenway and the AFL-CIO were not insuperable obstacles, but they could have been overcome only with great struggle and political risk. Prudence prevailed. Mondale chose to avoid that struggle by seeking reelection as attorney general.

The decision fitted the pattern of Mondale's career. His path of advancement never required the arduous, chancy business of pursuing a candidacy and building an organization from scratch as a nonincumbent. Whenever faced with an opportunity that would require taking that risk, Mondale found good reason for deciding to pass it up. His instincts were sound. By choosing not to knock himself out running for governor, he made himself available for an effortless ascent to the U.S. Senate in 1964. A decade later, the presidency beckoned—but too faintly to lure Mondale into pursuing it to the end. His forbearance was rewarded with the vice presidency. The formula's success was self-justifying.

It also suited Mondale's style. As became clear in 1962, he would not take the bold, dramatic steps that might capture the imagination of those who were not attracted by his quiet, intelligent, decent liberalism. Instead of practicing politics with flair or flamboyance, Mondale betrayed an inner defensiveness—a tendency to ward off those who might try to bore in too closely as either friends or critics, and to avoid conflict with those who held power within the party. Above all, Mondale was determined not to suffer the humiliation of losing.

There was not much chance of that in 1962 after Mondale removed himself as a possible contender for the governorship. The Republicans bowed to Mondale's obvious strength by choosing a pro-forma candidate to oppose him —a carpetbagger from Pennsylvania whose primary function was to keep Mondale on the defensive and thereby limit his effectiveness in helping Rolvaag.

By mid-October, the polls made it clear that the gubernatorial race was going to be very tight, with Andersen holding a slight advantage. The campaign's closing weeks were dominated by a furious controversy over a federal highway-construction project. It was a classic, last-minute election ploy involving grossly inflated charges by Rolvaag, Humphrey, and a DFL congressman, John Blatnik, of allegedly questionable road-building practices. Although a postelection report found the problems were negligible, the campaign ended on a note of scandal, with Andersen on the defensive.

Mondale did not question the DFL's smear tactics. Indeed, he played a minor role in sustaining the controversy. His staff—apparently without his knowledge—helped prepare the DFL's flimsy case against the Andersen administration's highway program. At Humphrey's insistence, Mondale agreed to appear on an election-eve telecast with Humphrey and Rolvaag. While the program was dominated by a free-wheeling discussion of the so-called scan-

dal, Mondale's remarks were limited to criticizing Andersen for punishing the Highway Department employee
who had revealed the alleged construction deficiencies.
Even that was an ambiguous issue. The employee was a
brother of a Rolvaag campaign worker and had eagerly
carried his accusations to the DFL before highway officials
had had time to evaluate their merits. The Highway Department subsequently granted the employee a short medical
leave for treatment of arthritis but then suspended him
when he used the time off to discuss the issue with reporters.

When the votes were counted, Mondale won handily, as
did his erstwhile gubernatorial supporter, Sandy Keith,
who—with Mondale's support—had captured the party's
endorsement for lieutenant governor over Rolvaag's stubborn opposition. The Andersen-Rolvaag contest ended in
a virtual deadlock. The outcome was not decided until after
a 139-day recount: Rolvaag won by ninety-one votes.

Rolvaag's belated installation as governor instantly
thawed what had been a chilly relationship between the
governor and attorney general during Andersen's tenure.
Separating the two offices in a wing of the domed State
Capitol building was a wide hallway; from 1961 to 1963, it
became an unbridgeable chasm of partisan suspicion.
Rather than entrust anything to Mondale, Andersen turned
to a private law firm for his legal advice. The one time he
did ask for the attorney general's opinion, Mondale found
a reason to remain silent, suspecting a political trap.

Almost from the day he took over, Rolvaag could count
on a steady stream of legal and political advice from his
young attorney general. Although that advice was not always heeded, it did not go unappreciated, either.

Mondale and Rolvaag also shared a love of the outdoors.
Indeed, Mondale would seek refuge several times a year
from the pressures of public life amid the lakes and forests
of northern Minnesota and Ontario. An indifferent hunter

and average fisherman, Mondale nevertheless found a re-
lease in those sports that no other pursuit seemed to offer.
Years later, when the vice-presidential nomination made
him an object of relentless media interest, Mondale would
tell reporters that fishing from a boat—or even through a
hole cut in the winter's ice—was therapeutic.

In early June 1964, however, a fishing trip with Rolvaag
almost ended in disaster. While Mondale was napping at a
cabin about three miles away, Rolvaag, who had been
drinking heavily, lost control of an outboard as he was
docking it on Rainy Lake, near the Minnesota-Canadian
border. One of Rolvaag's fishing companions was so badly
shaken up he required treatment at a hospital in nearby
International Falls. Rolvaag escaped serious injury only
because someone managed to shut off the motor.

Mondale, alerted by telephone, hurried to the scene to
help Rolvaag back to a cabin. He then left to catch a flight
south to the Twin Cities, as previously planned. That afternoon, Congressman John Blatnik, arriving at the International Falls Airport, encountered a much shaken Mondale.
"He was tense, pale, unsmiling," Blatnik recalled. "Something had happened. I sensed it at once. Out loud he said
he had been called back to his office. Then he whispered
in my ear. Karl was in a boat accident. It was a mess."

Blatnik added, "He was obviously leaving so he wouldn't
get involved in any way. The guys told him to leave, and he
probably wanted to leave anyway."

"It did shake me up," Mondale admitted. "I knew there
was trouble."

An unpleasant situation was confronting Mondale. Years
later, Rolvaag would resign from the Minnesota Public Service Commission, acknowledging publicly what had been
whispered for years in statehouse corridors—that he was an
alcoholic. But in 1964 the governor's drinking habits were
hardly a matter of open political discussion. As for Mondale, he drank just enough on social occasions to avoid

being thought a prude. Despite Mondale's own sobriety, full disclosure of the incident would not only be damaging to Rolvaag but also be embarrassing to Mondale. Aside from the political repercussions, there was a family consideration. His mother, proud of her son's accomplishments, was still bothered by the mixing of booze and politics.

Under the circumstances, Mondale found good reason to fly home at the first opportunity. In his haste, however, he neglected one detail. Neither Mondale, the Minnesota attorney general and the state's chief law enforcement officer, nor anyone else reported the boat accident to local police authorities as required by law. A couple of years later, the Republicans dredged up the incident in a politically inspired effort to embarrass Rolvaag. The GOP's charges of a coverup were never effectively rebutted, although their impact on the electorate did not seem significant.

8

A National Debut

The black woman spoke with a sorrowful, stark simplicity: "Mr. Chairman and the Credentials Committee," she was saying, "my name is Fanny Lou Hamer, and I live at 626 East LaFayette Street, Ruleville, Mississippi, Sunflower County, the home of Senator James O. Eastland and Senator Stennis."

With that simple introduction began one of the most stirring and far-reaching episodes in the history of American political conventions. It was a sultry Saturday afternoon in late August. A carnival mood had already captured the multitude of delegates, reporters, lobbyists, hookers, and other hangers-on who had flocked to the New Jersey resort of Atlantic City for the 1964 Democratic National Convention. Inside the cavernous hearing room, however, Walter Mondale and the ninety-nine other members of the convention's Credentials Committee sat riveted—many in spite of themselves—by Mrs. Hamer's account of police brutality and political repression in Mississippi, where she had lived and worked as a sharecropper on a white man's plantation.

It was a banal setting for an episode of such high drama —the long committee tables covered with cheap cloth, the glaring TV lights, the antiseptic room designed as a neutral meeting ground for Atlantic City's endless parade of con-

ventioneers. But for Mondale—and for other civil-rights
advocates—the symbolism of Mrs. Hamer's presence and
the simple, powerful imagery of her testimony endowed the
occasion with the quality of a religious experience, rather
than a political event.

Mondale was one of Minnesota's two representatives on
the committee that was to advise the full convention on
how to settle disputes over who was entitled to be seated
on the convention floor. Mrs. Hamer was the star witness
for the Mississippi Freedom Democratic Party (MFDP) delegation that had traveled to Atlantic City to challenge the
legitimacy of the lily-white delegation picked by their
state's Regular Democratic organization. But this was no
ordinary credentials challenge, and Mondale was no ordinary member of the committee. More than anyone else in
the room, he bore a special responsibility to mediate the
intractable and explosive issues being raised by the sharecropper at the witness table.

Mondale had not sought the mediator's role. But when
Hubert Humphrey asked him to lend a hand, he couldn't
say no. A lot was at stake. For Humphrey, it was quite
possibly the vice presidency itself. For Mondale, the U.S.
Senate. The long-range prospect was inspiring; the hours
ahead, unnerving.

Even the most sympathetic northern liberals, like Mondale and Humphrey, were forced to concede that legally
the Freedom Democrats didn't have much of a case. That
was true, even though the MFDP challenge went to the
heart of a system of terror and repression that had been
used since the end of Reconstruction to disfranchise the
black half of Mississippi's population. But in 1964, the evidence made it clear that the Regular Democrats had violated neither state law nor national party procedures in
selecting their delegations—the law and the procedures
were both still in a medieval state. Hoping to exploit the
technical defects in the MFDP's case, the White House

crafted a compromise proposal that was sheer tokenism. The plan was to let the Freedom Democrats on the convention floor as honored guests, exact a loyalty oath from the Mississippi Regulars, and promise that the party would not tolerate discrimination by state organizations in the future.

Johnson had prevailed on Humphrey to try to sell that package to the convention in the hopes of avoiding a messy racial confrontation on national television and averting a Southern walkout that would play into the hands of the Republicans and their nominee, Barry Goldwater. Humphrey had no choice. He was obliged to regard the assignment as yet another test of his worthiness to run as Johnson's vice-presidential running mate—an honor Humphrey desperately wanted. As the Democratic whip in the Senate, Humphrey had been the ramrod for Johnson's spectacularly successful legislative program earlier that year. Indeed, the supreme test of Humphrey's parliamentary skills had been the landmark civil-rights act of 1964—an accomplishment likely to increase his credibility in negotiating with the Freedom Democrats and their supporters. But Johnson was manipulating the process of selecting a vice-presidential nominee as part of a calculated strategy to extract maximum suspense and excitement from the convention. Humphrey could not take anything for granted. The president made it clear he might pick someone else. He might even pick Humphrey's comrade-in-arms from Minnesota politics, Gene McCarthy.

A swift solution to the Mississippi challenge, without any bloodletting, was what LBJ wanted. But by late Saturday afternoon on August 22, any hopes that Mondale and Humphrey might have harbored for a quick fix had evaporated. Token solutions and narrow legalisms were not going to get the Democratic party off the hook—not after Mrs. Hamer told a national television audience how she had been fired from her job and brutally beaten in a jail cell because of her voter-registration activities.

It was an ordeal that began when state troopers threw her into a patrol car, kicking her first as they arrested her. Later, three white men came to her jail cell. She recalled one of them saying, "We're going to make you wish you was dead."

She went on: "I was carried out of that cell into another cell where they had two Negro prisoners. The state highway patrolman ordered the first Negro to take the blackjack. [He] ordered me . . . to lay down on a bunk on my face, and I laid on my face. The first Negro began to beat, and I was beat by the first Negro until he was exhausted, and I was holding my hands behind me at that time on my left side because I suffered from polio when I was six years old. After the first Negro had beat until he was exhausted the state highway patrolman ordered the second Negro to take the blackjack. The second Negro began to beat. . . ."

Martin Luther King was the Freedom Democrats' last witness. "You, who must sit here judging their validity as delegates to this convention, cannot imagine the anguish and suffering they have undergone to get to this point," he told the Credentials Committee. "They come not to complain of their sufferings. They come seeking the actual fulfillment of their dream for democracy in Mississippi."

Mondale may have been a rookie in major-league politics —this was his first national political convention—but he knew as soon as King sat down that the MFDP had raised the ante for party harmony. The Freedom Democrats' lawyer was Joe Rauh, an old friend from SDA days and now a leading figure in Americans for Democratic Action and other liberal causes. Mondale admired the way Rauh had orchestrated the MFDP case. It had been a compelling moral indictment not just of politics but of a way of life in Mississippi and all Dixie. The national party was not immune from criticism either, having permitted state parties like the Regular Democrats to flout its ideals and responsibilities. But now the hard question remained: Would either side accept an accommodation that fell short of its original goal? Time was short. The convention's opening session was scheduled for Monday evening, August 24, and the report of the Credentials Committee would be one of the first orders of business. Failure to resolve the challenge within the committee would mean an inevitable floor battle —precisely the thing Johnson was anxious to avoid.

The next day—Sunday—the committee met privately for most of the afternoon. As a starting point, a delegate from Wyoming offered the weak White House compromise. It was worse than useless. Instead of providing a bridge to party reconciliation, the Johnson plan drove supporters of the rival Mississippi factions farther apart. The wrangling became embittered, the committee increasingly polarized. At one point, an Oregon delegate, Rep. Al Ullman, made a stab at compromise by suggesting that two of Mississippi's votes be awarded the Freedom Democrats. But that was swept aside when Ullman's own Oregon colleague in the U.S. House, Rep. Edith Green, stood up to answer him. In a cold fury, she compared the Regular Democrats to Hitler's Nazi party. She in turn was taken on by an enraged Mississippi state senator who likened the MFDP to the Ku Klux Klan—both had secret membership lists, he said— and insinuated that Hamer and her colleagues were pawns of Cuban revolutionaries. It was clear that the 75-year-old committee chairman, Gov. David Lawrence of Pennsylvania, had lost control. Taking charge of the Johnson administration's forces, Mondale recommended forming a subcommittee "that might develop an honorable and acceptable compromise." The committee, grateful for a respite, agreed. Lawrence promptly named two Southerners and two Northerners to this ad hoc mediating panel and installed Mondale as its chairman, with the deciding vote.

For the next forty hours, Mondale felt as if he were caught up in a huge floating crap game. The setting changed, as did the players, but the pressure grew more intense with every sleepless hour. What would the Freedom Democrats accept? What would the Regular Democrats give up? What would the South give up? Would any party give up anything? Would Mrs. Hamer and her comrades accept less than everything? Roll the dice and try again. Mondale learned all about smoke-filled rooms. From his room at the massive Shelburne Hotel, the scene shifted to Humphrey's suite down the hall, then to the third floor of the Pagent Motel—the White House command center near the convention hall—and back again to the Shelburne. Outside the door there would be a ubiquitous Humphrey aide to shoo away reporters; downstairs in the lobbies was an inevitable phalanx of Secret Service agents and blue-uniformed New Jersey state troopers to intercept troublemakers and snoopers.

The ambience behind the closed doors was unchanging —the stale odor of stubbed-out cigars and cigarette smoke; a faintly sweet scent of whiskey; the recycled mustiness of hotel air conditioning. There was no structure, no agenda, no Roberts Rules, no procedures. The internal tensions and contradictions of the national party—so dramatically underscored by the challenge itself—were built into the subcommittee. Charles Diggs, a black congressman from Michigan, clashed repeatedly with a former Texas governor, Price Daniels, who was the agent of the current governor, John Connally, who in turn was the agent of Lyndon Johnson. A Georgian named Irving Kahler was the agent of the South; he was paired off against an Iowa lawyer, Sherwin Markman, the agent of the North—but, as it turned out, also an agent of Johnson. Mondale was in the middle—the agent of Hubert Humphrey and the only vote that really counted. Sometimes he consulted with the subcommittee; often he did not.

Members of the two factions came and went. So did the representatives and leaders of the party's major power blocs—particularly organized labor—as well as influential

pols from different parts of the country. As they were ush-
ered into the room, they would be greeted by Mondale, tie
askew, shoes off, his mouth curling in a friendly smile
around a large cigar. Humphrey would often be at his side.
Or an important labor lobbyist. Much of Mondale's time
was also spent with a telephone cradled under his chin,
talking to Walter Jenkins, a top White House aide on the
scene in Atlantic City, or to Thomas Finney, a partner of
Clark Clifford, one of Washington's most prestigious lawyers. Talking to either was tantamount to talking to Johnson himself.

From his hotel window, Mondale could peer down on a
constant reminder of the dispute's moral dimension.
Throughout the weekend, civil-rights workers conducted a
sit-in on the Boardwalk. Theirs was a ragtag vigil in support
of the Freedom Democrats. Many of them were veterans of
the Mississippi Summer Project. They had gone to that
state as part of an assault on a social structure built out of
white bigotry and racial hatred. Three of their comrades
had been murdered that June near Philadelphia, Mississippi, while working with the MFDP on a black voter-registration drive.

Mondale worked through Sunday night. The next morning—only hours before the convention was to open—Humphrey called the participants together for a meeting at the
Pagent Motel. No solution was in sight. The two-hour
meeting only served to demonstrate that Humphrey and
Mondale were still hemmed in by the White House's determination to cling to its original formula and the MFDP's
equally rigid insistence that its entire delegation be seated.
Rauh and his clients did not care if Regular Democrats
were seated as well, with the state's votes divided among all
of them. Since Johnson would be nominated by acclamation, there was no significance attached to the act of voting.
The significance would lie in the symbolic presence of the
MFDP, officially recognized as part of the delegation that

would be seated around the standard of that unrecon-
structed bastion of the Old Confederacy—the state of Mississippi. The Regular Democrats were well aware of the
symbolism. They vowed an uncompromising struggle
against a step that would legitimize any notions of black
political equality in their state.

As Mondale and Humphrey struggled to reach a compromise, supporters of the two Mississippi factions exploited
the opportunity to posture in front of the national media.
Two MFDP backers on the Credentials Committee, Rep.
Robert Kastenmeier of Wisconsin and Edith Green, stalked
out of the meeting with Humphrey at the Pagent to demonstrate their displeasure over proposals that failed to meet
all of the MFDP's demands. On the other side of the dispute, Gov. Carl Sanders of Georgia warned darkly that any
solution seating Freedom Democrats as Mississippi delegates would trigger a massive Southern walkout and a hor-
rendous party split. Under the circumstances, many delegates from north of the Mason-Dixon line felt honestly
trapped in a hopeless dilemma. The convention's host,
New Jersey Gov. Richard Hughes, said that his delegation
had concluded that the Freedom Democrats had "no legal
basis under existing Mississippi law" to claim delegate
seats but added, "This does not mean we do not sympathize with the moral rightness of their cause."

By the time the Pagent Motel meeting broke up, it was
clear to everyone close to the situation that there was no
chance of resolving the challenge in an amicable way before
that evening. Lawrence and John Bailey, the Democratic
national chairman, agreed to give Mondale another twenty-
four hours and to open the convention with Mississippi's
seats vacant.

At this point, Johnson, who had been keeping an attentive eye on Mondale's progress from the White House,
escalated the pressure on the MFDP to call off the psychological warfare. Johnson enlisted Walter Reuther to help

settle the dispute. When Johnson placed the telephone call, the United Auto Workers' chief was deep in sensitive contract negotiations with General Motors. In pleading tones, Johnson prevailed on the reluctant Reuther to fly to Atlantic City as the president's personal mediator. Reuther brought with him Bayard Rustin, Dr. Martin Luther King's former assistant and a highly regarded black leader. But Reuther's intercession, in particular, represented an overt attempt to pressure the Freedom Democrats into moderating their position. During the turbulent months prior to the convention, the UAW had been a steady source of support and bail money for blacks as they mounted their historic assault on the Southern white establishment. The time had come to redeem part of that investment. In addition, Rauh was the UAW's general counsel—a relationship that Johnson hoped would give Reuther additional leverage over the MFDP.

Instinctively, Reuther perceived the emotional complexities of the situation. He was immediately impressed by Mondale's performance, particularly his ability to keep the two sides talking despite their passionate determination not to yield. After hearing Mondale's status report, Reuther was persuaded that the young Minnesota attorney general was right—the White House's original proposal did not go far enough toward meeting the MFDP's demands.

By now, Mondale had developed a different kind of compromise—one in which symbolism was again a key. The idea was to fashion a solution that would acknowledge a national responsibility for dealing with a historic problem. Mondale spelled out his plan over breakfast Tuesday morning in Humphrey's suite. Seated around the table as he talked were Humphrey, Lawrence, and two White House representatives—Reuther and Finney. They all realized there were only a few hours left for compromise. Otherwise, it would have to be fought out on the convention floor that night. As the breakfast dishes were cleared away, Mondale suggested that two Freedom Democrats be seated as at-large delegates representing the entire party, not just a single state. In this way, Mondale reasoned, the burden of the race problem would be spread around, and the white Mississippians would be spared the humiliation of being singled out for national opprobrium. One of the MFDP delegates would be Aaron Henry, a black pharmacist and head of the MFDP delegation. The other would be Dr. Edwin King, a white clergyman whose delegate status would signify the hope of liberals for the emergence of an integrated party in Mississippi and throughout the South. The remaining Freedom Democrats would be seated as guests, the Regular Democrats would serve as delegates subject to a loyalty oath, and the party would move to cleanse itself of bias in the future.

The plan represented a calculated risk, Mondale explained, because there was a high likelihood of rejection by the MFDP's rank and file, as well as by the Southerners, who would certainly bridle at the loyalty-oath requirement. The Freedom Democrats were indeed divided. King and Bayard Rustin understood convention politics and were willing to accept a purely symbolic gesture if coupled with guarantees of civil-rights reforms for future conventions. In fact, it was with their tacit encouragement that Congressman Ullman had proposed giving the Freedom Democrats two seats within the Mississippi delegation. There had been subsequent signals from King that two delegates would be acceptable. It was in that context that Mondale proposed his compromise as a variation on the earlier Ullman plan. But for others in the MFDP, any proposal that left some of their delegation unseated would be a sellout.

His explanation concluded, Mondale—eyes red-rimmed with fatigue and tension—asked for the approval of those gathered in the Humphrey suite. It was immediately given. As one of those present observed, no formula would be universally acceptable, so that a solution would ultimately have "to be imposed much as the Trieste settlement was imposed on Italy and Yugoslavia."

In other words, it was now time to play power politics. Mondale knew, as did everyone else in the room, that too much was at stake to let extremists on either side tear apart a hard-wrought, delicately balanced compromise. Mondale had been tremendously moved by Mrs. Hamer's testimony. But his training as a lawyer and instincts as a politician told him that her grievances could not be resolved at once. The MFDP would have to be recognized for what it was—a protest group operating outside of party procedures and law. Those could be changed only over time. Once Mondale reached that conclusion, the range of responses to the MFDP's demands was limited. A quixotic play to the liberal gallery might be morally satisfying, but seating all the Freedom Democrats would alienate the South, weaken Johnson, and quite possibly ruin Humphrey as a national candidate. Having decided on a limited response, the trick now was to ram the compromise through the Credentials Committee before either side—particularly the MFDP—could mobilize its supporters.

After the breakfast meeting broke up, Mondale returned to his subcommittee. As expected the plan was endorsed, three to two, over the dissenting votes of the two Southerners. But afterwards, Daniels and Kahler promised to try to sell it to the Southern delegations, or at least to dissuade them from a massive walkout. John Connally and Carl Sanders, governors of Texas and Georgia, also agreed to help out.

But minute-by-minute timing was now the key to the strategy of the Johnson-Humphrey-Mondale forces. The Credentials Committee was to meet later that afternoon. The objective was to present the compromise before the Freedom Democrats, who were meeting in a nearby church, had a chance to discover what the Mondale subcommittee had proposed. Once Fanny Lou Hamer and her followers learned the details, they would be certain to reject it. That action, in turn, would easily produce the eleven votes needed on the Credentials Committee for a minority report, the one parliamentary vehicle available to the Freedom Democrats for presenting their case on the convention floor. To Johnson and his men, the prospect was chilling. The MFDP had to be outmaneuvered.

Meanwhile, Joe Rauh, the fiery white liberal serving as the MFDP's counsel, was frantically trying to figure out what was happening. All his sources had dried up. They didn't know or weren't talking. Finally, Rauh walked to the meeting room where the Credentials Committee had gathered for its secret sessions over the past two days. As he was about to enter, he was stopped by Charlie Diggs, the black congressman on Mondale's subcommittee. A stout, round-faced man, Diggs was breathless, having run several blocks to catch Rauh with an important message. Rauh was to call his UAW boss, Reuther.

It was an abrupt conversation.

Reuther outlined the terms of the compromise and then added peremptorily, "The convention has made its decision. I expect you to accept it."

Rauh's head was swimming. As a man who understood the importance of symbols, he recognized the significance of the proposal. As a pragmatist, he realized that it was the best deal he could expect under the circumstances. But he also knew he was being caught in a squeeze play. With the committee due to debate and vote on the plan in a few minutes, he did not dare leave. When he asked for time to present the proposal to the MFDP, Reuther said no.

As he hung up, Rauh had one last hope. He intercepted Mondale in the doorway to the committee room.

"Look, I know what you people are going to offer us," Rauh said. "Just give me twenty minutes to present it to my people."

"That's fair enough," Mondale said. "Let's see if we can't do that."

At that point, Sherwin Markman, the Iowan on the Mondale subcommittee who was about to land a high-ranking job in the White House, appeared at Mondale's elbow.

"There'll be no further delays," Markman snapped. "It's been decided to go ahead with this offer."

With that Markman and Mondale, followed by Rauh, hurried into the room. Moments later, the doors closed and the meeting started.

Once inside, Mondale faced another in a series of tests that began when he agreed to come to Humphrey's aid. Could he sell the compromise? Never before had he faced such an audience—important members of Congress, governors, political professionals who could pick up a telephone and have the ear of the president of the United States. Keeping a dour eye on the proceedings was John Bailey, the national party chairman and a power broker who could destroy a political career with a single sentence. What they saw was an eloquent young man in complete command of the situation. Years later, Rauh was to say, "He blew me out of the water."

In his presentation, Mondale candidly conceded that Rauh and the MFDP had proven that blacks had been thwarted politically in Mississippi by a "clear pattern of discrimination and intimidation." Appealing to the handful of wavering liberals whose votes might be affected by the emotions of the moment, Mondale argued that the remedy to racial oppression was not to be found in overthrowing well-established party traditions and rules. The rule of law must be maintained. Despite Fanny Lou Hamer's damning evidence, the Mississippi Regulars had "the legal right to be seated as delegates if they, in good faith, support the nominees of this convention." Against that right, Mondale added, the Freedom Democrats could be regarded only as "a protest movement and not a political party." Even so,

Mondale urged the party to recognize the justice of the MFDP cause by making Aaron Henry and Edwin King delegates at large. That, Mondale said, would be a "strong and deep statement of appreciation to these leaders for stating their case as well and as bravely as they have." He added: "I can say and I think everyone knows we did not go as far as the Freedom Democratic Party wanted us to go, nor did we go as far as many of the Southern delegations wanted us to go. It would have been impossible to meet those extremes."

He then applied the soothing balm of eventual moral redemption to the troubled consciences of liberals and moderates. Having extracted a commitment to racial fairness in future party affairs, the Freedom Democrats could claim a "magnificent victory for the forces of civil rights . . . We have spelled the end of discrimination in state parties."

After Mondale finished, Rauh tried again to slow things down, only to be shouted down by an impatient and fatigued committee. Mondale had been careful to tell the committee that he had no assurances from either side that they would accept the compromise. But, moments later, a Maryland delegate, George P. Mahoney, arose to claim that Aaron Henry and Dr. Edwin King "are satisfied and happy about this situation." Mahoney, who two years later would run unsuccessfully for governor of Maryland using racist code words ("Your home is your castle. Protect it.") thus conveyed the impression that the compromise was acceptable to the MFDP delegates. Although incorrect, this assertion, unrebutted by Mondale or anybody else, undercut Rauh's final attempts to rally support for a minority report. After a futile attempt to demand a roll-call vote—which would have put some members on the spot with their liberal supporters—the committee roared its approval of the compromise.

Except for some of their leaders, the Freedom Democrats and their placard-carrying supporters on the Board-walk were incensed. But Rauh knew that the monolithic structure of white political power in the South had been struck a stunning blow. The reforms set in motion by the Mississippi challenge would transform the Democratic party—North and South—over the next eight years by opening it to groups that had never participated before—minorities, women, youngsters barely old enough to vote. Yet many within the MFDP felt betrayed by their liberal supporters in 1964. Despite pleas by Rauh, Rustin, and King—who described the deal as a "symbolic victory"—the MFDP rejected the compromise. Fanny Lou Hamer summed up the frustration: "We didn't come all that way just for two votes. It is all we get in Mississippi—a token of our rights. We want equal votes."

On the convention floor the overwhelming sentiment seemed to be with Mondale and Humphrey. The challenge was formally laid to rest early on the evening of August 25 —hours after Mondale had managed the compromise within the committee. After vainly trying to impose order on the kaleidoscopic sea of delegates on the convention floor, diminutive John Pastore of Rhode Island, the tempo-rary chairman, called for a voice vote on the compromise. Despite a chorus of noes from an odd assortment of South-erners and MFDP supporters, Pastore banged the gavel and declared the matter resolved exactly as Humphrey and Mondale had planned it.

With that, those Mississippi Regular Democrats who had not already done so began packing their bags. They were bolting the convention, if not the party, to demonstrate their displeasure over the loyalty oath and the general per-missiveness towards the renegades who were threatening their political survival.

Three Regulars did take the oath, but they disappeared after a number of Freedom Democrats, using borrowed credentials, infiltrated the convention and took seats under

the Mississippi standard. At first the sergeants at arms tried
to intercede, causing some scuffling. But that ended with a
call from the White House, and before long all the Mississippi seats were filled by Freedom Democrats. Despite
some grumbling among other Southern delegates, no one
walked out. In fact, Tom Harper, chairman of the Arkansas
delegation—a group thought to have been strongly in sympathy with the Mississippi Regulars—declared that the
Mondale formula was the best that the South could hope
for under the circumstances. Humphrey had passed the test
that had been thrust on the party by the Mississippi challenge—and then tossed to him by Johnson.

The convention went on to other business. On Wednesday night, a clamorous throng of delegates nominated Lyndon Johnson for the presidency by acclamation. The following night Hubert Horatio Humphrey was nominated for
vice president.

In November, the Johnson-Humphrey ticket was swept
into office by a landslide.

9

Chosen Again

And now the waiting began. Lyndon Johnson's selection of Hubert Humphrey as his running mate had rearranged Minnesota's political landscape, revealing new vistas for Walter Mondale. Although the Republican nomination of Barry Goldwater caused deep anxieties among liberals, moderates, and even some conservatives, the polls left little doubt in the minds of DFLers that the November election returns would open up one of the state's two U.S. Senate seats. Actually, that possibility had occurred to more than a few DFLers long before the actual convention. One member of Mondale's attorney general's staff had jotted down his thoughts moments after learning of President John F. Kennedy's assassination in Dallas on November 22, 1963. The first entry recorded the aide's grief and shock at the murder; the second was a prediction: Humphrey would become vice president and Mondale would proceed to the Senate.

But nothing could be taken for granted. In June, 1964, Johnson had appeared at the Minnesota DFL convention, providing an opportunity to raise funds for both the president's own campaign and the DFL coffers. Anxious to impress the president, Humphrey had entrusted Mondale with planning the most ambitious fund-raiser in DFL history. The main event was to be the party's first $100-a-plate dinner. Mondale, equally desirous of impressing the president, Humphrey, Governor Rolvaag, and anyone else who could affect his destiny, had spent prodigious amounts of energy and time making sure the president's visit would be a huge financial success.

As a test of his prowess as a political cardplayer, however, nothing could compare to the Mississippi credentials challenge that August—two months after the DFL's big dinner. The go-go-go pressure of the convention, however, offered little time to think about where the mad rush of events was carrying him. Even the hiatus caused by Miles Lord's resignation four years earlier had been resolved in less than a week. As the postconvention euphoria over Humphrey's good fortune faded, Mondale prepared himself for a prolonged period of uncertainty.

Karl Rolvaag, it seemed, was going to take his time. The Minnesota governor had grinned broadly when asked by Frank Wright, the Minneapolis *Tribune*'s political reporter, on the last day of the convention whether he was going to "play LBJ" in picking Humphrey's replacement, assuming a Democratic presidential victory in the fall.

"Ah'm a-gonna consult with lotta mah friends," Rolvaag told Wright in a poor imitation of Johnson's Texas drawl. In his story the next day, Wright did not fail to note that Rolvaag himself was a leading candidate for the job. Rolvaag never denied his interest in succeeding Humphrey. He had long dreamt of the day when his name might be enrolled in the U.S. Senate along with the great Populists and Progressives of earlier years—the LaFollettes, George W. Norris, and others.

That also happened to be a dream shared by Mondale, who once told a law-school classmate, Doug Head, that one of his grand ambitions in life was to emulate Norris's career, notwithstanding the fact that the great Nebraskan was a maverick Republican.

Rolvaag's possible designs on the Senate seat made maneuvering awkward. "It was a matter of enormous delicacy," Mondale recalled. "About all I could do was make certain that people whom Karl respected made him aware of their support for my candidacy." The most effective pressure was coming from organized labor, whose earlier support for Rolvaag's gubernatorial ambition was now annulled by the fear that he would be unable to hold the Senate seat against the Republicans. Rolvaag himself was amused by their transparent attempts at subtle persuasion: "Inevitably, they'd say, 'Well, you gotta go. But if you don't, then Mondale oughta go.' He was always second choice to me. What else were they gonna tell the governor? You know, I was realistic enough. I got the message."

It was an unpredictable situation, or at least it seemed so to Mondale at the time. In sweating out the attorney-general appointment, Mondale did not have to compete with the very man who would make the appointment. Freeman obviously had no interest in taking the job himself. If Rolvaag—a man known throughout the party as stubborn and strong-willed—was bent on sending himself to Washington, Mondale was powerless to dissuade him. And Rolvaag was only one of about fifteen prominent names of potential senators. Mondale was now on a much faster and more competitive track. The other competitors were people of substantial stature—Freeman himself; Congressman Blatnik, a giant in state politics and congressional power; Eugenie Anderson, the first woman ambassador in U.S. history and a charter member of the DFL; Walter Heller, one of the national Democratic party's top economic brains; Carl Rowan, the country's foremost black journalist and head of the U.S. Information Agency at the time; and even Miles Lord.

Even in that company, Mondale felt he had a strong claim, particularly in view of his cool handling of the Mississippi challenge. It was also an open secret among informed DFLers after the convention that Humphrey was now backing Mondale, although Humphrey remained publicly silent.

The other senator was not so reticent. On the final day of the Atlantic City convention, Gene McCarthy announced he was supporting Blatnik. Long-standing ties of mutual loyalty and respect bound the two men, stemming in part from Blatnik's willingness to stand aside in 1958 to allow McCarthy to run for the Senate. In addition, close friends were to say years later that McCarthy's feelings towards Humphrey, Mondale—and Lyndon Johnson—had been profoundly affected by his disappointment at being passed over for the vice-presidential nomination in 1964. During one encounter at Atlantic City, McCarthy lashed out in anger at Mondale for his zealous service on Humphrey's behalf.

Mondale was impatient to sustain his career's momentum. Rather than risk his future on an uncertain party fight, he had forgone the chance to run for governor in 1962. Now another major opportunity was at hand and there was no telling when another would crop up. If he failed to capture the Humphrey seat, it was unlikely that there would be another risk-free chance for advancement. A prudent man, Mondale was ever mindful of his family responsibilities. He and Joan were the parents of three children now —a son, William, had been born in 1962. Maybe the time had arrived when he should earn some money. During the summer and autumn of 1964, Mondale talked of this option with increasing frequency to friends and political associates.

Meanwhile, party regulars were lining up behind Mondale's candidacy, although their intercession was of dubious value. An iron curtain seemed to have descended between Rolvaag and major elements of the party, due in large measure to the events of 1962 and the governor's conviction that DFL ranks were riddled with his personal detractors. As it turned out, Rolvaag was right. The fact that one of the conspirators from 1962—Lt. Gov. Sandy Keith—had his office right down the hall from the governor only fed Rolvaag's suspicion.

Rolvaag had nothing but good will for Mondale, despite the younger man's earlier flirtations with the Keith forces. If anything, that episode seemed to give Rolvaag a keen appreciation of Mondale's party loyalty and political reliability.

"I was aware of Fritz's normal interests in the governorship," Rolvaag said years later. "Why shouldn't he have been interested?"

Whatever resentment might have lingered in Rolvaag's mind was effectively erased by Mondale's willingness to continue doing for him what he had done for Freeman— serve as a surrogate for the governor at party functions in an attempt to bolster his standing with DFL activists.

There were other considerations in Rolvaag's mind, though, aside from Mondale's much appreciated loyalty and ability to bridge the gulf between the governor's office and the party. One was the high likelihood he would get licked if he appointed himself to the Senate. With one exception, governors elsewhere who had tried that ploy were quickly turned out of office by the voters. Having won one statewide election that was virtually too close to call, Rolvaag was too much of a realist to tempt fate. Another factor was his determination not to turn over the governorship to Sandy Keith. Yet a third reason had to do with what Rolvaag later described as his first "glimmerings" of a drinking problem that ultimately was to shorten his public career.

In private, Humphrey was almost as circumspect about the appointment as he was in public. Despite his longstanding friendship with Blatnik, Humphrey let the powerful congressman know his belief that the DFL would be better served by Mondale—a younger man with an existing statewide base. However, Rolvaag and Humphrey did not discuss the matter at length. Rolvaag recalled briefing Humphrey on the situation while the two men were alone in a car on an airstrip waiting for a plane to take Humphrey back to Washington. In a conversation about six months before his death, Humphrey recalled that on at least one occasion he tried by indirection to dissuade Rolvaag from appointing himself. Humphrey said he broached the subject by asking Rolvaag in a somewhat disapproving tone, "Is there any substance to the story that you might be thinking about getting yourself appointed to the Senate?"

Humphrey said he was assured by Rolvaag that that was not the case. It was the governor, Humphrey said, who brought up Mondale. At that point, Humphrey said, "I told him that I thought he'd be an excellent appointee, that he'd fit in very well, that he is part of a younger generation and even then we were thinking about how to broaden the base of the party. It really was a Rolvaag appointment. I don't think anyone should take credit away from Karl on this one."

Rolvaag, however, was kept indirectly aware of Humphrey's feelings. The vice-president-elect had many agents who were now lobbying the governor for Mondale. A politician in Rolvaag's tenuous electoral circumstances could not ignore entreaties that came from such a powerful source. Humphrey's advocacy, direct and indirect, was not an act of friendship but of political realism. Filling the Senate seat was a major political move. The consequences could be felt for a generation or more. Personal considerations were largely irrelevant. Indeed, if intimacy was the test, Humphrey's candidate would have been Blatnik, a counselor and ally in frequent Washington battles. It's not that Humphrey was cool to Mondale. Until the 1964 credentials battle, the two simply hadn't worked together on anything since 1948. The election that year removed Humphrey from the state—and from the practical day-to-day political concerns of Mondale's life. Freeman became the man on the scene who could make things happen. By the time the vacancy occurred, Mondale had proven that he, not Blatnik, would be the best long-term guardian of the DFL's interests. He was younger than Blatnik by seventeen years and better known statewide; it could be a long time before the Republicans would have a chance of capturing that Humphrey seat.

As time passed, Mondale began to feel more confident of his prospects. But there were dangers in taking Rolvaag for granted. A bulletin on a Twin Cities radio station shortly after the election reported that Humphrey had ordered Mondale's appointment and that the Mondales were looking for rental housing in the Washington area.

Rolvaag responded indignantly.

"I don't get my marching orders from Washington," he declared.

An imminent announcement had been expected, but Rolvaag threw everybody into confusion—and Mondale into a state of acute anxiety—by leaving abruptly for a vacation in the Bahamas.

A short time later, Mondale called his top political associate, Warren Spannaus, an aide in the attorney general's office. The Mondales were rushing to catch a night flight to Florida. They were traveling under an assumed name. While they were away, Mondale said, Spannaus should tell reporters that the couple was relaxing at the home of Joan's parents on a bluff outside Afton, a hamlet in the St. Croix River valley. The Mondales' actual destination was Ft. Lauderdale, where they would meet Rolvaag. The governor had a piece of political business to discuss, Mondale told Spannaus.

Several days later—on November 17, 1964—Rolvaag told a crowded news conference at the State Capitol that he had decided to appoint Walter F. Mondale to the U.S. Senate. Rolvaag's announcement answered a question that had been pervading Minnesota politics for nearly a year: who would be the winners, and who the losers, in the scramble for higher office that would inevitably follow Humphrey's elevation to national office? Mondale was clearly a winner. As his career continued its extraordinarily smooth ascent, Mondale crossed the threshold of state politics and entered an arena where he could become involved in the great issues of the day.

In getting to that point, Mondale defied a law of political gravity which requires that politicians climb upward with struggle and sacrifice against the weight of competing ambitions. It's a way of testing the intensity of a candidate's aspirations for the office he seeks. In their own careers, Hubert Humphrey, Orville Freeman, and Karl Rolvaag—like generations of other American politicians —had submitted themselves to the exacting demands of the political process, whereby only the most durable survive. They had advanced by confronting challenges and overcoming risks. All three of Mondale's sponsors had lost at least one election in learning how the game was played, but the first time Mondale faced the voters, he did so with the advantage of incumbency. His own political advancements had twice been secured by winning the vote of only one man. Freeman in 1960 and Rolvaag in 1964 had cast the only ballots that counted. The office was seemingly seeking the man.

Above all, Mondale had been lucky. No one could possibly have orchestrated the events that made his rise possible —Lord's resignation, the Sister Kenny scandal, the chain of events set in motion by the Kennedy assassination. But at each of these points, good fortune intersected with Mondale's intellectual and political gifts. Neither Freeman nor Rolvaag was obliged to pick Mondale; indeed, both had understandable reasons for passing him over. Their decisions were made in light of the alternatives. On both occasions, Mondale clearly emerged as the most qualified candidate.

As Humphrey put it, after reflecting on Mondale's career, "I think this is one of the great elements of mystery in Fritz's life. He has the uncanny good luck of being able to be at a certain point at a certain time, and the time and the point are both right for the circumstances."

Once installed as attorney general, Mondale proved that he merited Freeman's confidence by his high standards of professionalism and integrity. In retrospect, the Kenny scandal may seem to have been a gratuitous windfall, and consumer protectionism, a low-risk, safe issue. In fact, both were murky areas where Mondale could easily have stumbled. Instead, his performance was skilled, resolute, and innovative.

Mondale also worked assiduously to cultivate a protégé relationship with those above him on the political ladder. His style was such that Freeman, Rolvaag, Humphrey, and other party seniors would find him politically reliable and personally compatible. Mondale's was the demeanor of a reasonable man who could be counted on not to offend or embarrass his allies. He possessed two of the most valued of all political gifts—caution and good judgment.

His handling of the Mississippi challenge also demonstrated an attribute that was to become the defining characteristic of his Senate career. Despite the clear moral issue at stake in the challenge, Mondale had no trouble resisting the temptation to throw political caution to the winds, even though such a move might have made a dramatic point about the nature of racism in Mississippi at the time. Instead, he worked on enlarging the compromise that would be acceptable to the center of the party and, in so doing, retained the good will of moderates on both sides of the issue, while disappointing those whose interests or grievances could not be satisfied by incremental reforms.

"The thing that is most evident about Mondale is that he

is nonabrasive," Humphrey said. "He was not a polarizer. He coupled all this with what was obvious talent: He was young, he was articulate, he was intelligent and clean-cut. He kept filling the bill. It's most amazing."

10

A New Face in the Senate

Washington 1965—the capital of an exuberant Great Society; the nerve center of a global, geopolitical giant; the massive, colorless workplace of an impenetrable bureaucracy; the new home of Walter and Joan Mondale. Their rented, split-level rambler in Chevy Chase was filthy when the family arrived on New Year's Eve, twenty-four hours after Gov. Karl Rolvaag had signed the papers officially installing Mondale in Hubert Humphrey's old Senate seat. The oven smelled of leaking gas, the dishwasher didn't work, the kitchen sink was clogged, and the bathroom shower wouldn't drain. Immediately after their arrival, Mondale had gone to the Senate to sign the necessary papers and confer with officials. When he returned to the house, everyone had gone to bed. Somehow, the kids had locked the bedroom where Joan was sleeping. Mondale spent his first night as a resident member of the Senate establishment on his living-room couch.

As she unpacked their personal belongings, Joan could not avoid comparing the modest dimensions of her new surroundings with the roomy Victorian house they had bought while Mondale was attorney general. In that house, located in one of Minneapolis's oldest and most gracious neighborhoods, Joan had once entertained seventy-one guests at a sitdown dinner in honor of composer-conductor

Henry Mancini. In their haste to find a house in Washington, they had chosen a suburban location, thinking they would find good schools—an important issue since Teddy was now seven, Eleanor almost five, and William two.

She was again disappointed. The schools didn't measure up to Minneapolis's, and the neighborhood was dull. Her merged interests in art and politics had led to an intensive involvement in DFL affairs and in her husband's campaigns. These facets of her life, in turn, had opened up a range of fascinating and diverse friendships in Minneapolis. Now, as a newly arrived senator's wife, she would try to brighten up conversation at Washington dinner parties with interesting anecdotes about DFL politics in Minneapolis. She recalled one glassy-eyed dinner partner inquiring blankly, "Milwaukee?"

On the positive side, there was the shining moment on Mondale's thirty-seventh birthday—January 5, 1965—when he had been sworn in. It was especially meaningful because Mrs. Claribel Mondale was in the gallery to watch as her son took his place in a back row—newly installed to handle the Democratic majority swept into office on the LBJ tidal wave of 1964. Since leaving its ancestral home 110 years earlier, the Mundal family had known years of poverty and hardship—the lockjaw, Reverend Mondale's various disappointments, his illness and death. For one of its descendants, at least, the odyssey had now led to a Senate seat alongside Fred Harris of Oklahoma, Joe Tydings of Maryland—and Bobby Kennedy of New York.

Once that moment was over, Mondale had to come to grips with the reality of Senate life. He coveted a seat on the Judiciary Committee but lost out to a conservative from Florida, George Smathers. Then, instead of pushing vigorously for another prestige committee—like Appropriations, Finance or Armed Services—he accepted assignments to committees on agriculture, on space, and on banking. Confined to these low-visibility forums, Mondale found little room for legislative maneuvering.

It was a dismal beginning—quite a contrast with his stunningly successful debut nearly five years earlier as attorney general. Things did not improve immediately, either. He had been spoiled by that earlier experience. The issues—Sister Kenny, consumer protection, antitrust lawsuits—had been ideally suited to state politics; there had been strong media interest and almost immediate feedback. His contact with the party and its grassroots was constant and direct. He knew and loved the state, and could sense its moods better than anyone else, perhaps even Humphrey. From his office in St. Paul, he could choose words and actions to suit the occasion; he was never out of touch. Surrounding him was a young, energetic, intelligent, loyal, and ambitious staff who protected his interests, performed chores, and supplemented his sources of political intelligence. He could not have asked for a more ideal political launching pad.

Now he was a lowly freshman in an institution that exalted seniority. The procedures were arcane, the legislative issues, extraordinarily complex. Mondale's keen political instincts helped him understand the way coalitions had to be built, but the process was infinitely more demanding, intellectually and politically, than anything he had known before. His failure to win the Judiciary assignment had been an initiation rite. It told him something about the clubbiness of the older members—mainly Southerners—who chaired the committees and formed a core of power organic to the institution. Smathers, a fourteen-year Senate veteran at the time, not only had a fistful of IOUs but he also could claim a record of conservative orthodoxy that was fully acceptable to the hierarchy. He would not be an ideological threat on the Judiciary Committee. The relationships that mattered were not laid out on an organizational chart; they could be learned only by experience.

Mondale had talked at some length to Humphrey about

what to expect in Washington. The older man had been happy to offer avuncular advice born of his own experience sixteen years earlier when—also as a thirty-seven-year-old freshman—he had offended the Senate establishment with his brash assertiveness and loquacious liberalism. Mellowed by the years, Humphrey told his protégé that Southerners don't take philosophical differences personally—if you don't. It was important to be on friendly terms with men like James Eastland and John Stennis, the two powerful Democrats from Mississippi, because you could never tell when you would want to ask them for a favor. They could help a young senator in all sorts of ways and yet no one would feel as though he were giving any ground. There was a time to fight and a time to be amiable. Mondale appreciated the advice, although it was not in his nature anyway to step on his elders' toes. He did not find it particularly difficult to become friends with those who espoused views—particularly on civil rights—that had always been anathema to Mondale.

Indeed, if anyone expected to see a latter-day version of Hubert Humphrey walk through the swinging doors on to the Senate floor in January, 1965, they were sorely disappointed. As became apparent during the Mississippi challenge, Mondale—both temperamentally and politically—was inclined not to lead frontal assaults but rather to work within institutions by seeking to reconcile moderates and isolate extremists. Times had changed since Humphrey, aflame with impatience at the nation's slow pace of social progress, had entered the Senate. In 1948, there did not seem hours enough in the day, or dollars in the Treasury, to right all the wrongs then agitating Humphrey. Outspoken, abrasive, unawed, Humphrey violated traditions and stepped on toes in his haste to write a liberal legislative agenda. But after a decade and a half of prodding, a nation seemingly inert and insensitive to civil rights had started to move—slowly at first but with gathering speed. The challenge by 1965 was to conserve earlier gains and to sustain the momentum.

Still, there was a kind of culture shock for Mondale in coming to the Senate. Over-confident and cocky, he had figured it would be easy to make his mark, but he soon discovered otherwise. For the first time in four years, his name disappeared from its accustomed place of prominence in the Minnesota media, as he found himself struggling with a dull bunch of back-bench issues. Within the Agriculture Committee, Mondale was the main spokesman for the administration's price-support program for feed grains, a position which put him in conflict with his chairman, Sen. Allen Ellender of Louisiana. Mondale also tangled with his friends in organized labor over his opposition to the requirement that 50 percent of the American wheat sold to Communist countries be carried in American ships. In both cases, Mondale pursued objectives important to a key voting bloc—farmers. He calculated that the benefits from currying favor in rural areas outweighed the costs of either angering Senate leaders or disappointing his labor friends. He polished his liberal credentials by speaking out strongly against the poll tax during the debate over the 1965 Voting Rights Act. He also identified himself as a vocal opponent of Sen. Everett Dirksen's unsuccessful attempt to amend the Constitution in order to negate the U.S. Supreme Court's one-man, one-vote decision on legislative reapportionment.

Mondale didn't kid himself. He knew it was an indifferent record, even for a rookie senator. He also did not have the luxury of a full six-year term to make up for his lackluster debut. The appointment was good only for the unexpired balance of Humphrey's term, meaning that Mondale would have to earn the right to retain the seat in the 1966 election. Along with his youth and popularity within the party, Mondale's proven abilities as a statewide candidate had been one of the major reasons why he had had Humphrey's support for the Senate appointment. Mondale found it disconcerting to be a thousand miles away from his constituency. Bob Hess recalled that Mondale would telephone him about once a week for a political status report and to inquire of the veteran labor leader whether he should be returning to Minnesota for more frequent political fence-mending trips.

"He was antsy and nervous. He was grasping to find *his* issue—the one great issue he needed to become a great senator," Hess said. "He was very impatient because he couldn't find it, and I kept saying, 'What's wrong with versatility?' "

Mondale's Senate staff felt the pressure more acutely than anyone else except Mondale himself. At times, his expectations seemed naïve and unrealistic. He would talk, for example, about how he needed to hire "a Sorensen"—someone who could do for his image what Ted Sorensen's soaring prose had done for John Kennedy. The pace in the office was feverish. "He was just go, go, go all the time," said one aide, Phil Byrne, who had worked on Mondale's attorney general's staff. "I think he drove himself and everybody for those two years after his appointment probably as hard as he had ever pushed anyone in his whole life. It was a much more intense, time-consuming, hard-driving work relationship than it had ever been in the attorney general's office."

For many, Mondale's Senate office was not an easy or pleasant place to work during those early years on Capitol Hill, partly because he did little to establish a bond of warmth or intimacy with those under him. If anything, he was even more aloof and impersonal than he had been as attorney general, when his closest staff associates were talented lawyers close to his own age. It was not uncommon to hear members of his Senate staff mutter unhappily, "We might as well be working for him in Minnesota."

Just as their predecessors on the attorney general's staff

did, Mondale's staff aides urged their boss to walk through
the staff work areas in the morning rather than popping
into his office through a private door.

"It was a disaster," recalled one former aide. "The idea
was to stop by people's desks and make small talk. He just
wasn't good at it. But to make matters worse, he would paw
through their papers, and once he came across a letter that
should have gone out days earlier and he wound up chew-
ing the person out. So instead of being happy to see their
boss up close and informal, the staff was terrified he'd come
through again."

Some DFLers were surprised when Mondale failed to
offer a top Washington staff job to his closest political associate, Warren Spannaus. Spannaus had a relaxed, informal
manner that seemed a perfect complement to Mondale's
hard-driving intensity. Spannaus was politically gifted, too,
and he would later win the attorney general's office in his
own right. "Mondale has a tendency to pigeonhole people," said one DFLer with extensive Washington staff experience. "He saw Warren as a Minnesota political type and
he wanted a Washington staff. He didn't realize Warren
would have been perfect for his needs."

Spannaus himself was irked by the slight. During a going-
away party in late 1964, Spannaus uncharacteristically expressed his pique to Mondale. Later in the party, Mondale
tried to make amends by thanking him for a set of luggage
purchased by the staff as a going-away present.

"They even have padded handles," Mondale said, pointing to the suitcases.

"So what?" Spannaus retorted. "You'll never carry
them."

Cold, impersonal, exacting—he was a boss who demanded that he be overprepared on all issues confronting
the Senate as insurance against being embarrassed by a
question he couldn't fully answer.

That was the tense, uptight Mondale, trying to cope with

the pressures of high elective office. There was also the irrepressible Mondale for whom humor remained an essential trait and a formidable political asset. When the Washington Press Club assembled in 1966 for its traditional midwinter congressional banquet, many of its influential members formed their first impressions of Mondale by listening to his droll, off-the-cuff, irreverent discourse on the subject, "Resolved: It's easier to be appointed than elected to the U.S. Senate."

Mondale's congenial wit and accommodating nature helped overcome the prickly reserve of Southerners like Richard Russell of Georgia towards Northern liberals. During one encounter, Russell offered Mondale a superb Cuban cigar—a rare delicacy Russell customarily shared only with trusted friends.

Mondale stepped back in mock dismay.

"Dick, I'm shocked a good, patriotic American like you would deal with Communist merchandise," Mondale said.

"Damn, you're just like all them other Yankees," Russell retorted. "You jump to conclusions. We know nothing about where this cigar came from. All we know is what's written on the wrapper."

Enduring the tedium of a long-winded debate one afternoon, Mondale was occupying his time by signing photographs of himself in company with a large group of constituents. His seatmate, Robert Kennedy, impulsively reached over at one point and grabbed several of the prints. "You're a fine group and I'm with you all the way," he scrawled, followed by his signature.

"That's great; I appreciate that," Mondale told Kennedy. Then, in a gibe at Kennedy's standing as the nation's foremost Catholic politician, Mondale added, "You'll go over big with Planned Parenthood of Minnesota."

There was yet another side of Walter Mondale. One miserable March night in Minneapolis, a large group of senior citizens braved the cold weather to meet their junior sena-

tor. A Washington aide, used to being treated "like a typewriter or a piece of furniture" by his boss, was astonished
at the rapport that Mondale established with the audience,
as he shared with them his own frustrations over his
mother's entanglements with the Social Security Administration. Afterwards, Mondale relentlessly pushed his case-
workers until each problem reported that night had been
taken care of.

As the Eighty-ninth Congress convened for its second
session during the election year of 1966, Mondale was still
searching for a national issue that would vault him to prominence and assure his victory in the fall. When his press
secretary, a former Minneapolis newspaper reporter
named Dick Conlon, tried to persuade his boss to capitalize
on his earlier experience as attorney general in the area of
consumer protection, Mondale resisted. He felt consumer-
ism lacked political glamour. But Conlon and others on
Mondale's staff persisted. And so did a frequent visitor to
Mondale's offices in those days—Ralph Nader. Nader's ex-
posés were making auto safety one of the hottest topics on
the legislative agenda, and finally Mondale's interest was
rekindled. The idea for a specific piece of legislation glim-
mered during a chat in Minneapolis with Bill Mullin, his
former consumer-protection aide in the attorney general's
office. Mullin had been fascinated by the news that several
Minneapolis auto dealers had been ordered by a manufac-
turer to repair certain safety defects whenever a particular
model was brought into their garage.

"What about the fellow who never brings his car in?"
Mondale asked Mullin.

"I guess he's out of luck," Mullin replied. "He's driving
an unsafe car."

Two months later, Mondale introduced the Fair Warning
Act of 1966, a major legislative initiative to require auto
makers to notify car owners of dangerous defects. He
scored a solid triumph when the Congress accepted the

measure as an amendment to the Johnson administration's National Traffic and Motor Vehicle Safety Act, even though Mondale was not a member of the Senate Commerce Committee, which had jurisdiction over the issue. Mondale won the crucial support of the committee's chairman, Sen. Warren Magnuson of Washington, while Nader stoked the political fires with charges of new auto defects. When Mondale accused Detroit in April, 1966, of failing to warn millions of car owners that their vehicles were unsafe, the response was overwhelming. The volume of mail and telephone calls from all over the nation overwhelmed the office staff of this obscure Minnesota senator. One woman, about to leave on vacation in a 1961 Buick, wanted Mondale to reassure her that she would be safe on the road. Detroit's protests about the law's financial costs were swept aside. "We cannot continue to permit people to drive time bombs which can cause fatal or crippling accidents without warning," Mondale declared. "Human life is more important than corporate profits."

Meanwhile, internal warfare had erupted in the Minnesota DFL party. Discontent with Gov. Karl Rolvaag as a party leader had now ripened. Unlike the abortive draft-Mondale movement four years earlier, the anti-Rolvaag forces now had a willing power seeker. Instead of being a conspirator, Sandy Keith, the lieutenant governor, was the open challenger to Rolvaag's grip on the governorship in 1966. The party that Mondale had helped build was in shambles. Mondale watched from afar with a sense of helplessness. Seemingly, there was nothing either he or Humphrey could do to avert the fraternal bloodletting. It was amazing how quickly he had become irrelevant to the ongoing, practical life of the party. Rolvaag's appointment had converted Mondale into a remote figurehead—more of an ambassador from a distant kingdom than an indigenous party leader. The same thing had happened to Humphrey in 1948 when he left for the Senate, letting Freeman grasp practical control of the DFL. By the same token, Mondale was no longer in a position to sense and influence subtle shifts in the party's mood—to fine-tune the DFL to suit his own political needs. Like Humphrey, his name still evoked tremendous loyalty, but the rift within his political base alarmed him.

Mondale personally did not have to agonize over whom to support. He would, of course, back the man who had appointed him to the Senate—Gov. Rolvaag, but the topsy-turvy developments still left him acutely anxious about his own political situation. He realized that the election that fall would in many ways be the most crucial of his career—more so even than 1960, when he had been far less certain of his political skills. There would be no Sister Kenny case to help him out in 1966, however. Indeed, a scandal of similar dimensions was now embarrassing the Rolvaag administration. It involved a high-risk auto casualty firm, the American Allied Insurance Company, which went bankrupt in mid-1965. Eventually, the state insurance commissioner and sixteen others were indicted for bilking American Allied policyholders of $3.7 million in premiums. Amid the blizzard of charges and countercharges was the allegation that Mondale had ignored a state insurance examiner's report in August, 1964, that gave early warning of American Allied's financial problems. The Republicans also gleefully noted that Sandy Keith was a director of an American Allied subsidiary, although the evidence showed that he was merely a figurehead. Nevertheless, there were whispers throughout the campaign that Mondale and Rolvaag had allowed American Allied to go down the drain to embarrass Keith.

Far more serious to both Mondale and Rolvaag was the fact that a fund-raiser—working on behalf of both their campaigns—had accepted an illegal $2,000 corporate contribution from the man suspected of being the chief swindler in the American Allied case. The key question was

V.P. and Vice Premier Deng in Washington *(White House photo)*

With Anwar Sadat in Alexandria, Egypt
With Prime Minister Menachem Begin in Jerusalem *(White House photos)*

The Scheduled Monday Lunch

(White House photo)

Two Minnesota vice presidents

(White House photo)

whether Mondale knew the true origin of the contribution. The Republicans were determined not let the issue die. Mondale's integrity, never before challenged, was on the line.

The contribution had been solicited by a St. Paul lawyer and Rolvaag fund-raiser. Mondale's campaign officials never saw the $2,000 check and returned the money as soon as the receiver for the now-defunct insurance company alerted them as to its illegal source. Unfortunately, the answers never seemed to catch up with the volley of questions being fired by the Republicans. The scandal gained added momentum only days before the election when the Rolvaag fund-raiser went on trial, charged with violating the state's corrupt-practices act. Finally, late in the campaign, Mondale went on Sunday-night television to defend himself. His aides had never seen him so upset. His hands were fluttering, and his voice trembled and broke. He looked flushed. One assistant, a lawyer, thought to himself as he watched Mondale that honest men make the least credible witnesses when their integrity is challenged. They always overreact. In this case, the insinuations and accusations cut through the tough political crust Mondale had acquired from years in politics. More was at stake than his political position; his personal worth was involved—indeed, everything he had ever been taught, including his father's whipping when he had been caught filching from the collection plate. "You can make mistakes around here, but you can't lie or steal. Your integrity is everything," his father had told him.

What was being exposed was the seamy side of politics —fat-cat money, quid pro quos, under-the-table deals. Watching all this was his mother, Claribel, who had always been put off by the crasser rites of politics. Mondale knew that she would be particularly bothered by the fact that the entire unfortunate episode was centered on a fund-raising cocktail reception. The event was an intrinsic violation of the Methodist taboos against liquor and greed. His denials of complicity in any illegal deal had merely provoked more charges from his Republican adversary, who asserted, "We have good reason to believe Mr. Mondale was not telling the truth . . ."

"My opponent has virtually charged that I lied," Mondale told the Sunday-night news conference. "He has hit a new low in Minnesota politics. He has slandered my name and cheapened this campaign."

It was an overwrought performance. Several of Mondale's closest friends and aides—people like Warren Spannaus and Harry MacLaughlin, Mondale's former law partner—feared their young champion had blown the election. They recalled former Gov. Elmer Andersen's overreaction to Democratic charges of irregularities in his administration's highway program and wondered whether history was repeating itself.

Their worries were unfounded, or at least premature. On election eve, the Rolvaag fund-raiser was acquitted. And, despite the disarray among DFLers over the Keith-Rolvaag struggle, Mondale's personal standing in the state was unmatched by anyone except Humphrey. When he needed it most, the reserve of goodwill, built over the years by attending to the hard, undramatic tasks of politics, cushioned him against political adversity. And while Mondale's performance as a senator during the two preceding years might not have been studded with legislative victories, it had nonetheless reflected his usual painstaking attention to political detail. Mondale was also fortunate in having had Gene McCarthy as Minnesota's senior senator, even though the personal ties were not particularly close or warm. McCarthy, who had won a landslide reelection victory two years earlier, disdained the more mundane aspects of Senate politics. As a result, he had offered little competition in currying favor with constituents, and Mondale's office soon became the clearinghouse for announcements regarding government actions in Minnesota. Conlon, Mondale's press secretary, churned out an unending stream of press releases in which Mondale would proclaim the details of the latest pork-barrel project for Minnesota. Humphrey had been an enormously helpful expediter, and Mondale had called on him frequently whenever any Minnesota project had become bogged down in the bureaucracy. An inquiry from the vice president was almost always sufficient to get it going.

At one point in early 1966, Mondale had almost called off his first junket—a fact-finding trip to India as an Agriculture Committee member combined with a visit-the-troops stop in South Vietnam. The schedule conflicted with a prior commitment to speak in Moorhead, a small city in northwestern Minnesota. Mondale had agreed to go abroad only after his staff had arranged for him to address the Moorhead gathering over a trans-Pacific telephone hookup from the ambassador's residence in Saigon.

That kind of attentiveness to the voter paid off in 1966. While Rolvaag and several other DFLers were going down to defeat at the hands of Republicans, Mondale won his first election as a U.S. senator with 53.9 percent of the vote. It was Mondale's lowest victory margin in a statewide race but enough to sustain his career.

11

A Tough Assignment

Ralph Nader was startled. Was this really quiet, cautious Fritz Mondale saying these angry things? The man whom he had to prod into taking up politically easy issues like auto safety? "Hey, this guy is really angry," Nader thought. The two men were talking over dinner about the unleashed racial fury that—even at that moment—was devastating cities across the nation. "This country has got to change," Mondale declared, his fists clenched, voice throaty with emotion. "We're so goddamn rich we can build these spaceships and fight somebody else's war, but our cities are hellholes."

It was the summer of 1967. Certain things had changed in the Mondale family's life over that past year. Mondale had won an arduous election and could devote the next six years to improving his mediocre Senate record. That had been a postcampaign promise to some of his top aides and supporters. He had also moved the family out of the suburb where they had lived for the first two Senate years. The Mondales, along with the mortgage company, now owned an old stucco house in Cleveland Park, a gracefully aging Washington neighborhood, much like the one they had left behind in Minneapolis. Joan was happily involved in writing a book that would explore the interrelationships between art and politics—an outgrowth of a series of talks she gave across Minnesota to stir interest among women in working for the DFL. At the same time, their lives had been saddened by Claribel Mondale's death of cancer at the age of seventy-four.

As the Ninetieth Congress convened, Mondale's independence was circumscribed in one major area. He might carp privately to friends about the costs, but he remained publicly committed to supporting Johnson's war policies, in part out of loyalty to Humphrey. That was a commitment many would hold against Mondale as ignoble. Mondale himself would confess years later that his timidity in criticizing the administration was his single most serious mistake as a senator. But he was acutely aware of having come to Washington at least partly under Humphrey's sponsorship. Humphrey had seriously damaged his own standing within the administration in early 1965 by attempting to warn Johnson privately against the folly of adopting war policies that only aped those advocated a few months earlier by Barry Goldwater during the presidential campaign. The last thing Humphrey needed was a defection in the Senate by the man who was widely regarded as his protégé.

The cities were something else. Mondale's guts told him they were crying out for national leadership. Just as he had been with Nader, Mondale was in a dark mood when he arrived in Minneapolis to speak to the American Trial Lawyers Association in late July during its annual convention.

"Maybe America is as sick as it has ever been," Mondale said. "We can do nothing and accept the fact of growing rebellions and learn to live with it, or perhaps die with it. Or we can build walls around the ghettos and patrol those walls with troops. That is, commit ourselves to an armed police-state against the Negroes.

"As great Americans, I think we will require social order and social justice and serve social progress by giving the slum ghetto resident a stake in our society."

There were no quick fixes. But already the nation had

made great strides. Over the past decade, Congress had passed a series of civil-rights laws leveling long-standing discriminatory barriers and revolutionizing race relations. As a result, blacks were guaranteed the right to mingle freely with whites in public places, to vote, and to compete for jobs. And now, while charred buildings smoked in Detroit, Newark, and other cities, Mondale was working on one of the last great untouched issues on the civil-rights agenda—open housing. Politically, it was perhaps the most controversial. When the House had passed a watered-down open-housing bill in 1966, conservatives on the race question had had no trouble killing it in the Senate. Their tactic had been the filibuster—they simply talked the bill to death. Meanwhile, many of the bill's supporters had lost their seats in the off-year elections that autumn, as the balance in the Congress shifted to the right.

Notwithstanding the country's increasingly conservative mood, President Johnson revived the issue in his civil-rights message on February 15, 1967, asserting that open housing "is decent and right. Injustice must be opposed, however difficult or unpopular the issue." Several days later, a small group of senators, led by Phil Hart of Michigan, met on Capitol Hill to plan the strategy for passing Johnson's multifaceted civil-rights package. On one crucial point, there was very little disagreement: The country was not ready for open housing. That being the case, there seemed little point in tacking such a provision on to an omnibus bill. That would only complicate—and perhaps doom—the task of passing the other, less controversial, initiatives sought by the president. Gazing around the room for someone to offer a separate open-housing bill, Hart's eye fell on Mondale, the most junior senator present.

"Fritz, why don't you take it on?" Hart inquired.

Mondale readily agreed. It was an awesome, frightening assignment. But it was also an opportunity. Washington is an echo chamber in which disparaging remarks, secretly whispered, soon end up reverberating in the public ear. Mondale was not unaware of those who criticized him as one who wore a bleeding heart on his sleeve but would not back up his commitments by taking political risks. Gene McCarthy, still angry over Mondale's role in helping Humphrey capture the 1964 vice-presidential nomination, had welcomed Mondale to the Senate by describing his junior colleague to friends as a transparent politician, whose values had a mass-produced quality lacking either courage or subtlety. McCarthy said Mondale reminded him of "the new brand of Senate liberal. He's like the toothpaste in a plastic bag with a brush—you get it all at once."

Mondale and his principal Republican ally on open housing, Sen. Edward Brooke of Massachusetts, worked carefully through the long, violent summer to lay the groundwork for the bill that would outlaw discrimination in the selling and renting of most of the nation's 65 million housing units. Mondale and Brooke, the lone black in the Senate, won an early procedural victory when the bill was diverted from the Judiciary Committee, where Chairman James Eastland of Mississippi and a like-minded majority would have quickly buried it. Instead, their measure was referred to the Banking and Currency Committee, which had jurisdiction over housing legislation. The committee chairman, Sen. John Sparkman of Alabama, didn't like open housing any better than Eastland, but the membership was more liberal on racial questions. Since both Mondale and Brooke sat on the panel, Sparkman felt obliged to promise hearings on the bill.

That, at least, was a start toward building support for a civil-rights measure that, for the first time, would confront the indisputable fact that racial bias pervaded all sections of the country, north and south. In addition, the bill's sweeping scope—containing only a very minor exemption for religiously sponsored housing developments—would

almost certainly be perceived by opponents as a frontal
attack on the sanctity of neighborhoods and a threat to the
property values of millions of homeowners. It was shaping
up as a classic collision between property rights and human
rights.

The three days of hearings in late August were designed
to answer those charges and to show that the nation's highest ideals were at stake. A society that partitioned its citizens behind artificial and exclusionary barriers would be
fatally flawed. There could be no true racial, social, and
economic justice unless people were free to choose where
to live. As crusty George Meany, national head of the AFL-
CIO, told the senators, the Mondale bill was "absolutely
essential" in order to achieve the other collateral national
goals of desegregated schools and equal employment opportunity.

"Until open housing becomes an operating fact, much of
the statutory civil-rights progress of recent years . . . will be
no more than inoperative theory," Meany said bluntly.

The hearings behind them, Mondale and Brooke now
faced the procedural problem of bringing their bill to the
Senate floor. They had the support of a majority on the
committee but they also knew that Sparkman would never
permit a vote on the bill. As a Southern conservative, the
chairman had been as helpful as they could reasonably
expect. The rest was up to them. They bided their time.
There was nothing else they could do.

In late December, Mondale reported back to the civil-
rights caucus. He had carried open housing further than
anyone in the group thought possible or likely. Rather than
quietly bury it, Mondale had worked for the president's
proposal. Now he had a strategy. Since he could not bring
a separate bill to the floor over Sparkman's opposition,
Mondale's idea was to present the open-housing plan as an
amendment to what remained of the president's civil-rights
proposal. The White House bill, already passed by the

House, would be awaiting Senate action when Congress returned from its long holiday recess. The measure was basically aimed at protecting civil-rights workers from initimidation and harassment. Mondale was well aware of the reasons for dumping open housing from the bill in the first place, but he felt the situation had changed. He had built a case for open housing, as was indicated by the willingness of a majority of the Banking Committee to sign a document summarizing the findings of the hearings. Protecting civil-rights workers was important, but open housing was more important. With a presidential election looming in the fall and a possible change in the nation's leadership, it might be years before Congress would have another opportunity to pass open housing. Mondale even told the caucus he was—reluctantly—willing to weaken his proposal somewhat by exempting those who live in their house but rent out up to four rooms or apartments. Known as the "Mrs. Murphy exemption," the change would reduce the bill's coverage to about 91 percent of the nation's housing.

Mike Mansfield, Senate majority leader from Montana, was peeved. He had been unable to break the previous year's filibuster of an open-housing bill that covered only 40 percent. "I don't think we have the votes for an open-housing amendment," Mansfield told interviewers the day before the Senate reconvened. What point was there in jeopardizing a limited but necessary civil-rights bill with Mondale's albatross? Mansfield was supported by Ramsey Clark, Johnson's attorney general. Even Phil Hart, perhaps the most dedicated civil-rights fighter in the Congress, gently suggested to Mondale that perhaps the timing was bad.

Mondale and Brooke discussed the situation. As a low-ranking senator, Mondale did not relish the idea of crossing his majority leader, but other interests were at stake. It might be true that the less urgent civil-rights objectives would be jeopardized by their amendment, but it was also true that open housing would never become a reality unless pressure was maintained. In addition, the Leadership Conference on Civil Rights—an umbrella group comprising about 115 labor, church, civil-rights, and civic groups—was heavily involved in the open-housing struggle by now. Its chief lobbyist, Clarence Mitchell, who was also the Washington head of the National Association for the Advancement of Colored People, was reporting inroads among the Republicans. That was especially important, because the key to ultimately passing any controversial civil-rights measure in the Senate lay with Everett Dirksen, the Republican minority leader. Dirksen's opposition a year earlier had been fatal to open housing. But Dirksen could be swayed, if enough other GOP votes could be won. There was also a surprising lack of lobbying on the part of the natural opponents of open housing. The real-estate interests, which had led earlier attacks on open housing, were not taking the latest move seriously. Finally, towards the end of January, Hart was convinced by Mitchell that the time had come for an all-out push. With Hart finally at his side, Mondale introduced his open-housing amendment on February 6.

By then, debate on the civil-rights bill had dragged on for nearly three weeks. Immediately, the battle's focus shifted. Open housing became the issue. As the amendment's floor manager, Mondale found himself going up against a formidable foe. The leading strategist for the anti–open-housing forces was Sen. Sam Ervin, a cherubic-looking North Carolina Democrat with a back-country drawl, a reputation as the Senate's leading constitutional lawyer, and a firm mastery of Senate procedures. Both knew the battle would be won or lost on cloture—a filibuster-killing motion. In 1968, the cloture rule, first adopted by the Senate in 1917, required a two-thirds affirmative vote of all senators answering the roll call. If all members were to vote on the eventual open-housing cloture motion, Mondale would need the support of sixty-seven out of the hundred senators to shut up the opposition. It was a tough assignment. There had been fifty-eight cloture votes in fifty-one years; seven had been successful. Cloture had been attempted thirteen times on clear-cut civil-rights issues; it had carried only twice.

The outcome of the first cloture vote showed that Mondale and Brooke's legislative spadework had not been in vain. Fifty-five senators voted for cloture, seven short of what would have been required on that particular vote. Thirty-seven voted in opposition. Compared with the cloture vote two years earlier, the tally showed growing support for open housing, even though the Mondale amendment was considerably tougher than the earlier proposal.

The gap was still wide. The attempt to close it would be time-consuming and, quite possibly, futile. The day after the cloture vote, Mansfield, the majority leader, moved "with regret" to kill Mondale's amendment. Mansfield said that the Minnesotan was engaging in a doomed venture that could only endanger the other carefully crafted civil-rights proposals in the pending bill. It was time to get on to other business. The Senate disagreed. Open housing was kept alive, as the Senate voted down Mansfield's motion to table the Mondale-Brooke initiative. Four senators —two Democrats and two Republicans—who had voted against Mondale on cloture now supported the attempt to keep open housing alive.

Even more significant—and more surprising—was the message Mondale's supporters received following Mansfield's unsuccessful attempt to clear the calendar of open housing. Everett Dirksen, the eloquent Republican minority leader from Illinois, was ready to negotiate. His troops were restless. Senate Republicans, under intense pressure from civil-rights lobbyists, were moving in increasing numbers to support open housing. Six more members of the Grand Old Party supported cloture in 1968 than two years earlier. Dirksen felt he could not afford to be left behind.

For the next several days, Mondale courted Dirksen assiduously. It was an obligatory ritual calculated to help Dirksen execute a dignified political about-face. The point of the charade was to cast Dirksen as the man of the hour: He alone could bring order out of the chaos on the Senate floor and assure victory for the civil-rights forces. It had happened four years earlier when Humphrey shamelessly flattered Dirksen in order to secure passage of that year's monumental civil-rights law. Timing was the key. If there was to be a breakthrough on open housing, Dirksen wanted to be at the president's elbow as he signed the bill.

The civil-rights forces were ecstatic about the outcome of the negotiations. Mondale described the compromise as a "miracle," given the emotional and political obstacles involved. After considerable bluster about making the open-housing proposal "more workable," Dirksen wound up insisting on only one change exempting another 10 percent of the nation's housing units from the requirements of the revised Mondale plan. One other concession did not need discussing, because it was understood from the outset to be part of the price of Dirksen's support. The amendment would bear the name of the senior senator from Illinois.

The fight was not over, however. While his opposition would have assured defeat, Dirksen's support did not guarantee victory. In the midst of bargaining with the minority leader, Mondale and his allies lost a second cloture vote, thirty-six to fifty-six, six less than required under the formula. Open housing had picked up the support of only one senator between the first and second cloture roll calls. But the defeat was not unexpected, since Dirksen was still on the opposing side.

Expectations of victory were high when Mansfield called for a third cloture vote on March 1. It was no longer just a liberal Democrat and a black Republican who were asking the Senate to accept open housing. Backing them up now was the Republican floor leader, well known as a staunch defender of property rights. Even that was not enough, though. Mondale's heart sank as the roll was called. Dirksen had managed to switch only two other Republicans, one of them his son-in-law, Howard Baker of Tennessee. In the cloakroom afterwards, there was speculation about the vote's significance. Dirksen was seen as having suffered a humbling personal defeat; his power was seemingly on the wane. Open housing was in grave danger and possibly doomed. Mansfield, his patience now at an end, made it clear that he would allow only one more "go for broke" vote and that then it would be time for the Senate to move on to something else.

In the late afternoon gloom, a small group of senators from the civil-rights caucus and key aides gathered for a final strategy session in Mondale's office. Lists of names were passed around, as they pondered their problem. Where would the additional votes come from? One was easy. Sen. Albert Gore, a Tennessee Democrat, had voted for cloture the first two times, but switched on the third try because he said he felt the Senate needed more time to digest the compromise. Another possible convert was a Kansas Republican, Sen. Frank Carlson, who had indicated he might vote for cloture if his support was needed. But that still left open housing several votes shy of survival. Finally, Mondale hit his desk with his fist and headed out the door to find Hubert Humphrey. It was now time for the administration to join the trench warfare. For the next twenty-four hours, Mondale and Humphrey worked on wavering senators but, as the vote neared on March 4, they still needed at least two more votes.

"Call the president," Humphrey said.

Lyndon Johnson was returning from Puerto Rico aboard Air Force I when Mondale got him on the telephone. The president understood the situation immediately. Joe Califano, Johnson's top domestic-affairs adviser, made sev-

eral strategic calls to political supporters of one key Democrat, Sen. E. L. Bartlett of Alaska. The plane was circling
Andrews Air Force Base by the time he was finished. Then,
as Califano gripped a table in the president's cabin, Johnson placed two calls himself. One was to Bartlett. The other
was to Sen. Howard Cannon, a Nevada Democrat who opposed cloture as a matter of principle. A defender of unlim-
ited debate as a means of protecting the rights of small
states, Cannon voted for cloture once in his career in order
to help save the 1964 civil-rights bill. Open housing would
be his second.

Hours later, the Senate convened. The galleries were
packed. No more debate was necessary. The issues were
firmly fixed in everyone's mind and all that remained was
to count the votes. As the roll call wound to its conclusion,
Mondale and his allies were one vote shy of cloture when
Bartlett approached the clerks tallying the vote at the desk
in the front of the chamber.

"Aye," he said, unleashing a moment of exhilaration and
triumph in the galleries and on the floor. The filibuster was
broken. With the opposition in full retreat, the Senate went
on to approve a civil-rights bill that contained the first
open-housing provision to pass that chamber in the twen-
tieth century. The vote was seventy-one to twenty. The
House did likewise about a month later, sealing Walter
Mondale's most significant achievement in three years as a
U.S. senator.

The open-housing fight stamped Mondale as a serious
legislator. For the first time, he now commanded real respect within Capitol Hill's clannish little world of politicians, lobbyists, aides, and reporters. He could no longer
be dismissed as just another pretty liberal face. One power
group in particular was impressed. For all their ideological
differences, Southerners had by now grown to admire
Mondale's professionalism, skill, and intelligence. As connoisseurs of the legislative craft, they were prepared to

accept him as a coequal, despite his role on open housing. Mondale was shocked and flattered the first time J. S. Kimmitt, secretary for the majority, appeared at his elbow late one afternoon and whispered that "Jim" wondered if Mondale would care to join him and some of the boys for a drink in a back room.

"Jim" was none other than James Eastland, chairman of the Senate Judiciary Committee, implacable foe of civil rights and guardian of the very political establishment in his home state of Mississippi that Mondale had successfully attacked during the credentials battle of the 1964 Democratic National Convention. No one better epitomized the conservative Southern patriarchy than Jim Eastland, plantation owner from Sunflower County, home of Fanny Lou Hamer. It would have been hard to have imagined two more dissimilar types, and yet a curious friendship developed between Mondale and Eastland. Implacable foes on almost every human-rights issue, they still could enjoy each other's company in the clubby atmosphere of Kimmitt's office. There, they would rib each other, occasionally bargain over an issue, swap political tales, and discuss their profession. It was Eastland's preserve. Other senators would drift in, but Mondale became a regular.

By every empirical standard, Mondale had proven himself an energetic, dedicated liberal with a deep commitment to New Deal traditions and a philosophy of government activism. Despite the stubborn opposition of powerful vested interests, Mondale played a key role during the Ninetieth Congress in cracking down on slaughterhouses that had been exploiting a legal loophole to sell diseased and putrid meat to retailers. Mondale also collaborated with a low-ranking Republican member of the Banking Committee, Sen. Charles Percy of Illinois, to enact a mortgage-subsidy program that would enable 480,000 low-income families to purchase their own homes. Mondale's concerns about redressing the social and economic balance in favor of the disadvantaged pleased his old friends in Americans for Democratic Action. An ADA report card placed him in a select group of ten senators who voted correctly on ADA issues over 92 percent of the time during the 1967 session. The following year, he won a perfect score from the political analysts for the AFL-CIO. On the other hand, Americans for Constitutional Action—the right wing's answer to ADA—gave Mondale a zero for his work during the 1968 session.

From a more neutral perspective, voting studies by *Congressional Quarterly,* an independent research and reporting service, showed that Mondale was among those senators who voted most consistently in support of President Johnson's programs and in opposition to what *CQ* defines as the conservative coalition—a voting alliance of Republicans and Southern Democrats in Congress. Other *CQ* analyses demonstrated that Mondale could be counted on to support proposals for expanding the federal role in American life, and that he was a strong party loyalist on key issues.

12

HHH and the War: A Delicate Balance

By 1968, Walter Mondale felt comfortable with his record on domestic issues. He had no apologies to make. The policies he had pioneered as attorney general rested comfortably on his conscience. As a senator, he was a liberal, a progressive, a reformer, a believer in human dignity. Perhaps he had only touched a few people in small ways, but at least he had been true to himself.

Foreign policy was a different matter. Unlike the immediate post–World War II era, global political issues seemed ambiguous and complex to the new young senator from Minnesota. What a change from the early 1950s, when policy choices involved such easily understood options as the Marshall Plan, the containment of Communist aggression, and the Korean War. The ADA, the Democratic party, Truman—all agreed Communism was no joke. The battle for control of the DFL in 1947 and 1948 left no doubts in Mondale's mind on that score. Like Humphrey, Mondale's reflexive anticommunism was hardened by the soft-on-Communism charges that were flung at many domestic liberals after mainland China fell in 1949 to Mao Tsetung's Red armies. These factors, together with his political fealty to Humphrey, made his support of the war predictably certain when he arrived in the Senate in 1965. A personal briefing by Lyndon Johnson several months after

Mondale's swearing-in cemented his loyalty. "I have never been more impressed by a man," Mondale said later. "I have great confidence in his handling of this matter."

Mondale would later regret that allegiance in a way that he would never regret a vote or a commitment on a domestic-policy matter. On the most significant issue of the 1960s —one that intermingled questions of morality and national interest—Mondale waffled. Privately, he was troubled by doubts about the Johnson administration's war policies. Publicly, he was a loyal soldier. Neither committed hawk nor committed dove, Mondale's confusion was curious considering how frequently his mind focused on that early parental admonition: "Your integrity is everything." Put to the test on the war issue, Mondale sought political safety by developing a position built out of loyalty to Humphrey.

By April 27, 1968, however, Mondale had become sharply aware of the limitations of that commitment. It was on that date that Humphrey declared his candidacy for president before a mob of supporters that overflowed a huge ballroom in Washington's Shoreham Hotel. Humphrey was greeted by a thunderous chant: "We want Hubert, we want Hubert, we want Hubert." Grinning broadly, Humphrey clasped his hands high in a victory salute and shouted back, "You've got me, you've got me."

Still, the moment seemed flawed. The year 1968 was not the best of times to proclaim the politics of joy—as Humphrey had just done—and may well have been the worst of times. Lyndon Johnson's shocking decision a month earlier not to seek another term in the White House demonstrated how seriously polarized the nation had become over Vietnam. Less than a week after LBJ's bombshell, Martin Luther King was gunned down in Memphis. The resulting riots spread to within blocks of the White House. The deepening dissension within the Democratic party mirrored the country's malaise. First Humphrey's old ally from DFL politics, Gene McCarthy, and then Robert Kennedy were drawn into the Democratic campaign. Now each was attracting growing and impassioned constituencies determined to seek new leadership for a nation mired in war, political dissent, and racial bitterness. Nonetheless, when Humphrey beckoned, Mondale responded, and now he was cochairman of United Democrats for Humphrey, along with Sen. Fred Harris of Oklahoma.

Contemptuously dismissed at first by one politician as "two brass boy scouts," Mondale and Harris soon won the respect of even the hard-bitten professionals in the Kennedy campaign. The son of a sharecropper and husband of a lovely Comanche, Harris was a stumpy man who exuded a sense of animal energy and dynamism. Jowly even at thirty-seven, his hair slicked back in an oily mane, Harris crisscrossed the nation that spring as Humphrey's huckster —cajoling, wheedling, humoring, and pressuring national convention delegates into giving the vice president a chance to become his own man. Mondale, meanwhile, concentrated on setting up an organization and laying the groundwork for a campaign that would secure the nomination without irreparably splitting the party. Or so he hoped. Humphrey's worst problem in 1968 was his image as a captive of Lyndon Johnson. Not only had LBJ's war policies divided the nation, but his general style as a political operator was under attack. First there was McCarthy, with his hordes of college volunteers out working the precincts for "clean Gene." Then followed Kennedy, in his shirtsleeves, plunging into crowds of adoring migrants. The imagery of these campaigns signaled a sharp break with the sleazy, special-interest, influence-peddling practices of the "old politics." Humphrey had to free himself from that legacy, without antagonizing the main-line Democrats—and their bosses—who were still the core of the party's strength.

For Mondale, that was more than just a pragmatic acknowledgment of a compellingly new political consciousness. The perception arose from the same part of his political soul that was humiliated and outraged when his Republican opponent in 1966 insinuated that he had accepted dirty campaign money from a suspected swindler. Mondale's reaction was similarly violent when a Johnson operative visited the United Democrats headquarters in Washington to tell of arrangements for a $40,000 payoff to public officials in West Virginia to secure their cooperation in the campaign. Mondale leapt to his feet in a rage, shouting, "Get out, get out, get out of this room." After the ashen-faced politico fled, a livid Mondale jabbed his finger at a staff member and said, through gritted teeth, "I don't ever want to hear that kind of talk again. Never."

Mondale and Harris pursued Humphrey's nomination with flair and skill. When the Democrats in Delaware selected a pro-Humphrey slate, the cochairmen picked up the national convention delegates in a jet for a round-trip ride to a thank-you party in Washington thrown by the vice president himself. A major battleground for Humphrey was Pennsylvania, which would send the third largest delegation—behind New York and California—to the convention. Almost as important as securing the delegates was a psychological war against Kennedy, who had won primaries in Indiana and Nebraska. The New York senator was headed for a West Coast showdown with McCarthy on May 28 in Oregon and June 4 in California. In a move that enraged the Kennedy forces, Mondale and Harris slickly persuaded the Pennsylvania Democratic leadership to schedule a delegation caucus on May 27—the day before the Oregon balloting—in order to canvass the presidential preferences of the delegates. Assured of the support of the bosses, the Humphrey forces were determined to underscore Kennedy's minimal strength in a major industrial state and to increase the vice president's momentum at a time when uncommitted delegates were pragmatically judging the drift of events.

Sen. Edward Kennedy of Massachusetts, the youngest of

the Kennedy brothers, was dispatched to Pennsylvania to take command of his brother's forces. There was only one problem. By the time he landed in Harrisburg, Mondale was installed in the Penn-Harris Hotel's presidential suite, where he personally lobbied the delegates, both in groups and singly. From his spies, Mondale learned that the Kennedy and McCarthy forces were planning a joint countermove to keep much of the delegation uncommitted, obscuring Kennedy's lack of support. In a hasty telephone call to a McCarthy strategist in Washington, Mondale warned that only Kennedy would benefit from the ploy. Moments before the caucus started, the strategist called McCarthy's top lieutenant in Pennsylvania and ordered him not to cooperate with the Kennedy camp. By the time the two-and-a-half-hour caucus was over, Humphrey had eighty-three firm commitments, with another twenty or so likely to wind up in his column. Kennedy could claim no more than six votes out of the 130 that would be cast by the Pennsylvania delegation. Humphrey was in Minnesota, celebrating his fifty-seventh birthday by carving up a cake decorated like a map of the United States, when Mondale and Harris called to give him the news of the caucus results. Al Barken, the chief national political operative of the AFL-CIO, grabbed the telephone and shouted, "Hubert, we did it, we did it, we did it for you." As they were rejoicing, Kenneth O'Donnell, a top national aide in the Kennedy camp, was holding a news conference to denounce the "Pennsylvania railroad" that had just run over the Kennedy bandwagon.

Delegate counts, however, became irrelevant after Kennedy's murder in a kitchen passage of Los Angeles' Ambassador Hotel on the night of his narrow victory over McCarthy in the California primary. Now it was simply a mechanical process of securing the nomination. As clearly as anyone, McCarthy now realized that his campaign was over—that the drift toward Humphrey was irreversible.

There yet remained a more difficult question. Could

Humphrey survive the convention in good enough shape politically to win the general election? Would the nomination be worth anything? It all went back to whether Humphrey could free himself of entanglement in Johnson's policies, in which case there was a chance he might unite the party. As Johnson's puppet, never. McCarthy and Kennedy had proven that the disaffection was too deep. Mondale knew he would have a fight on his hands—that Johnson would not willingly allow Humphrey to declare his independence. To strengthen his own position, Mondale insisted on a clear grant of authority from Humphrey for the running of the campaign. Mondale made the demand because of Humphrey's inability to say no to cronies whom he would permit to drift in and out of his campaigns, leaving everyone confused as to who was in charge.

Nonetheless, about a week after having been installed as cochairmen, Mondale and Harris were chagrined to discover that another Washington organization, Citizens for Humphrey, was raising and spending money. They also became aware of a third group located in Humphrey's vice-presidential office and headed by his chief of staff, Bill Connell. With some exceptions, Connell's group and Citizens for Humphrey took positions on issues considerably to the right of Mondale and Harris. Connell, in particular, urged Humphrey to mute his liberalism in an effort to preempt the center of the political spectrum. That strategy ignored the concerns of liberals who, Connell argued, could safely be taken for granted in the absence of a reasonable alternative.

The infighting was fierce. There was a bitter confrontation in Humphrey's office between Connell and Mondale-Harris over whether Humphrey should make an appearance at the Lincoln Memorial overlooking Resurrection City—the encampment for the Poor People's March. It was June, 1968, and the aggregation of welfare mothers, community organizers, ghetto militants, black separatists, civil-rights workers, and rabble-rousers was becoming a public irritant. Connell argued that it was needless for Humphrey to risk alienating white conservatives by dignifying a ragtag mob. Mondale and Harris, however, saw the issue in terms of Humphrey's liberation. They argued that he had strayed from his liberal origins and was now seen as the captive of special interests—of big business, big labor, the party bosses, and, ultimately, of Lyndon Johnson himself. How could he convince a nation of cantankerous and skeptical voters if he could not convince himself of the nobility of his motives and values? So, persuaded by his two young friends, Humphrey made the visit. Similarly, Humphrey's speeches on domestic policy rang with renewed concern for social justice. By appealing to his lifelong ideals, the cochairmen had weaned Humphrey from the temptation to invoke strident racial code words like "law and order" and "crime in the streets."

However, the major issue was the war. By 1966, America's involvement had been escalated sharply. Like other senators, Mondale was having to explain why it was necessary to send thousands of young American men to their death in the hostile jungles and rice paddies of a backward Southeast Asian country. The political ground under the administration's Vietnam policy was shifting. Mondale played no public role in the early stage of the growing debate, but privately he was beginning to doubt the policy he had so loyally endorsed. When Duane Scribner, a University of Minnesota teaching assistant, met with Mondale in late 1966 before being hired for the top staff job in Washington, the war was the first subject they discussed.

Scribner had barely settled in his chair when Mondale asked, "How do you feel about the war?"

"I don't know how I feel," Scribner admitted.

"Neither do I," Mondale confided.

At another point, Mondale called Arthur Goldberg, Johnson's ambassador to the United Nations, in despair and told him he was considering breaking with the administration over Vietnam. Goldberg attempted to calm Mondale by putting him in touch with Joseph Sisco, an assistant secretary of state.

"I called Joe and spent a lot of time with him. His advice was to just stay cool for a while and there were going to be developments. This is the way we just kept going," Mondale said.

Ultimately it was Mondale's loyalty to Humphrey that held him in line. Chatting with Ralph Nader in his Senate office one day in 1967, Mondale interrupted the conversation to receive a telephone call from the vice president. After hanging up, Mondale turned to Nader and said, "Boy, he's taking so much abuse. He's so misunderstood."

He could not betray Humphrey, although that did not mean remaining mute. He repeatedly criticized the administration for failing to insist that the South Vietnamese government undertake a broad and effective program of social reform. He also spoke out when U.S. bombers strayed from narrow military objectives and embarked on missions that might kill civilians, endanger Russian shipping, or provoke the Chinese. In addition, Mondale publicly urged that the National Liberation Front, as the Viet Cong were officially known, be included in peace negotiations. A prior suggestion to that effect by Robert Kennedy in early 1966 was denounced by Humphrey, who likened the idea to "putting foxes in the henhouse."

If Mondale from time to time made dovish noises, he was still no dove. One issue cut across the debate: Anyone who did not support demands for an unconditional halt to bombing over North Vietnam was considered in league with Johnson. For all his agonizing over the war and its debilitating impact on the Johnsonian dream of a Great Society, Mondale could not cross the line and espouse the one step that the North Vietnamese said could lead to a negotiated political settlement.

Mondale's loyalty caused some to judge him harshly. After Mondale had an emergency appendectomy in early 1967, one DFLer remarked, "I hope they stuffed him with some guts before sewing him up."

Later that year, Mondale arrived at his alma mater, Macalester, to deliver a major speech defending his position on the war, only to be greeted by pickets with placards expressing the same dissatisfaction with his equivocating. "SEN. MONDALE, PEOPLE ARE DYING FOR YOU TO DECIDE," was one message. A couple of others read, "SEN. MONDALE, YOUR FENCE IS MOVING," and "ARE YOU A DOVE, HAWK, OR FLYING SQUIRREL?"

The exasperation was mutual. As Mondale told friends, "With those people, unless you fall on your sword, you're no damn good. Well, I don't intend to fall on my sword." His speech at Macalester that night was an attempt to bridge what he described as an "emotion gap," opened by the massive distrust and atmosphere of recriminations that was poisoning the political debate over the war. "I cannot see a world with only one issue and one position that can be taken on that issue," Mondale said. It was an apt and succinct formulation of Mondale's unhappiness over the disintegration of common civility in the country's political discourse.

The emotion gap showed no signs of closing. Nor was there any slackening in the war's murderous intensity. When Mondale appeared at the University of Minnesota, one theatrical professor leapt to a table and, throwing his arms wide in a gesture of supplication, pleaded, "Senator, from the bowels of Christ, I beseech you to make the president stop this madness."

Then, on January 30, 1968, the Communists took advantage of a ceasefire during Tet, the Vietnamese New Year, to mount a massive attack, striking at virtually every significant population center in South Vietnam. Before the Tet offensive had run its course, friends in both Minnesota and

Washington noted a subtle shift in Mondale's attitude. No end seemed in sight. The Communist strength had not been sapped despite the introduction of over 500,000 American troops, saturation bombing of military targets in the North, years of search-and-destroy missions in the South, and rural pacification. For the first time, Mondale privately began expressing fundamental doubts tinged with bitterness towards administration policy-makers. In one significant remark to a friend, Mondale said it was easy for political leaders to make brave combat decisions when their lives weren't in jeopardy. The friend became convinced that Mondale had decided before Johnson's withdrawal that it was time for a dramatic step to bring peace.

That was still Mondale's opinion on July 25, 1968, when he and Harris met privately with Humphrey to discuss a speech on Vietnam. The text was certain to draw headlines. Drawing on extensive staff work by some of the best foreign-policy brains available to the Democratic Party, Humphrey was prepared to declare his support for an unconditional bombing halt and a deescalation of the war. The two cochairmen were ecstatic.

"Don't change a word of it," Mondale told Humphrey, as he and Harris were leaving the vice president's ceremonial office just off the Senate floor.

As it happened, not a word was changed. The speech was preserved verbatim. It was just never delivered. Johnson pulled the leash tighter, and Humphrey spent the next several weeks with the draft in his pocket, its contents a secret to all but a few innermost advisers.

A similar fate befell a subsequent attempt to write a peace plank for the Democratic platform that would have the support of the more moderate backers of Humphrey, McCarthy, and the slain Robert Kennedy. The core of the proposal involved a call for an unconditional bombing halt and a ceasefire. Those had now become the basic elements of Mondale's own position on the war. Delicate negotiations to bring the various party elements into balance foundered on the eve of the convention. Alerted to what was afoot, Johnson was furious. If Humphrey was determined to repudiate the administration, then Johnson would have to repudiate him. That was the clear message from the LBJ ranch as delegates assembled in Chicago for the convention's opening session on August 26. With a sinking feeling of inevitability, Mondale watched as the last hopes for a united party—never more than a glimmer in any case—were snuffed by a renewed gust of suspicion, hostility, recrimination, and, ultimately, street violence.

"I have not been so relieved at getting away from a place since I left Saigon," Mondale said in Minneapolis several days after the convention's disharmonious conclusion. He had helped guide his old friend to the nomination but now it seemed a tattered prize. Despite some successes on domestic issues, Mondale never freed Humphrey from the clutches of others—particularly Johnson. He and Harris already had handed over much of the day-to-day operation of the campaign to Larry O'Brien, who had been one of Kennedy's top political aides before the shooting. Now O'Brien would be entrusted with the campaign's overall leadership. There was a hint of defeat in Mondale's voice when he said he would concentrate in the fall on producing a magnificent vote for Humphrey in Minnesota. Besides Humphrey's victory, all he now wanted, Mondale said, was to become the best possible U.S. senator he could be.

There was really nothing left for Mondale to do but declare his own independence on the most critical issue of the day. On September 17, he called for an unconditional bombing halt over North Vietnam.

"I think if we're serious about peace talks in Paris, we have to recognize that the talks are on dead center," Mondale said. "If we offer to stop the bombing . . . it may result in serious negotiations. One can only guess at that, but I think it's worth the risk."

Humphrey, campaigning in Rochester, New York, paused in the midst of a hectic day to respond. "Mondale," Humphrey said enigmatically, "is a good friend. . . . [He] has a right and responsibility to speak out and I welcome his view."

13

No Easy Solutions

Freddy was a nine-year-old ghetto kid when Mondale heard about him—a kid like thousands of others from fatherless homes. It was his mother who put food on the table, holding down different jobs at different times, but always working. She had to leave the younger kids home alone, while she went off to work and Freddy went to school. Lots of Freddy's friends in Washington came from such homes. While his classmates were eating lunch at school, Freddy would disappear. He wasn't supposed to leave the schoolyard but he would anyway, clutching a paper bag filled with his lunch and whatever else he could snitch from the food line when no one was looking. He would scamper home to share his lunch with his siblings. It held down the food bill, and besides, they were too young to fix lunch for themselves. Then he'd run back to school before anyone noticed he was gone.

One lunch hour, Freddy was run over by a truck and killed. Newspapers wrote stories about him, and for a brief moment a ghetto boy was singled out for special attention.

Mondale never forgot that story. Freddy was very much on his mind when Sid Johnson walked into Mondale's office in early January, 1969, for a job interview before being hired as a poverty and education specialist. Mondale talked mostly about "cheated children." His meaning became apparent when he stood to gaze out the window, telling Freddy's story as he did so. When he turned back, his eyes were glistening. "Kids are being mutilated," Mondale told Johnson. Poverty, malnutrition, bad schools, medical neglect—all were ravaging their bodies and spirits. He said he was prepared to work seriously on the problem. It would be a good investment. Maybe candidates for future welfare rolls could be turned into productive citizens instead. More importantly, it was the only moral and humane thing to do.

The intensity of Mondale's feelings reflected a maturing of his political commitments. Since coming to the Senate in late 1964, Mondale had been searching for an issue that would be his alone. Now, four years later, Mondale was on the verge of a unique and solitary expedition into largely uncharted legislative areas where he would confront a number of unique or neglected issues. One constant theme, however, was the plight of children—the children of migrants, of welfare mothers, of broken homes. He began by wrestling with the problems of the politically powerless and then embarked on an intensive study of how to educate their disadvantaged kids. Finally, all of Mondale's concerns fused in an effort toward strengthening the American family.

As he set out on this path at the start of the Ninety-first Congress, he faced numerous uncertainties. What he knew for sure was that things were likely to get worse for kids like Freddy and for everybody else bereft of power. He based that conclusion on the outcome of 1968's tortured politics: The election of Richard Nixon to the presidency. Nixon's victory banished Humphrey to temporary political exile and signaled the end of the Great Society, which, despite the blight of war and urban riots, had offered a major federal commitment to eliminating poverty in its various forms from society. By electing Nixon, the country had turned to the right, away from the domestic concerns that preoccupied Humphrey and Mondale.

But the events of 1968 also liberated Mondale. Having called for an unconditional bombing halt, Mondale was no longer encumbered by Vietnam. Had Humphrey been elected, he could not have strayed far from administration policy. With Nixon in the White House, however, he could move towards an uncompromising antiwar position. Among Minnesota Democrats he became the leading dove, eclipsing even McCarthy, who was nearing the end of his Senate career.

Mondale was able to steer clear of Humphrey's inhibiting shadow on other issues as well. There was now a more uncompromising tone to Mondale's social commentary. With the Nixon administration as a backdrop, Mondale could project a liberal, social-reformist image without having to apologize for the record of a Humphrey presidency. He did not have to worry about the political consequences to his long-time mentor of telling a church group in an affluent Minneapolis suburb in June, 1970, that the United States "is not as compassionate, as understanding, as sensitive as we think we are. Our priorities are screwy; our priorities are pretty close to being obscene."

In the Nixon administration, Mondale had an inviting target. He also now had a forum. Several forums, in fact. Robert Kennedy's death opened up a seat on the Labor and Public Welfare Committee. The Senate leadership filled it with Mondale, tacitly acknowledging that there should be a continuity of concern for the disadvantaged. When the Ninety-first Congress convened, he was named to the Labor Committee's Subcommittee on Migratory Labor. He was also appointed to the newly formed Select Committee on Nutrition and Human Needs and to a seat on the Special Committee on Aging. That latter assignment led to his second subcommittee chairmanship when he was appointed head of the Subcommittee on Retirement and the Individual. A year later, Mondale thrust himself into a bitter fight on the Senate floor over school desegregation and

busing. As a result, he was made chairman of a select committee to study the problem of assuring every youngster a
reasonably equal opportunity for a sound education. His
other subcommittee assignments covered general education; labor legislation; employment, manpower, and poverty; veterans' affairs; and the specialized problems of Indian education. Mondale was not exaggerating when he
said, "I spend most of my time in the Senate on human-
problem committees. Perhaps I'm on more of them than
any other member of the Senate."

In taking over the Migratory Labor Subcommittee, Mondale was stepping into another void left by the death of
Kennedy, who had gone to Delano, California, in 1966 for
widely publicized hearings. These gave an enormous boost
to Cesar Chavez's national farm workers movement.
Chavez was struggling against the growers and rival labor
groups to organize field hands into an effective union when
Kennedy was killed. Like Kennedy, Mondale found himself
struggling with a paradox: The remedies for the miseries
of powerless groups like the migrants were political and
therefore unobtainable by those whose lack of power con-
signed them to the lower rungs of society. He took on the
assignment not as a facile or self-serving demonstration of
his liberalism but as a challenge. He studied the literature
on migrants, interviewed experts like Robert Coles, a child
psychiatrist and student of migrants, and made field trips.

The latter were particularly depressing. As a member of
Sen. George McGovern's Hunger Committee, Mondale
toured Collier County, Florida, which had been singled out
in a report, *Hunger, USA,* as a place where malnutrition was
scandalously widespread, particularly among migrants.
Mondale would long remember being physically staggered
by the stench of a dark, dank home of a family of ten living
on field-hand wages of $1,500 a year. He was appalled by
the mother's account of her family diet. Asked about food
stamps, she gave a look of blank bewilderment. Meanwhile,

county officials were telling the committee that the migrants were "federal people"—not the responsibility of local welfare authorities. The editor of the Immokalee *Bulletin* ridiculed assertions that a photograph of a child with a distended stomach was evidence of hunger. The picture actually depicted "symptoms of a healthy Negro child with a full tummy and bare buttocks," he suggested.

A week after returning to Capitol Hill, Mondale was on the road again—this time traveling to Delano to meet with Chavez, the charismatic leader of the farm workers. Unlike Kennedy visiting there three years earlier or McGovern going to Florida, Mondale deliberately avoided calling attention to himself. There had been enough media events. The issue was the economic and social exploitation of migrant workers, and Mondale did not want to be guilty of their political exploitation, as well. But in taking a low-keyed approach, Mondale was forfeiting the possibility of stirring up public opinion and forcing reluctant politicians to face a tough and otherwise unrewarding issue. Mondale was relying instead on his abilities as a junior senator to achieve legislative remedies. There is no question that Mondale quickly mastered the complexities of the migratory-labor problem and that he was deeply moved by what he learned.

For nearly two years, Mondale and his subcommittee probed the dark and widely ignored story of the migrant. His work was underscored by an NBC documentary on how large employers, like Coca-Cola, abused migrants. When Mondale ordered hearings, Coca-Cola promised to improve the pay, housing, and medical care of the thousand migrants who worked for its subsidiaries—Minute Maid, Hi-C, and Snow Crop.

When a spokesman for the Florida growers tried to discredit NBC's portrayal of a particular migrant child, Mondale erupted. "What kind of system produces that kind of tragedy?" Mondale demanded, his voice rising to a near shout as he pounded his fist on the polished hearing-room table. "That was a child whose life was being ruined. I'd like to see some expression of concern out of you. These people are being mangled and destroyed."

The exchange was replayed on a network evening-news program, prompting Robert Lewis Shayon to suggest in *Saturday Review* that television "would do well to put him [Mondale] on camera more frequently. . . . It was quite a welcome shock to see a politician acting like a man and not a politician."

The record compiled by the Mondale subcommittee was shocking. Even though migrants at the time were three hundred times more prone to work accidents than the average U.S. worker, they were excluded from worker's compensation. Migrants were unemployed much of the time, working only an average of seventy-eight days a year to earn $891, yet they didn't qualify for unemployment compensation. And child-labor laws failed to forbid the practice of entire families—including youngsters of grade-school age—working as a unit in the fields.

Indeed, it was the impact of migrant life on children that stood out most vividly amidst the volumes of testimony, statistics, and government exhibits compiled by Mondale and his investigators. Particularly devastating was the testimony of Dr. Raymond Wheeler, a Charlotte, North Carolina, physician, who, along with fourteen other doctors, studied 1,400 families in Hidalgo County, Texas. He reported discovering children whose intestines were crawling with parasites, children with oozing sores from chronic skin diseases, children going deaf because of recurring ear infections. Few who heard Wheeler could forget his description of an emaciated three-month-old infant, lying on a bed, pulling at a bottle of sour milk, while pus poured from its right ear. Despite the penicillin and hastily arranged formula feedings, the team was too late.

Mondale levied a harsh judgment on what he had discovered as chairman of the subcommittee: "A migrant camp is a microcosm of nearly every social ill . . . every injustice . . . and everything shameful in our society: Poverty almost beyond belief, rampant disease and malnutrition, racism, filth, squalor, pitiful children drained of pride and hope, exploitation and powerlessness, and the inability or unwillingness of public and private institutions at all levels to erase this terrible plight on our country."

Despite his revulsion and outrage over the abuses of migrant life, Mondale's cautious pragmatism restrained him from undertaking a futile legislative venture. Nixon's election had undammed a tide of reaction against social-reformism. Reinforcing that trend was the clout of growers and others who profited from the exploitation of migrants. Few senators were willing to stand up to the farm lobby in their states for the sake of a pitiful handful of migrants, who never stayed in one place long enough to register as voters. It was apparent that the range of practical legislative options was hopelessly narrow. Mondale saw no effective way to widen it. Just as he had in his last high-school track meet, Mondale sprinted through the investigation, then slowed to a deliberate walk at the political finish line. Rather than try to write new laws to deal with the unique status of migrants, Mondale proposed to strengthen those already on the books. His main initiatives were to extend unemployment compensation and Social Security coverage to migrants, but these were defeated in Congress. His attempts to obtain increased funding for migrant health, education, and legal-service programs were similarly fruitless. The Immigration and Naturalization Service ignored pressure from him to tighten up its border surveillance so as to cut off the flow of aliens which Mondale felt was the core of the migrant problem. He did succeed, however, in extending occupational-hazards coverage to farm workers. But it was a discouraging and disheartening experience, and Mondale finally relinquished the subcommittee chairmanship to become head in February 1971 of a newly created Subcommittee on Children and Youth. In ironic tribute to the powerlessness of the migrant, the subcommittee was abolished. "This is no environment for liberals," he remarked in late November, 1969. "This is no time for liberals to win many arguments and we're not winning any of them."

Mondale elaborated on that theme in an interview with Albert Eisele of the St. Paul *Pioneer Press.* Mondale described many of his colleagues as too cautious and too willing to compromise for the sake of their survival.

"I think that prior to 1968, I was more of an organization man because I thought more could be achieved through a political organization than I do now. I still think political organizations are terribly important, but when I see the unbelievable mess nationally that we're in, I think one should spend more time debating issues rather than in organizational politics," Mondale said. "I think I'm still a practical man. I'm not a messiah. I like to be persuaded of the sound nature of a policy before I pursue it. I think I'm a pragmatic liberal. I'm still problem-oriented. I'm not a radical. I'm a reformer. I haven't rejected the system—just want to see it work."

Mondale clearly regarded the Nixon presidency as a challenge to liberalism and a chance to make a national reputation for himself as a battler for humane causes. It was also a time when many liberals could not resist a chance to posture for different constituencies, and Mondale did that as well. In a New York speech on May 7, 1971, before the NAACP Legal Defense and Education Fund, Mondale spoke darkly of an "American apartheid—which victimizes white and black, rich and poor, city and suburb." In an applause line near the end of his speech, he declared, "The sickening truth is that this country is rapidly coming to resemble South Africa." It is unlikely Mondale ever really believed that, because otherwise his commitment to pragmatic liberalism would have been untenable. What he was describing was a country and a national character so flawed by racism that it would soon be beyond redemption by gradualist reformers like himself.

Mondale was more optimistic in a long interview two years later with Elizabeth Drew of *The New Yorker*. "There are so many human problems in the midst of our wealth that need a country that cares and a government that tries," Mondale said in language almost identical to the standard rhetoric of Jimmy Carter's "government filled with love" campaign speeches several years later. Mondale continued: "I don't think the average American is that selfish, and I think this is where the Nixon approach is going to go wrong. I think the average American is more just and more compassionate than Nixon thinks he is."

The early 1970s were dominated by epochal struggles between Congress and Nixon over the war and Watergate. In neither instance was Mondale more than a bit player. Operating with no fanfare in the background, he was pursuing new issues that evolved from his experiences with the migrants. With a full-length Senate speech on December 9, 1970, entitled "Justice for Children," Mondale undertook a legislative effort that would earn him the reputation of being a children's senator.

"Our national myth is that we love children," Mondale said. "Yet we are starving thousands. Other thousands die because decent medical care is unavailable to them. The lives of still thousands of others are stifled by poor schools and some never have a chance to go to school at all. Millions live in substandard and unfit housing in neighborhoods which mangle the human spirit."

At the outset, it seemed an inconsequential issue. Like motherhood, no one could possibly oppose fair treatment for children. But just as there was no obvious bloc of opposition, neither was there any bloc of active support. That all changed, however, when Mondale's newly created Subcommittee on Children and Youth produced the Comprehensive Child Development Act of 1971. The heart of the bill was a provision establishing day-care centers for the children of working mothers. If children were being cheated because of the stresses and demands society placed on adults, then there should be a way to relieve the pressure and to provide a voluntary source of supplemental support for families with special problems. Again, Mondale had Freddy in mind. The bill was an attempt to fill a void by offering warm, friendly places where kids could be left in skilled hands, while mothers went to their jobs. The emphasis would be on preschool training, but the staff would also be equipped to deal with health, nutrition, and other child-development problems. There was also a provision for prenatal care.

At an annual estimated cost to the taxpayers of about $2 billion, it was an expensive program. Poor kids would be admitted free. Other parents would pay on a graduated scale according to income. Partially offsetting the cost was the expectation that the program would cut welfare rolls by freeing many mothers to take jobs.

It was a sweeping bill, perhaps as significant in scope as Medicare. The response, Mondale said, was "like spontaneous combustion." Suddenly, he found himself marching at the head of a broad coalition encompassing the woman's liberation movement, organized labor, the mayors, major church groups, civil-rights organizations, and even zero-population-growth advocates.

The only real opposition came from Nixon—and he had the power to kill it. In a patronizing veto message, Nixon faulted the program for its "fiscal irresponsibility, administrative unworkability, and family-weakening implications." The president seemed particularly upset by its "radical" provisions for "communal child rearing." Mondale denounced the veto as a "totally indefensible act." The Senate fell seven votes short of overriding Nixon.

Twice Mondale tried to resurrect the program, but it was finally buried after somebody or some group sent out a mysterious flier, hysterically attacking the bill as an attempt to break up the American family. The nationwide mailing triggered such an avalanche of hostile letters on Capitol Hill that Mondale had no choice but to drop the bill.

On other children's issues, however, he was more successful, winning passage of a bill authorizing pioneering attempts to treat child abuse as a social disease and another establishing a three-year, $9 million effort to probe causes of crib death.

Mondale's exposure to hunger, the problems of the migrants, and child neglect finally coalesced into one overall issue—the destruction of the American family. What Mondale saw in 1973 was a welter of pressures, many of which were fed by the government, putting unbearable strains on the family. Welfare programs penalized two-parent homes. Tax laws provided no real benefits for families of average means during child-rearing years. New expressways disrupted neighborhoods. Urban renewal uprooted extended families and left communities segregated by age, with grandparents imprisoned in high-rises. And so on.

"I wonder if we shouldn't have a family-impact study," Mondale told Elizabeth Drew in the *New Yorker* interview. "When we pass tax laws or welfare laws or housing laws or transportation laws, we ought to say, 'Well, what will this do to the families?' "

While Mondale and his subcommittee never figured out how to draft a family-impact statement, he showed a fresh and inquiring mind. Some critics sneered at his work on family legislation and other such social issues as being politically risk-free. To them, he seemed to lack a cutting edge. For example, when Mondale worked unsuccessfully for legislation aimed at strengthening the government's ability to analyze and diagnose social ills, columnist George F. Will ridiculed Mondale's objectives and concluded, "A man of such mushiness has a great future in the Democratic Party.''

It was certainly true that Mondale was a do-gooder. Tackling the problems of crib death and child abuse did not exactly seem like astounding acts of political courage. It is also true that Mondale saw these problems in a larger context and that he had a more complicated set of objectives than simply aligning himself with motherhood issues. However, he was discovering that some problems are beyond easy legislative solution. That was the lesson of the migratory-labor hearings, which shed new light on migrant hardships but yielded no coherent or politically feasible line of attack. Similarly, Mondale's study of the trends and pressures operating on the American family suggested a theoretical framework for political action, but one that was too complicated to be immediately realistic.

14

Busing: Frontline Fighter

Politically, John Stennis and Abe Ribicoff were an odd couple. But their alliance in February, 1970, on the issue of school integration was more than a mere curiosity. Walter Mondale, at least, viewed it as a signal that a reactionary trend—sixteen years after the U. S. Supreme Court's landmark school-desegregation decision—was gaining overwhelming momentum. On the face of it, the amendment offered by Stennis to an education bill seemed fair enough. As prepared by the courtly Democrat from Mississippi, it would simply declare, as a matter of policy, that the federal government would apply desegregation guidelines evenhandedly to school systems all over the country. Ribicoff, a liberal Democrat from Connecticut and a former Secretary of Health, Education, and Welfare under John Kennedy, embraced the amendment as a chance to end a hypocritical legal distinction that was forcing the rapid desegregation of Southern school systems, while Northern schools in many cases seemed to mock the goals of integration. The difference hinged on two Latin phrases. One was "de jure" segregation, which referred to racially discriminatory policies purposefully adopted by state and local education authorities, mainly in the South. The other was "de facto" segregation, wherein the races were unintentionally separated—as in many Western and Northern cities—due to housing patterns, economic development, neighborhood loyalties, and the like.

To Ribicoff, the distinction made no sense.

"We're just as racist in the North as they are in the South. De facto, de jure, I don't want to hide behind those two phrases," Ribicoff said.

To Stennis, it wasn't fair.

"I would [like to] see a genuine national policy based on reason and common sense and live and let live. . . . If you have to do that [integrate] in your area [the North], you will see what it means to us."

But to Mondale, Stennis and Ribicoff were colluding in a hoax.

"I would rather lose my public career than give up on civil rights. For ten years as attorney general of my state and as a U.S. senator, I have regarded it as a religious responsibility to treat every man as an equal and I am offended by racial segregation wherever it exists," Mondale declared during a biting exchange on the Senate floor with Ribicoff. "I know an amendment that does not do anything when I see it. . . . The amendment offered by the senator from Mississippi would do nothing about de facto segregation. Its sole and obvious purpose is to paralyze and hamper efforts to eliminate the dual school systems wherever they exist."

Northern politicians had found it easy and satisfying to pass civil rights laws when the target was the South. They were now confronting, however, the agonies and anxieties stirred by desegregation as yellow school buses began picking up the children of their constituents and carrying them miles away to racially alien schools.

As clearly as anyone, Mondale felt that the spreading national hostility to busing was eroding support for civil rights. "I sense that [civil rights] is less popular than it's been for a number of years. Unless we sustain it, the cause of our country will be lost."

But the question of de facto segregation in Northern schools could not be ignored—a fact which Mondale recognized well before the debate over the Stennis amendment. A week earlier, Mondale had proposed an alternative to the Mississippian's maneuver that involved setting up a select committee to do a nationwide study of the school-integration problem. After the Senate adopted the Stennis proposal, Mondale renewed the idea, assuring his colleagues that the study would not overlook racial isolation and imbalance in the North. The motion carried and Mondale was installed as chairman of the Select Committee on Equal Educational Opportunity. While originating in the battle over school integration, the committee's charter was much broader—to study how well public schools were fulfilling their role in the American dream of self-betterment through equal access to a decent education.

The assignment offered an intellectual challenge that Mondale met in a serious-minded way. Even his partisan opponents were impressed by his efforts to master some of the most complex issues in American education. "The first thing he did was to read like a crazy man," recalled one of his staff assistants, Bert Carp. Later he met for hours with the best brains in the field—academicians, theoreticians, school administrators, principals, teachers. By the time the committee was ready to start public hearings in the spring of 1970, Republican as well as Democratic committee aides acknowledged that Mondale was a rare example of a senator who knew more about the issues under study than the professional staff.

Mondale was aware that he was not operating in a vacuum. There were two powerful Southern Democrats on the select committee—John McClellan of Arkansas and Sam Ervin of North Carolina—as well as two conservative Republicans. While the moderates formed the largest bloc, three of them—Adlai Stevenson of Illinois, Jacob Javits of New York, and Edward Brooke of Massachusetts—were worried about inner-city busing problems in their own states. Mondale realized the importance of quickly grasping the offensive. As he had done with the migrant-worker investigation, he made an unannounced field trip—to Mississippi, Louisiana, Alabama, and Texas. He returned prepared to keep the pressure on the South. He had discovered a massive fraud in progress. Millions in public funds were being diverted to support private academies that were springing up across the South as alternatives to integrated public schools. Fleets of repainted buses had been pressed into service for the ironic purpose of busing white students past their old neighborhood schools to new schools with the same old color barriers. There were other dodges, as well. In Homer, Louisiana, desegregation meant crowding entire classes of black pupils into the basement of an abandoned industrial-arts building in a supposedly "integrated" school complex. Meanwhile, the National Education Association estimated that 5,000 black principals, teachers, and school employees had been fired or demoted regardless of qualifications as nominal desegregation occurred.

Mondale was a realist, nonetheless. He well knew that "forced busing" was becoming a code word in the North, as well as in the South, for a coercive and hated government attempt at social experimentation, with kids as the guinea pigs. Even in Minneapolis, whose minuscule black population lived in two neighborhoods, a backlash was developing against schemes to disperse the black school population. After eight years with a liberal mayor, the city sent the politicians a message by overwhelmingly electing an ultra-conservative police detective to the office Hubert Humphrey once held. In fact, it was Humphrey himself who was the surest barometer of the changing political climate. Campaigning against Alabama Gov. George Wallace in Florida's 1972 Democratic presidential primary, Humphrey repeatedly denounced plans that would bus children

solely for the sake of achieving a racial balance in the classroom.

Mondale's own thinking went through a subtle evolution.
When he took charge of the select committee, he talked
hopefully of building a national constituency for integration. There was an urgent need to overcome what he described as racial isolation. His rhetoric was insistent, even
impassioned. Kids were being "maimed" by bad schools,
their cultural horizons narrowed by lack of exposure to the
majority culture that would surround them all their lives.
This flaw, fatal to young developing minds, could be overcome only by mixing kids from different backgrounds and
races in the classroom. That meant busing.

By 1972, however, Mondale's legislative emphasis had
shifted. Attempts to circumscribe or outlaw busing were
growing in number and picking up increasing support.
Mondale himself faced reelection that fall. No major opponent was in sight, but there were nonetheless pockets of
antibusing feeling in Minneapolis, St. Paul, and Duluth.
Mondale began talking less about busing as a means of
overcoming racial isolation and more about broader remedies. As the select committee said in its report a year later,
busing was but one of many ways to attack the problem of
unequal educational opportunity. The issue had now become the constitutional authority of the courts to order
busing as one method of implementing legitimate desegregation orders. He argued repeatedly that the Congress
could not repeal the Constitution, and that the courts had
a responsibility to overturn official acts of discrimination,
even if it meant the use of busing to desegregate schools.

The fight reached a climax in early 1972 as the Congress
prepared to dispose of an emergency school-aid bill
freighted with a number of House-passed antibusing
amendments. In an eloquent speech on February 18, Mondale implored the Congress not to "stand in the school-
house door," referring to Wallace's infamous act of de-

fiance when he had physically tried to block the integration of the University of Alabama.

"The country is at a crossroads," Mondale declared. "School desegregation in the South is largely completed. But we from the North are now beginning to feel the pressure, which our colleagues from the South felt for so many years, to abandon the course set by the Fourteenth Amendment. If we do, we will deal a blow to public education in the North and South from which it may never recover."

The New York *Times,* which reported the speech on page one, noted, "Two years ago, so open an advocacy for integration from a Northern liberal would not have been unusual; today, such talk is scarce."

The two-year battle was resolved—for Mondale, at least —when several months later Congress passed a bill containing many of the provisions sought by his select committee. The two-year bill authorized $2 billion to deal with the learning problems of kids from racially isolated and poor neighborhoods. Special-education projects, integrated magnet schools, innovative use of educational television, bilingual education—all were funded after initially having been recommended by Mondale's subcommittee.

Mondale also succeeded in stripping the bill of the more far-reaching amendments to eliminate court-ordered busing. At the same time, his opponents won a moratorium on certain busing orders until they had been appealed in court. Another provision put restrictions on the use of federal funds to pay local busing costs.

The fight also focused national attention on Mondale at a time when some liberals at least were looking for new national leaders. In early August 1970, the *New Republic*'s TRB column approvingly noted Mondale's work on behalf of equal educational opportunity.

"He looked into migrant workers, now into the new chapter of school desegregation," TRB wrote. "We think Mondale is of presidential caliber."

15

Testing the Presidential Waters

"Some people in this town wake up in the middle of the night hearing 'Hail to the Chief,' " Dick Moe said in late 1974. "Mondale never did." That may have been true, but, for about fourteen months immediately before Moe's remark, Mondale's ears were straining.

There never was a precise moment when one could have said for sure that Walter Mondale had become a candidate for president. He certainly was careful never to say flatly that he was running, although others were freely assuming that he was. Among those who so assumed were a number of national political reporters, many of whom had traveled with him during the time when the presidency was most on his mind. The impressions gathered from those trips had prompted many of them to write stories indicating that it was only a matter of time before this young, attractive, liberal Minnesota Democrat would formally declare his candidacy for the job so long sought by another not-so-young Minnesota Democrat named Hubert Humphrey. That was why it stunned most of the reporters who crammed a Senate hearing room—just down the hall from Mondale's office in the Old Senate Office Building—to hear him announce on November 21, 1974, that he would not seek the 1976 Democratic presidential nomination.

In fact, Mondale had been on the verge of making that

announcement several months earlier but he had been
talked out of it by Dick Moe, his top Senate aide and political adviser, and by his two other most trusted political
helpers, Mike Berman and Jim Johnson. These three were
the main drafters and implementers of a plan devised to
help Mondale explore his prospects of running successfully
for president. Aside from Mondale's misgivings, the plan
was coming off about as they had hoped. Every few days,
Moe would rise from his desk in a cramped back office and
jab a flag pin into a wall map of the United States. Each flag
represented a Mondale appearance as part of the master
plan. By the time Mondale called things off, about thirty
states on Moe's map had sprouted flags; one state, California, was fairly bristling. The map also showed that Mondale
—or certainly Moe—was working hard at developing a base
of support in the Midwest and in states like New Hampshire, Iowa, and Arizona that would draw intense media
interest as political harbingers because of their early starting dates for picking national-convention delegates. Like a
shy suitor, Mondale's tentative winks and diffident smiles
seemed to betray a White House yearning. There were only
so many ways reporters could phrase the question, "Senator, are you going to be a candidate in 1976?" It was incon-
venient to have to translate his answers from the subjunc-
tive into the declarative mood, but he seemed to be saying
yes when he declared:

• In Albuquerque on August 14, "From the encouragement I've had, I believe I will."
• In Duluth on September 25, "I'm ninety-nine percent
of the way there, but I have not yet decided."
• In Washington on October 1 that he would "get into
New Hampshire because that's the first" presidential primary.
• In Newark on October 30, "I'm probably going to
run."

It was as though he had raised the starter's gun over his

head and called out, "On your mark, get set . . ." Everybody paying any attention could almost hear the word forming on his lips. Even Joan Mondale was surprised when that word turned out to be no.

"Suddenly, I remember sitting there in my red president suit, saying to myself, 'I am unemployed,' " she said in an interview. "And I was indeed, because I had cleared my life to go campaigning with him. I had gotten everything off the boards. I had stopped all my volunteer work. I just unburdened my life so that I could go with him and do whatever he needed."

Meanwhile, Moe was making tentative plans to resign from the Senate payroll to join the campaign staff. The two other members of Mondale's political triumvirate were also proceeding on the assumption that their boss would become a full-fledged candidate. There was Berman, a lawyer and a logistical wizard who rigged up a flawless communications system for Humphrey at the 1968 convention, while McCarthy's people were groping desperately for ways to pass messages. On the week of Mondale's press conference, Berman was in Washington to find office space for a national headquarters and to begin hiring an enlarged staff to raise funds for a serious campaign budget, beyond the $100,000 that had come in during the exploratory phase.

Meanwhile, Johnson had taken a leave of absence from the Dayton-Hudson Corporation in Minneapolis, where he was a rising thirty-year-old executive. Before going to Dayton-Hudson, Johnson had been an activist in the campus peace movement, an aide in Sen. Edmund Muskie's 1972 presidential campaign, and a graduate student at Princeton. But, like Mondale, Johnson's roots were the small towns of rural southern Minnesota. A DFLer at birth, Johnson learned his earliest lessons in politics from his father, a former speaker of the Minnesota House of Representatives. On Mondale's political forays, Johnson would collect the names and addresses of people they met who might be

potential campaign workers. He would then record that
information on an index card. By late October, Johnson
had a file of over twelve thousand cards.

There were plenty of reasons for a quickening in the
collective pulse rate of this minuscule Mondale staff as its
forty-six-year-old champion undertook an intensified
schedule during the fall of 1974, leading up to the congressional elections and a Democratic party conference in December. A pitiful seedling of a candidacy suddenly acquired
growing space and a long-denied place in the sun when
Teddy Kennedy chopped down his own stand of presidential timber. Kennedy's announcement on September 23,
1974, removed the one rival who could be regarded at that
early stage as a near cinch for a first-ballot nomination. In
the aftermath of Kennedy's move, it seemed as though
Mondale was well positioned to inherit the support of the
party's liberal and moderate wings.

No one expected Mondale to become a political titan
overnight. Even so, Mondale and his aides were privately
disappointed when nothing much materialized. Kennedy's
removal did quicken the flow of campaign contributions to
Mondale and awakened some interest on the part of political professionals now cut adrift. Yet, among the voters at
large—and even among Democrats—Mondale remained
an obscure figure, lacking any independent identity. The
first Gallup Poll after Kennedy bowed out showed George
Wallace in first place as the preferred candidate of Democrats. Mondale was stuck at 2 percent, almost precisely
where he was six months earlier. Moe, Berman, and Johnson tried to stiffen Mondale's resolve, citing other measure-
ments of strength that were either too subtle or too premature to be reflected in Gallup's samplings. A straw poll of
Iowa Democrats at their Jefferson-Jackson Day dinner in
early October, they pointed out, gave him a substantial
37-to-16 percent lead over his closest competitor, Scoop
Jackson. Gov. James Earl Carter of Georgia was not listed,

although two years later, he would use the support of some of those same Democrats to vault into an early lead for the nomination before New Hampshire had even voted in its primary. (It is obviously futile to speculate what would have happened if Mondale had challenged Carter for the nomination. But if Mondale's strength in Iowa's precinct caucuses had materialized, as Moe and others thought possible, Carter might well have been denied the early victory there that contributed so substantially to the gathering momentum of his campaign.)

Meanwhile, a poll of Democratic national committee members, state party leaders, and governors showed that Mondale was preferred even over Kennedy. And a nationwide Lou Harris poll published three days after Mondale's withdrawal put him in a virtual dead heat with Jackson. Both trailed President Ford by sixteen percentage points.

As evidence of a potential base that could eventually be developed into broad public support, those indicators were not invalid. In the vernacular of Wall Street, Mondale's campaign had growth potential. Nineteen months after aborting it, he described that earlier decision as having been based on a pragmatic assessment of his presidential prospects and the conclusion that his would be a hopeless pursuit. It was an odd explanation to offer Carter, whose own prospects in late 1974 were as bleak as any candidate's. On the other hand, the determination of the Carterites to overcome all obstacles made it inadvisable for Mondale to stress the other major reason for scuttling Mike Berman's plans to open a national Mondale-for-President headquarters in Washington. That had to do with Mondale's admission that he lacked the burning ambition—or the overweening ego—to endure the life-wrenching pressures standing between him on November 21, 1974, and the presidential nomination on July 14, 1976.

In an interview with Frank Wright of the Minneapolis *Tribune* on the day of his I-am-not-a-candidate decision,

Mondale conceded that he had "a reasonable chance," given the lineup of other contenders, to win the nomination. There was, he agreed, "no front runner." It was certain to be "the most wide-open race in years." But he also realized he was at a point of no return. The campaign could not be run indefinitely on the backs of Moe, Johnson, Berman, and Susan Tannenbaum, his twenty-nine-year-old scheduler, a veteran of Kennedy campaigns. To match the rapidly growing efforts of other rivals, Mondale was going to have to hire a substantial national staff, as well as develop an apparatus in such states as Iowa, New Hampshire, Wisconsin, and Illinois that were critical to a strategy of building early momentum and a strong Midwestern base. That also meant that the fund-raising operation was going to have to be expanded and accelerated. Time and money— lots of people were going to have to part with lots of both if Mondale was going to make a serious bid.

"In order to be a serious presidential candidate, I was going to have to ask others to commit themselves—to pledge part of their lives to my campaign," Mondale told Wright. "Being uncertain myself as to whether I really wanted to seek the office, I just didn't feel I could ask others to make the commitment. Up until this point, I don't think I've hurt anybody, but, if I stay in, and I'm uncertain, I'll not be as good a candidate as I should be and I'll occupy part of the road. If a person is not certain he wants to be a candidate, then probably he shouldn't run."

And so it came down to his admission at the press conference that he did not have the "overwhelming desire to be president which is essential for the kind of campaign that is required." He also said, "I don't think anyone should be president who is not willing to go through fire."

That was not a casual or facile conclusion. He had struggled with himself for months before deciding that both he and the Republic could survive with somebody else in the White House. After he had been dissuaded from dropping out in the summer of 1974, there had indeed been moments when he was 99 percent certain he would run for president—moments when he could feel himself in tune with a crowd and when there seemed to be an emotional surge that carried them forward together. For example, he would remember an evening with a small group of supporters at a Phoenix party when he moved several of his listeners to tears with a quiet talk about cheated children. Another major campaign theme was spelled out in a Senate speech on September 17, 1973, in which he warned of the emergence of an imperial, "bloated" presidency that had "become larger than life, and larger than the law." He was referring, of course, to Nixon, Watergate, and the need to restore faith in tarnished public institutions. He also zeroed in on the heartlessness of Republican economic policies, and the arrogance and unbridled power of Big Oil. After he wove these thematic strands into a campaign pitch, people would often press forward, offering to help out in the presidential quest they assumed lay ahead.

As he approached the momentous decision, however, Mondale became increasingly ambivalent about moving into the final phase—total commitment to a presidential campaign. Humphrey, once again a U.S. senator from Minnesota, had been at least partially responsible for getting Mondale involved as a potential presidential aspirant. On election night 1972, while Mondale was coasting to an easy reelection victory over an obscure Republican, Humphrey dragged him in front of a national network TV crew to proclaim the beginning of "a truly great national career that can take Fritz Mondale to the office which I long sought."

Fourteen months later, Mondale still hadn't committed himself. He told one aide that he had changed his mind five times the night before the fateful press conference. Finally, however, what lingered were the memories of the petty humiliations and frustrations, of weekend after weekend away from his family. An example was his visit to Fremont, Nebraska, on August 19, nearly two weeks after Nixon had resigned. It was the time of summer when the Mondale family would usually retreat to a fishing resort beneath the cool pines of northern Minnesota. Now, however, he was in Nebraska to address the nineteenth annual convention of the state AFL-CIO. In the midst of a stifling heat wave, Mondale found himself stranded at a reception attended by just fifteen people, counting Jim Johnson. Their host insisted then on taking them twenty miles out of town to a barbeque. Only five hands to shake there. Besides, the food was terrible, so they broke free without having eaten. When they finally hitched a ride back to the motel, they were frustrated and fatigued, hungry and hung up.

"We had to walk about two miles along the highway and the heat was just merciless, and then we got to this restaurant that was just closing," Mondale recalled. "It had been a Holiday Inn but it must have lost its franchise. They said all they could serve us was catfish.

"And I said, 'Tell me again, Jim. Why are we here?' "

Mondale was also nagged by the helpless sense that he was slipping out of touch with his constituents and that he was discharging his Senate duties by rote, without his customary careful preparation. He seemed caught on a political ferris wheel, his life already badly out of kilter. He felt as if he was being drained of his intellectual juices as the tempo of his physical activities picked up. As a youngster, he was always taught not to brag about himself—unless he was ready to endure one of Reverend Mondale's famous switchings. But now every time he went somplace new, that was what people expected. He had to sell himself constantly. In Minnesota, where everyone knew him as Fritz, all he had to do was speak his mind. His style was low-key, conversational. If he came on too strong, "I think they'd grab their billfolds and start counting the silver," Mondale confided.

His Minnesota manner was not enough now. To get strangers to listen and to persuade them of his sincerity, he had to wave his arms and infuse his rhetoric with an emotional intensity that never was his style. He even had a speech professor from the University of Wisconsin follow him for three days in early 1974 on a swing through California. The fellow said he was doing just swell and disappeared. But the suggestions continued. Go to Hollywood. Look resplendent. Loosen your necktie. Cut your hair. Let it grow longer. Try the dry look.

Meanwhile, Mondale was being nudged from various directions to escalate the campaign. One nudger was Humphrey, who was quoted by syndicated newspaper columnists Rowland Evans and Robert Novak as wondering whether Mondale had the "fire in the belly" to undergo the rigors of a sustained national campaign. That irritated Mondale. While Humphrey was musing about Mondale's political toughness, Mondale saw in Humphrey the immeasurable costs of being seduced into constant pursuit of the presidency. Humphrey's quest for the 1972 Democratic nomination had been strident and graceless, and he had suffered a loss of respect among Senate peers. Already, outsiders were trying to mess with Mondale's personal style, as had happened earlier with Humphrey. Humphrey's was not an isolated example. As Dick Moe said years later, "Mondale saw too many of his colleagues go down that road. Somehow they were never the same when they returned."

All those impressions and experiences were on Mondale's mind as he prepared to take himself out of the running at his press conference on November 21. He lacked the ultimate lust for power. Boredom overcame his competitive instincts and cut short his final high school footrace. He had forsworn running for governor in 1962 out of a concern for party harmony, a desire to maintain good relations with senior party leaders, and a commitment to

Karl Rolvaag. The pattern was clear. For every prize, there was a price. Mondale would stop bidding where others might continue; the decision was based on subjective calculations of personal costs and political risks. In 1974, the sacrifice was too great, when humiliation might be his only reward.

16

Gaining Influence

Life now returned to normal. The decision to strike his name from the list of Democratic presidential contenders had not been an easy one, but Walter Mondale was relieved once he made up his mind and put the campaign behind him. There would be no more weekends spent skyhopping across the country to strut his stuff in front of political powerbrokers. No more worrying about his speaking style, hair style, clothing style, or any of the other styles that intrigue the practitioners and connoisseurs of big-time politics, American style. Mondale had not felt comfortable in the role of presidential candidate, particularly since he could not convince himself that all the posturing and political hyperbole would lead anywhere except to ignominious defeat.

Now Mondale could focus his undivided attention on the work of the Senate. That was a mixed blessing. However flawed his candidacy might have been in other ways, it kept him from getting bored. In the past, once having explored an issue and carried it as far as he could, Mondale would impatiently move on to a new challenge. Now there was nothing to distract him from the frequent tedium of legislative life. What he needed was a good stirring fight to ward off the post–presidential-campaign blahs.

The convening of the Ninety-fourth Congress on January

14, 1975, offered just such an opportunity. The issue was the filibuster rule. The fight started when Mondale and Sen. James Pearson, a progressive Republican from Kansas, filed a resolution seeking a change in the Senate rules that would lower the cloture requirement to end a filibuster from two-thirds of all senators voting to three-fifths. The Mondale-Pearson plan meant that at least sixty, instead of sixty-seven, senators would have to vote for cloture, if all one hundred members were to take a position on the issue. Ever since the open-housing fight, Mondale had been looking for an opportunity to tackle cloture. He knew the venture was an uncertain one. Since the late 1950s, liberals had made repeated assaults on the filibuster—all futile. The Southerners were as skilled in its defense as they were in its use as a weapon to obstruct civil rights. Now, as Mondale and Pearson pressed the issue, they found themselves opposed by one of the sliest foxes in the Senate, James Allen of Alabama. Allen's great strength lay in his awesome mastery of the parliamentary mumbo-jumbo that sometimes confused even other experienced senators. To prepare for the fight, Mondale had immersed himself for days in a detailed study of the complex procedural rituals that could determine the fate of his and Pearson's resolution.

For six weeks after filing the resolution, the fight was joined. The tenacity and skill with which the Mondale-Pearson forces fought Allen alerted the filibuster defenders to the seriousness of the challenge. To an uninitiated or casual visitor, the proceedings must have seemed arcane, even bizarre. Here was the world's greatest deliberative body solemnly voting to table the Lord's Prayer. At another point, the Senate became polarized over a murky motion to table a motion to reconsider a vote to table an appeal of a ruling that a point of order was not in order against a motion to table another point of order against a motion to bring to a vote a motion to call up a resolution that would change the rules. At least, that's what it sounded like.

It was a cat-and-mouse game in which both sides sought to play the cat's role by executing a lightning parliamentary thrust that would clinch it. A major break occurred in late February when Vice President Nelson Rockefeller, presiding officer of the Senate, surprised everyone, including President Ford, with a series of rulings in favor of Mondale's side. That triggered a furious counteroffensive by Allen. The gaunt-faced Alabamian used every imaginable parliamentary trick to prevent a final vote or to provoke Mondale into a procedural misstep. Tempers were fraying. In the midst of a dispute over one of Rockefeller's rulings, Sen. Russell Long of Louisiana, an Allen ally, leaped to his feet, shouting, "He [Rockefeller] does not own this body." In the next breath, however, Long proposed a compromise calling for a rigid formula under which the antifilibuster forces would have to muster the support of three-fifths of the entire Senate to end debate. With one-hundred members, the magic number would always be sixty, regardless of how many senators might play hooky when a cloture vote was called. In an institution where truancy is common, Mondale's proposal—three-fifths of only those answering a roll call—meant that the magic number would often be considerably less than sixty.

The Senate's heavyweights immediately lined up behind Long. Senate Majority Whip Robert Byrd, a Democrat from West Virginia, became the floor leader for the compromise. He was backed by Senate Majority Leader Mike Mansfield, who fretted about the Senate's image and its long agenda as the Mondale-Allen fight dragged on.

Mondale and his allies were in a quandary. The leadership's heavy artillery had been wheeled onto the floor, and the question was whether to fight on two fronts—against the Long compromise as well as against the Allen forces. Or should they trim their hopes and accept a limited victory? Some, like Sen. Ted Kennedy, felt that total victory would ultimately be theirs.

The decision was Mondale's. After considering the floor situation overnight, he announced his support of the Long compromise. In his mind, it was a significant improvement over the old rule. He was also impressed by the mood on the floor. Rejection of the compromise would have thrust him into the middle of a fight that was no longer a routine parliamentary hassle. Personal and political relationships were already being strained. Mondale's move put an end to that, assuring adoption of the change proposed by Long. Mondale had always been skilled at working cooperatively with political leaderships. His record of helpfulness to Humphrey, Freeman, and Rolvaag played no small role in shaping his career. It would have been uncharacteristically quixotic of Mondale to have risked the good will of Mansfield, Byrd, and Long when a limited victory was at hand. Day after day, Mondale and Pearson fought Allen on his own terms, building support for their effort as they did so. Finally, the momentum they generated swept a reluctant leadership into the fight, making possible the first easing of the cloture rule since its adoption fifty-eight years earlier. Later, leaving the Senate for the vice presidency, Mondale would list the filibuster change as the capstone of his legislative career.

The cloture fight marked Mondale's emergence as a moderately influential figure in the Senate. Although still years away from a committee chairmanship, Mondale was nonetheless respected as an intelligent, serious-minded, pragmatic liberal. Enhancing his stature were committee assignments that drew him closer to the center of action in the Senate. The critical step in that process had actually occurred two years earlier. Returning to the Congress in early 1973, after an easy reelection campaign, Mondale decided to try for a seat on the Finance Committee, the Senate's tax-writing panel. As he reviewed his prospects one afternoon with J. S. Kimmitt, the secretary to the Democratic majority, Mondale concluded that the conservative opposition would be fatal. This would be his second try, having failed two years earlier.

"Have you asked Jim for help?" Kimmitt asked. Sen. James Eastland was a member of the Democratic Steering Committee, which handed out committee assignments to fellow Democrats.

"Jim?" Mondale asked incredulously. "That's out of the question. We haven't agreed on an issue since I got here."

"Can't hurt to ask. All he can say is no," Kimmitt said. "And he might surprise you."

Feeling faintly foolish, Mondale approached Eastland to ask for the ultraconservative's vote. Eastland's eyes twinkled as he listened to Mondale's request.

"Yup," Eastland said with his customary brevity. That assured Mondale of an appointment to what many believed was the most important committee in the Senate.

Mondale's good fortune was not accidental. Partly it was due to the long hours in Kimmitt's office with Eastland when the boys would gather for a drink and political talk during slow, late-afternoon sessions. But more important had been Humphrey's advice to maintain good personal relationships even with strong political adversaries. In Eastland's case, that had paid off. Indeed, Mondale seemed to leave few scars on his political opponents in the Senate. His appointment to the Finance Committee was received as big news by lobbyists and others who study federal tax legislation, largely because he was viewed as one of the few liberals smart enough to take on Russell Long, the tyrannical but brilliant chairman. For tax reformers, Mondale was seen as an inside man who could use his leverage to fight vigorously for their broad goals of eliminating loopholes in the federal Internal Revenue Code. These are provisions that lower the effective tax burden on wealthy individuals or flourishing businesses. The confrontation never took place. Mondale's unwillingness to play the role of the self-immolating liberal had changed little since the Vietnam-

protest days, when he had spurned pleas of the antiwar left
to sacrifice himself politically for their cause. He did not
abandon the tax-reform goals he had long espoused before
joining the committee. But a do-or-die crusader he was not.

Nonetheless, there was an overall consistency in his
efforts to infuse greater equity into the tax code and to
oppose the more egregious attempts to confer unwarranted tax breaks on special-interest groups. He was the
most persistent and effective spokesman in Congress for
the use of income-tax credits as a kind of poor-man's loophole. For several years, he worked to educate his colleagues
about the relative value of credits, as opposed to deductions or exemptions, to taxpayers with different incomes.
As Mondale pointed out, deductions and exemptions are
financial benefits that increase in value as taxpayers grow
richer. The bigger the income, the bigger the savings. That
is true because a $100 deduction for a taxpayer whose
modest income is taxed at 22 percent produces a $22 sav-
ings. Compare, Mondale said, with the fat cat whose wealth
pushes him into the 70 percent tax bracket. His savings
from the $100 deduction will be $70. Credits have the
reverse effect, because they are flat sums subtracted equally
from everyone's tax liability, regardless of income. Each
dollar of credit saves a dollar of taxes. A $100 credit, Mon-
dale pointed out, is a proportionally larger savings for a
taxpayer with $15,000 in income than it would be if his
income was $150,000. That, Mondale argued, is consistent
with the progressive intent of the American tax system,
under which the tax burden is supposed to rest more heavily on the rich than on the poor.

Despite his repeated denunciations of a tax system that
allows some of the super-wealthy to escape huge taxes by
exploiting various legal dodges, Mondale's overall posture
toward Long was one of accommodation—to the displeasure of tax reformers. Their dissatisfaction with Mondale
peaked in early March, 1975—just as the filibuster fight was

approaching a critical stage. A small band of liberals on the Ways and Means Committee, the House's counterpart of the Finance Committee, passed a measure repealing the oil-depletion allowance, the granddaddy of all tax loopholes. The liberals' strategy was to sugarcoat oil-depletion repeal by attaching it to a $21.3 billion tax-cut bill. The ploy worked in the House. Robert Brandon of Ralph Nader's Tax Reform Research Group then visited Mondale in the hopes of enlisting him as an ally. Mondale, already heavily committed to the filibuster fight, declined. Later, Mondale made no special effort to oppose Long within the committee when the chairman moved successfully to detach the oil-depletion repealer from the rest of the tax bill. Mondale did support the assault on the huge loophole when the matter reached the Senate floor. While the depletion allowance was not totally repealed, its benefits were substantially reduced. However, the leaders in that fight were Ted Kennedy and Fritz Hollings of South Carolina, neither of whom were Finance Committee members.

A year after winning the Finance Committee seat, Mondale was appointed to the newly created Budget Committee, which had been given broad responsibilities over Senate tax and spending policies. For the next two years, he was the only Democrat to sit simultaneously on both committees. It meant he was in a position to deal with some of the most intricate and significant public-policy issues facing Congress. No longer was he fated to sit in nearly empty hearing rooms as a lone senator chairing forlorn inquiries into the plight of the powerless. Now he could make things happen. By early 1974, he was working to reshape an antirecession tax-cut bill so that its benefits would be liberally distributed to those in low-income brackets by offering a $200 individual credit as an alternative to the $750 personal exemption. He lost that fight but was successful in another when he fended off Long and the Nixon administration in order to insure that $2.5 billion in annual benefits from a social-service program would go to the needy. Designed to help welfare recipients become self-supporting earners, the program's strategy was conceived as a targeted attack on particular circumstances that might be blocking an individual's or family's efforts to break free of poverty and a dependency on the dole. For some, the answer might lie in family planning. For kids from troubled or broken homes, the need might be for foster care. There was also money to help provide day-care services for working mothers, as well as other kinds of services tailored to the needs of the aged, the blind, the physically disabled, the mentally retarded, alcoholics, and drug addicts.

Then, about a month before his nomination as vice president, Mondale redeemed some of his standing with tax reformers when he whipped Long on the Senate floor. The fight involved an attempt by the Finance Committee chairman to reduce the maximum tax rate on investment income —a move that would have benefited the wealthy.

These efforts were consistent with his lifelong interests in helping underdogs. However, by 1975, Mondale was beginning to try to blur his ideological image in an effort to broaden his Minnesota base in a way that would be attractive to moderate Republicans. Mondale's strategy was to show that he was not so antibusiness as his GOP foes claimed. Always a free-trade advocate, Mondale had steered a bill through Congress in late 1969 liberalizing restrictions on commerce with Communist-bloc countries. It was the first such trade bill to pass since World War II. His efforts had been deeply appreciated by some of his powerful corporate constituents—Control Data, Honeywell, Minnesota Mining and Manufacturing. They all claimed to have lost substantial business because of Cold War trade restraints. But it was the Finance Committee that held the greatest opportunity for doing an occasional favor for a corporate constituent. Once committed to eliminating a tax subsidy for American exporters, Mondale backed off in 1976 under intense business lobbying. He wound up supporting a measure that merely reduced the subsidy, but did not eliminate it. He even attempted to punch two additional loopholes in the federal tax code. One was calculated to benefit Honeywell. The other beneficiary would have been Investors Diversified Services, Inc., a huge Minneapolis-based financial-services company. Both were dropped by the Finance Committee after Mondale was nominated to become Jimmy Carter's running mate.

As part of his effort to retailor himself politically, Mondale also dropped from his rhetorical wardrobe earlier sweeping assertions about the need for fundamental social change. His laments about the "curse of racism" and the plight of the powerless were broad social indictments, implicating Democrats as well as Republicans. Presidential campaigning taught him to become more narrowly partisan, to focus on traditional economic issues that would unite and not divide his party. Even though he had spent two years in the front lines of a pitched battle over school busing, he seldom discussed the topic unless specifically questioned.

Life as a candidate and high public officeholder had left its mark on Mondale in other ways as well. The demands of politics require, as a prime rule of survival, that one keep an eye out for one's own interests before anything else. Friends, aides, allies, and even opponents sometimes must be used—perhaps they even expect to be used. That Mondale understood this early in his political life was demonstrated by the abrupt way he left the law firm that had hired him fresh from school. He left in search of greater freedom to pursue a political career, even though it might well be argued that he owed the firm more service in return for the training and opportunities it had provided. Having left, Mondale placed a major professional burden on his partner, Harry MacLaughlin, who nonetheless willingly undertook the challenge of launching a new practice with one whose interests and energies were being directed toward politics and not the law. For MacLaughlin, the gamble eventually paid off with an appointment to the federal bench.

Later, Mondale depended on young lawyers in his attorney general's office to help him with speeches and to drive him around the state to various engagements. Those chores were not part of their official duties. No one's legal career would have suffered by refusing to give up evenings and weekends in order to help advance Mondale's fortunes. Nonetheless, those interested in politics could be counted on to make themselves available—eagerly, in most cases.

As he grew older, some of Mondale's closest friends were hunting and fishing companions. For Mondale, the woods and lakes of northern Minnesota were an escape from the pressures of public office and its constant demands. In public, he was constantly on stage, always performing, always projecting an image. At all times—on the Senate floor, in committee, along the campaign trail, in his office—he had to be mentally sharp, alert to nuances and intrigue. The one respite was in the wilderness where there would be a crude equalitarianism and where—except for occasional discussions about busing or gun control—no one would call him to account for his political positions. In that totally masculine environment, he became known as a good "bull cook"—the one who does the menial tasks of peeling potatoes, slicing onions, cleaning the pots and pans.

Of those who hunted and fished with Mondale, none was closer than Fran Befera, a rough-spoken Duluth television-station owner whose habits and interests were not shared by anyone Mondale knew in Washington. Yet, over the years, Befera became a constant in Mondale's life, a friend of almost total and unquestioning loyalty, whose boisterous gregariousness was a contrast to the inner tautness of Mondale's personality. There was something else about Befera. "I suppose in all the years I've known Mondale, I've never asked him for a favor," Befera said.

Like others in Mondale's life, Befera, too, was on call. Befera remembered going to a New Year's Eve party six weeks after Mondale aborted his presidential-campaign plans. Befera got a midnight telephone call at the height of the party. It was Mondale.

"I assumed it was to wish me Happy New Year," Befera recalled. "He not only wished me Happy New Year but said he would be in Duluth on New Year's Day at seven o'clock in the morning. And I said, 'You've gotta be kidding.' And he said, 'I'm all packed. I'm leaving on the first plane out of Washington and we're going [ice] fishing.' I was completely shocked at suggesting going fishing on New Year's Day. And he said he just had to get away at that time. I've got two snowmobiles and a trailer, and he said, 'Get the boys and we'll go up to the shack.' Sure enough. He was there at seven o'clock in the morning and we were ready with the machines and we went fishing for five days in Canada."

Befera and Mondale clearly have a close personal relationship. Mondale obviously knew that he could count on Befera not to be outraged at such a patently presumptuous suggestion—that Befera drop whatever he was doing on a New Year's holiday to accommodate Mondale's impulse. Doubtless, Befera appreciated the extreme pressures that had been tormenting his friend during that presidential campaign-tryout period. Still, the timing of the call—coming in the midst of a New Year's Eve celebration—and the shortness of the notice are evidence that Mondale himself was not entirely innocent of the imperial attitude that he found so alarming in the presidency. Implicit in his approach to setting up the fishing trip was the expectation that some degree of deference was his due.

However, as a boss, Mondale by now had become less demanding, more willing to live within the capabilities of his staff—which, anchored by Moe, was judged to be one of the best on Capitol Hill. Mondale attracted solid, bright professionals. Meanwhile, having acknowledged his own limitations as a politician by dropping out of presidential contention, he now became more tolerant of the limitations of others. "I think after he made that decision he felt a great weight lifted," said Gail Harrison, who joined the staff in 1969 and later became one of his top issues experts. "You could see him digging in, in a number of areas. I think he reacted by saying, 'OK, now there's some stuff I'm going to do.'"

One of those projects was to write a book—*The Accountability of Power*—describing the things "we as Americans must do to protect our system and our liberties from the encroachment of an unaccountable presidency." It was a serious attempt to lay out an agenda of institutional reforms—affecting the executive branch, Congress, the political parties, and the media—that might restrain the agressive tendencies of an "imperial presidency."

Inspired by Watergate, Vietnam, and his own political experiences, the book anticipated the final chapter in his own Senate career. For, by 1975, a new scandal was unfolding. The newspapers were filled with horrifying accounts of how the country's two most powerful intelligence and investigative agencies, the CIA and the FBI, had strayed from their legal charters to spy on Americans, attempted to discredit minority political leaders like Martin Luther King, disrupted dissident protest groups, and plotted the assassinations of foreign heads of state. Mondale had not been a central participant in the battles over Vietnam or efforts to unravel Watergate. Now, he became an important figure in Congress's response to this latest crisis. As the third-ranking Democrat on the Select Committee on Intelligence, he managed to carve out major areas of influence. He took on the chairmanship of an FBI subcommittee, a role in which he personally investigated the bureau's vendetta against King. Although outranked by the committee chairman,

Frank Church of Idaho, and by Phil Hart of Michigan, Mondale found himself increasingly in control of the overall investigation. By the early spring of 1976, Church was running for president, while Hart was battling the cancer that would eventually kill him. As a result, Mondale was effectively running an investigation that raised fundamental constitutional questions. As a pragmatic veteran of thirty years in competitive politics, Mondale had shaped a career characterized by an ability to make tradeoffs. But this was different. This was not the Finance Committee, which dealt with complex and ambiguous issues. Nor was it like the task of balancing the competing demands of rival political factions from Mississippi to seats at the 1964 Democratic Convention. What was at stake, Mondale said in a major speech in early October, 1975, were illegal attempts by the CIA, the FBI, and other intelligence agencies "to chill political dissent in this country and to stifle the constitutional right to the free expression of views essential" to democracy.

"Those bastards . . . have got to figure out that there are some rules in this society that they're going to have to live with, along with everyone else," Mondale told *Time* magazine. "They're going to tell the truth, they're going to obey the law and they're going to listen to people. . . . But the idea that you can defend this nation within the Constitution, under the law, and tell the truth is still considered a sort of childish, feminine position." There were echoes in Mondale's words of lessons learned during a much earlier period of his life, when his father would unlimber a switch for violations of a moral code that valued personal integrity above everything.

Mondale's anger and frustration surfaced during a hearing on December 11, 1975, when Attorney General Edward Levi told the select committee of a proposed set of guidelines that would bar the FBI from investigating dissidents unless there was a "likelihood" that they were involved in violent and illegal activities. Mondale interrupted. No domestic security investigation should even be considered by the FBI unless there was "unarguable evidence that an exception is needed," Mondale asserted. Would Levi's guidelines stand up if the president ordered the FBI to violate them? Mondale answered his own question: "They would mean nothing." He then asked Levi whether the FBI would give the intelligence committee access to internal reports of possible wrongdoing. "The CIA gave us their reports," Mondale noted.

"I'm not in the CIA," Levi answered.

"Do you think that's a good answer?" Mondale inquired.

"The answer is as good as the question," Levi retorted.

"I think that kind of arrogance is why we have trouble with the executive branch," Mondale exclaimed.

Levi later apologized—sort of. "I didn't mean to be arrogant. I thought someone else was being arrogant. I apologize."

Mondale and the committee pursued the intelligence agencies until one afternoon in late May, 1976. Fifteen months of work ended when the Senate declared it would no longer avert its eyes to the CIA's and FBI's dirty work. On an overwhelming vote, Mondale and his colleagues established a new committee with extensive legislative and budgetary authority over intelligence agencies. The new committee was also to have broad investigative authority backed up by subpoena power. It was a resounding defeat for the handful of the most powerful senators who for decades had alone been privy to CIA and FBI secrets. "No nation has quite done what we've just done," Mondale declared proudly.

Afterwards, a lawyer for the CIA paid tribute to Mondale. "He's got a first-rate mind," the attorney said. "He was no patsy—that's for damn sure."

It had been a sobering experience, but Mondale had not lost his sense of humor. Church scheduled a public hearing to highlight revelations about a CIA cache of highly toxic shellfish poisons. At one point, as Church was approaching the climax of his interrogation of a key CIA witness, Mondale scribbled a note to a staff assistant: "I think Frank is zeroing in on the smoking clam."

Meanwhile, Jimmy Carter was zeroing in on the Democratic presidential nomination. It was also about this time that Dick Moe sat down in his back office to draft an extremely confidential memo. The subject: Jimmy Carter, Fritz Mondale, and the vice presidency of the United States.

17

At the Center of Power

The presentation of the John Nance Garner Award took place in Minneapolis's Leamington Hotel amid the hubbub of election night 1976. Walter Mondale had just been elected vice president of the United States. While raucous DFLers celebrated their hero's good fortune, CBS reporters Jed Duvall and Bill Plante and producer Charles Wolfson presented Mondale with a brass cuspidor in memory of Garner, whose experiences as vice president under Franklin Roosevelt inspired him to describe the job as not being "worth a pitcher of warm spit."

Mondale appreciated the irony. As he well knew, his illustrious predecessors also included Thomas Marshall, who decided that serving as Woodrow Wilson's vice president was "like a man in a cataleptic fit: He cannot speak, he cannot move, he suffers no pain, he is perfectly conscious of all that goes on, but has no part in it." Then there was Mr. Dooley—satirist Finley Peter Dunne's fictional mouthpiece—to remind him that "The prisidincy is th' highest office in th' gift iv th' people. Th' vice-prisidincy is th' next highest an' th' lowest. It isn't a crime exactly. Ye can't be sint to jail f'r it, but it's kind iv a disgrace. It's like writin' anonymous letters."

Mondale had more intimate teachers at hand than Garner, Marshall, or Mr. Dooley. The critical question for

Mondale was posed by Hubert Humphrey, who had propounded something called Humphrey's law: "He who giveth can taketh away—and often does." Nearing the end of one of the most productive political lives in the nation's history, Humphrey's relationship with Mondale had now changed. No longer were there the minor frictions and inevitable rivalries between two nimble politicians seeking the approval of the same constituency. Their paths had separated, the 1976 election having dissolved a Senate partnership. Humphrey was now reconciled to a career unfulfilled by the White House. He had become an elder statesman anyway, and he seemed to take an almost paternal solicitude in the political well-being of others. With their shared experiences in Minnesota politics, Mondale had a special place in the older man's affections. Having encouraged Mondale to seek the vice presidency, Humphrey now spent hours with him detailing the personal and political humiliations of having tried to serve Lyndon Johnson in that office. Humphrey recalled how he never recouped his standing after he enraged Johnson by arguing privately within the administration against plans in early 1965 to launch heavy bombing strikes against military targets in North Vietnam. Even more pathetic had been the petty indignities. Going out of town required submitting a written request to Johnson for use of a presidential airplane. If the manifest included the names of reporters, they would be stricken. Aside from one or two top aides, Humphrey's staff had little access to the White House. Norman Sherman, Humphrey's press secretary, estimated that he made about five visits in four years to the White House West Wing, perhaps fifty yards from his office in the Old Executive Office Building.

These were matters of great concern. But Mondale soon discovered he had little time to worry about his fate. He was too busy helping Carter put together a new government. After a short Caribbean vacation with Joan, Mondale took a position at Carter's side as one of his key planners during the ten-week transition period preceding the Inauguration. As Carter's talent scouts began screening and recruiting Cabinet members and other top policy-making officials, Mondale found himself standing near the apex of a selection process, one step below Carter himself. Aspirants for top-echelon jobs discovered that an interview with Mondale meant they were among the finalists. The ultimate decision usually was made when the president-elect and the vice president-elect would meet alone. At least two eventual Cabinet appointees—Bob Bergland at Agriculture and Joe Califano at Health, Education and Welfare—won their jobs on the strength of Mondale's advocacy. The selection of Charles Schultze as chairman of the Council of Economic Advisers was also heavily favored by Mondale.

Mondale and Carter had their first substantive discussion of the vice presidency on that sweltering July morning in Plains when Mondale presented himself for a job interview. The question, eclipsed by subsequent campaign pressures, remained unresolved until Mondale presented himself on the evening of December 9 at Blair House, Carter's transition residence. Sitting in the elegant second-floor drawing room—where visiting heads of state normally receive callers—Carter and Mondale gazed out the window at the White House, bathed in floodlight, across Pennsylvania Avenue. In Carter's lap was a memorandum, drafted under Dick Moe's supervision, spelling out Mondale's ideas for a successful vice presidency. As they talked, the history of that office passed in review: Truman assuming the presidency ignorant of the atomic bomb and of FDR's wartime diplomacy; Ike asking for a week to think of maybe one contribution by Nixon to the Eisenhower presidency. When Mondale got up to leave, Carter assured him: "This time it's going to be different."

"The history is pretty grim," Mondale replied. "I'd be surprised if this works out any differently."

Campaigning with Bobby Kennedy, 1966

Inspecting flood damage in Minnesota with Gene McCarthy, Karl Rolvaag, and Lyndon Johnson

Mondale withdraws from presidential contention, 1974

The Mondale-Dole vice-presidential debate, 1976

Mondale's pessimism was not based on anything Carter had said. In fact, Mondale had just received sweeping approval of everything he proposed in the written memo, including his becoming an intimate and general adviser to Carter. In Mondale's mind, an important advisory role should be the core of his relationship to Carter. It meant one thing: Influence. Indeed, Mondale had some reason to be hopeful even before presenting Carter with the memo. He recalled that earlier conversation in Plains when Carter had insisted that he would not be threatened by an activist and politically savvy vice president. The power of the presidency is constitutionally indivisible, Carter had said. No one in his administration could usurp it. Influence, however, was an attribute he could bestow on others; Carter also realized that his success in office might well depend on how the influence was exercised—and by whom. His lack of familiarity with Washington and its various power centers alone required that he be influenced by someone with the kind of insider's knowledge he lacked.

That meant Mondale. Carter's Cabinet-level nominees gathered on December 28 in the sun-filled room of a Carter friend's house on St. Simons Island, a vacation spot off the Georgia coast, for their first joint working session. They were handed a twenty-nine-page memo outlining Carter's weekly schedule through March. "Fritz has done some good work," Carter said, nodding towards his vice president-elect seated on his left.

The agenda, prepared by a Carter-Mondale staff team under Mondale's supervision, allocated the president's time among fourteen main concerns during the administration's first hundred days and then laid out a more general work plan extending into early summer. The document also sketched broad themes to lend coherence to a Carter presidency. At one point, for example, the Mondale agenda stressed the importance of depicting Carter as "a president who will unify the country, healing past divisions, so that we can get on with meeting the problems of the future, rather than debating those of the past." It was in part an exercise in image-making, but it resulted in a dramatic move the first day Carter took office. The new president issued a "full, complete, and unconditional pardon" for those who violated the Selective Service Act during the Vietnam War.

Another early initiative, foreshadowed by the Mondale memo, was Carter's request that Congress revive the Legislative Reorganization Act as part of fulfilling a much ballyhooed campaign promise to shake up and streamline the bureaucracy. The memo also sketched out Carter's economic-stimulus package and suggested a ten-day vice-presidential tour of Western Europe and Japan to lay the groundwork for a spring summit conference.

One significant early presidential action not mentioned in the Mondale agenda was Carter's abrupt move in mid-February to cut off federal funding for eighteen water projects. Notwithstanding Carter's contention that the projects would be environmental disasters and economic boondoggles, the administration's heavy-handedness betrayed gross inexperience and insensitivity in dealings with Capitol Hill. Congress was outraged. For one thing, Carter was attacking—as he had said he would—the time-honored custom of pork-barrel politics. For another, Carter failed to consult beforehand with many of the senators and representatives directly affected by the cuts. Mondale, aghast at the self-inflicted damage to the administration's legislative program, helped persuade Carter to strike a compromise with Congress, although Carter would later regret having softened his position.

The episode did demonstrate the limits of Mondale's influence. Where his advice might collide with Carter's will, the outcome was predictable. In the early days of the administration, it was not altogether clear who had Carter's ear, although the vice president was certainly one of those with the greatest degree of access. But there was also Carter's old Georgia friend and budget director, Bert Lance, as well as his young Georgia friend and political troubleshooter, Ham Jordan. Lance and Jordan could approach Carter on the basis of years of loyal and close association. So could press secretary Jody Powell and Atlanta lawyer Charles Kirbo, who functioned as a general adviser without portfolio in the Carter White House. On economic policy, Carter was likely to turn to Lance, Charles Schultze, and Treasury Secretary Mike Blumenthal. Stuart Eizenstat, Carter's domestic-affairs chief and another Georgian, was also influential on issues of economic and social policy. The formulation of foreign policy was equally complex, involving Secretary of State Cyrus Vance, National Security Adviser Zbigniew Brzezinski, Intelligence Director Stansfield Turner, and Defense Secretary Harold Brown.

As an economic conservative, Carter was determined to curb inflation and balance the federal budget by the end of his term. Those commitments alone were certain to lower Mondale's batting average as an advocate of liberal programs. He fought to salvage the $50 tax rebate as the centerpiece of Carter's economic-stimulus package—and lost. He fought for a higher minimum wage—and lost. He fought for higher farm price supports—and lost.

The defeats hurt because they raised questions about Mondale's influence and refueled the familiar debate about his political toughness. They did not, however, seem to retard the institutional and personal relationship that was developing between Carter and Mondale. Aside from the largely ceremonial duties of the presiding officer of the U.S. Senate, the vice president has only one constitutional responsibility—to be ready to assume power in case the presidency becomes vacant, or the president is incapacitated. Mondale had been assured that, whatever happened, he and the nation would not be doomed to relive Truman's harrowing experience, if Carter's presidency were foreshortened. That assurance took on substance during the transition when Carter invited Mondale to pick an office in the West Wing. He settled on a suite less than fifty paces from the Oval Office and located between Jordan's and Brzezinski's offices. Mondale's window looked out on the Old Executive Office Building across West Executive Avenue—a gray-walled fortress with a huge second-floor office representing the closest advance by his predecessors on the seat of power. Now he had become the first vice president to establish a permanent beachhead within the presidency's inner sanctum.

The office assignments were significant. "You might as well be in Baltimore," Mondale told visitors, gesturing out his office window towards the old EOB. Proximity to Carter made access possible, although not guaranteed. In his memo, however, Mondale had listed specific steps that would help him function as an effective counselor.

One was to prevent the poisonous staff rivalries that had made Humphrey's life miserable. In this respect, Mondale started with an enormous advantage over Humphrey and other vice presidents. The successful meshing of the campaign staffs had made it easy to take the next logical step. Carter agreed with Mondale that the two staffs should continue functioning as one. The working relationship between Moe—who became chief of Mondale's vice-presidential staff—and Jordan continued through the transition and into the presidency. Other top campaign aides, like Jim Johnson, Mike Berman, and Gail Harrison, moved with Moe into important staff positions after inauguration. Their contacts with counterparts on Carter's staff also continued. The administration's relations with the press generally were strengthened when Mondale hired a press secretary. He was Albert Eisele, a highly regarded Washington correspondent for the Ridder newspapers and author of a joint biography of Hubert Humphrey and Gene McCarthy. Distinctions between the staffs were further blurred by presidential assignments that often involved collaborative efforts. "I consider I work for Mondale," Jordan said. "He's my second boss, the way Carter is my first boss." Other staff decisions extended Mondale's influence. David Aaron, a foreign policy specialist from his Senate staff, was named Brzezinski's top deputy. Bert Carp, another long-time Mondale aide, became head of the Domestic Council staff under Eizenstat. Although no longer on his payroll, Aaron and Carp were Mondale loyalists now in high, sensitive positions under Carter. Their involvement in important administration decisions meant that Mondale's interests would not be neglected. Carp's and Aaron's affection for Mondale was well known. Their hiring was a sign of Carter's good faith.

Other recommendations in the memo were also faithfully executed. Thanks to advice from both Humphrey and Nelson Rockefeller, Mondale avoided one of the deepest traps of his office. Unlike both those former vice presidents, Mondale was not burdened with time-consuming—but politically insignificant—operational or managerial assignments. Humphrey, for example, was made chairman of the National Aeronautics and Space Council. Under Gerry Ford, Rockefeller headed the Committee on the Right to Privacy, the Commission on Productivity and Work Quality, and the Federal Compensation Commission. Mondale's assignments involved substantive issues of short duration, giving him real flexibility. In addition, a Monday lunch became a fixture on both men's schedule. Mondale also was included at the president's regularly scheduled intelligence briefings with CIA Director Turner and National Security Adviser Brzezinski. And when Brzezinski and Secretary of State Vance gathered on Fridays for their ninety-minute foreign-policy breakfast with Carter, Mondale was there. He was also expected to participate in all National Security Council and Cabinet meetings.

To make sure that Mondale missed nothing else of significance, Carter directed his staff to supply the vice president with detailed, advance copies of his presidential schedule. Mondale was to feel free to join any meeting involving Carter. Nothing was to be off-limits—not even the most sensitive negotiations with foreign leaders or strategy sessions involving the most crucial national security question—the attempt to reach agreement with the Soviet Union on a Strategic Arms Limitation Treaty. Of at least equal significance was Mondale's location at a major sluice gate in the enormous paperflow generated by Carter. Mondale was in what the White House bureaucratically called the "loop": every piece of paper Carter saw, he would see. It meant he could study sensitive foreign-intelligence reports before they reached Carter and then later read the presidential directives and notations they inspired. The process bolstered Mondale's clout enormously. When Vance sent Carter a text of a speech he was to deliver in late September, 1978, to the United Nations, it routinely wound up on Mondale's desk as well. What attracted his attention was a section containing language certain to inflame the Israelis. The offending portion involved the West Bank and the Palestinians—two Middle East issues that were highly sensitive following Carter's Camp David summit with Egyptian President Anwar Sadat and Israeli Premier Menachem Begin. Mondale argued unsuccessfully with Vance and Brzezinski for softer language. Finally, he appealed to Carter, who had already tentatively approved the original draft.

As Carter recalled the incident in an interview, "One evening—I think it was probably nine-thirty, ten o'clock—Fritz called me on the phone and said he wanted to appeal my decision, and asked me to reexamine it.

"I think I was in a movie theater with a group of guests." (The scene was the White House theater and the movie was *Paint Your Wagon.*) "I left the theater and went up to my study and reread the text to look at Fritz's comments and

I agreed with Fritz. I called Vance in New York and told him to modify the text.

"And I might say that both the Arabs . . . and the Israelis accepted the revised text with a great deal of appreciation."

In terms of his constitutional position in the line of succession to the presidency, Mondale's situation enabled him to watch and understand every step taken by Carter. If not exactly a bully pulpit, the vice presidency was at least a great pew for learning how to lead the congregation someday himself.

He was not just an observer. As chairman of the obscure White House Executive Management Committee, Mondale was also in charge of the president's long-range planning. The committee was established six months after Carter took office. The idea was to provide a tool for helping the president unclog a glut of issues that could otherwise immobilize the White House. By Thanksgiving, 1978, the process was working smoothly. Mondale presented Carter with a thick preliminary draft of a memorandum on domestic and foreign policies. The memo set forth Carter's options for assigning the next year's priorities, based on his overall objectives of controlling inflation and completing a strategic-arms treaty. It covered everything from congressional relations to overseas travel. After receiving Carter's reaction, the committee prepared a final list of about twelve high-priority issues for his attention. A second list was prepared for the Cabinet's attention, subject ultimately to Carter's review. A third list involved matters of lesser importance, either to be initiated by Congress or the agencies themselves, but not rated significant enough for extensive White House lobbying.

Theirs was more than just a working relationship. Thirty years of political craftsmanship had led Mondale to this point. Now he was applying the lessons of those years to perfecting his White House role. Like any successful politician, Mondale was a man of many faces. One was the public figure seen by cheering crowds—exhorting, haranguing, imploring, inspiring. This was the man who was always up —never vexed, never doubting. But behind the scenes was a different man who ran his staff with varying degrees of civility and crabbiness, depending on his mood, and who, in earlier days at least, regarded aides as expendable resources. Then there was the bureaucratic man who had learned to work with peers and superiors by accommodation, and who in particular had mastered the secret of deference. In this guise, Mondale did not burn bridges unnecessarily—not even with someone like James Eastland, seemingly an archenemy. He had managed to work with Freeman, Rolvaag, Humphrey, and now he was working with the president. Jimmy Carter's one complaint about Mondale early in the administration was that he didn't speak up enough. But otherwise he had done everything right, beginning with their first meeting in Plains when Mondale had prepped himself like a schoolboy. Carter and Mondale had become friends.

Formed at middle age during a period of intense political pressure, their friendship did not have the deeply enduring personal quality of Carter's ties with Bert Lance—or Mondale's with Fran Befera. Nonetheless, there developed a strong bond of respect, admiration, and fondness that made their constant proximity and occasional disagreements tolerable. When Mondale submitted a memo on September 6, 1977, reviewing their relationship, he noted that during one particular week, 48 percent of his office hours were spent in the president's company. Carter scribbled in the margin, "Fritz, I'm pleased." It was signed "Jimmy." One day, fourteen hours were spent together. When reporters in the early fall of 1977 began asking Jody Powell skeptical questions about Mondale's influence, Carter stepped in to deflate the stories that he saw coming. In an extraordinary presidential gesture, Carter made two lengthy telephone calls to bureau chiefs of influential newspapers—Hedrick Smith of the New York *Times* and Jack Nelson of the Los Angeles *Times*—to argue that the vice president's role was growing stronger. He told Nelson, "On thirty minutes' notice, I would be perfectly willing to say, 'Fritz, I can't go to the Soviet Union because of some reason, would you go and do the final arrangements in the SALT negotiations with Brezhnev.' He has complete knowledge of the subject and of my position." In a subsequent news conference, Carter estimated that he was spending more time with Mondale than with all his other senior staff advisers combined.

Mondale also knew when to fade from view. While Carter was agonizing over disclosures about Lance's questionable banking past, Mondale stayed in the background. He let the president know his view—that Lance's usefulness to the administration had been destroyed. He recognized Carter's personal trauma—and stood clear as Lance, a rival source of influence, was swept from office by events.

"Fritz doesn't waste his influence," Carter said. "He does excellent background study. And his staff is superb. He also uses my staff, some of whom are his former staff members, very effectively.

"In general, Fritz stays quiet during meetings and listens to the debates and arguments both ways.

"Almost invariably, when Fritz is present, when I'm approaching the time for a decision, I turn to him last and say, 'Mr. Vice President, what is your assessment?' And that's when he is always thoroughly prepared and he weighs in on the few items about which he feels very deeply.

"And it's really kind of a rare thing for me not to go along with his position because Fritz tries to put himself in the role of a president and not just espouse a fairly radical argument, one way or the other, in an irresponsible way.

"But, when he does speak on an issue, everybody gets quiet, everybody listens to him, because they know that he's approaching the point of making the judgment from the same perspective as if he were president.''

Although intended as working sessions, the format of the regular Monday lunches would occasionally break down, and they would spend the time discussing books instead of the items on Mondale's agenda. Carter often ribbed Mondale in front of others. One Cabinet session in late July, 1977, opened when Carter declared that ''a very serious thing occurred'' the previous week during a state visit by West German Chancellor Helmut Schmidt. Mondale, who had earlier been criticized by a fashion designer for wearing tuxedo pants that were too short, had gone to a German embassy dinner in ''formal clothes with his trousers up to his knees,'' Carter said.

''It embarrassed me and the Cabinet,'' he added.

''Mr. President, wait a minute,'' interrupted Mondale. ''Those pants fit me when I assumed office. But I've grown a lot.''

''Up until this week,'' Carter corrected him.

About six months later, when Carter returned to Washington on January 6 from a seven-nation tour, he was met by Mondale with this greeting:

''When you left, Mr. President, you asked those of us who stayed behind to take care of things. These have been nine successful days in the history of the country. And we are proud of it. We have avoided war. We have continued government services with no increase in taxes. The Congress [it was then in recess] has not turned down a single suggestion during these past nine days. I have aged a year [Mondale had turned fifty the previous day], and Amy is now an accomplished skier.''

''Maybe I should have stayed gone longer,'' Carter responded.

Aside from the fact that they got along, the questions persisted: How much influence did Mondale have? Did his presence in an office so close to the Oval Office really make a difference? How seriously was Carter taking his advice?

Early in the administration, Mondale had been warned by Humphrey not to antagonize the three special-interest groups that most prominently supported both of them— the blacks, organized labor, and the Jews. As Carter's term passed the halfway point, what was the situation?

• The blacks wanted a comprehensive jobs program to lower the stratospheric unemployment rates among inner-city residents. What they got was a bill named after Humphrey—but watered down drastically and passed after his death.

• Organized labor wanted Congress to pass several union-security bills and act on Sen. Edward Kennedy's ambitious plan for national health insurance. What happened? The administration could not flex enough muscle to help labor win its objectives and called Kennedy's health program too expensive.

• The American Jewish community wanted assurances that Israel's security would not become a bargaining chip in U.S. efforts to assure long-term access to Middle East oil supplies. Instead, Jewish anxieties grew as the Carter administration pressed for an Egyptian-Israeli peace agreement that would affect Israel's security along the West Bank.

Publicly, Mondale was Carter's cheerleader, just as Humphrey had been Johnson's. Meeting with reporters at a White House breakfast in mid-December, 1977, Mondale ignored a string of setbacks and proclaimed Carter's legislative record at the end of his first year in office "one of the most successful . . . in a long, long time." The following spring, Mondale—like almost every other modern vice president—undertook the assignment of campaigning for administration-favored candidates in the off-year elections. In fact, however, he was campaigning for Carter. And, while remaining stoutly enthusiastic about his president, he also was defensive. Social Security tax increases, prolonged haggling over natural-gas prices, the Senate fight over the

Panama Canal treaties—there was not much in the Carter record to excite the party faithful, let alone the nation. While tacitly acknowledging Carter's difficulties, Mondale put the best possible face on things. "I predict that before this is over Jimmy Carter is going to be one of the most respected and popular presidents in American history because he was man enough to do the job," Mondale told loyal Democrats in Dubuque on March 29. In a Detroit suburb the next day, Mondale elaborated: Restoring the Social Security System's solvency was painful, Mondale said. "After many years of ignoring the problem, and it was there for everybody to see, we stood up to the problem. . . . Do you think we wanted to? No. It had to be done."

Carter—the president who takes on the tough ones. That was Mondale's theme through the fall. Carter's victories late in the Ninety-fifth Congress did help. An administration bill reforming the Civil Service system was passed, while two big vetoes were upheld. One was of a weapons-procurement bill; the other, a public-works measure. Meanwhile, the outcome of the Egyptian-Israeli summit at Camp David seemed for a while to promise an early peace treaty, thanks to Carter's persistence. Mondale's portrait of a courageous leader in the White House, tackling intractable problems, seemed now to take on substance.

But by early December—when the Democratic party held a midterm conference in Memphis—Mondale was back on the defensive. Inflation-fighting had become the administration's top priority. Carter was putting the finishing touches on a budget that would reduce the federal deficit to less than $30 billion by restraining spending on social programs, while increasing defense spending. The liberals were enraged. Their leader, Senator Kennedy, declared that the budget would be the administration's Vietnam. Mondale retorted that a failure to deal with inflation would drive the Democrats "out of public office just as our predecessors were for failing to stand up to the problem of the Vietnam War."

For a politician who had spent much of his adult life championing the oppressed and the victimized, Mondale was in an odd position. From the outset, he had privately opposed the rigidity of Carter's $30 billion deficit target. He had been equally distressed by a proposal to increase the Pentagon budget by 3 percent over the rate of inflation. For years as a senator, he had assailed the "screwy, almost obscene" priorities of a Republican administration that slashed social spending while investing heavily in hardware for space and defense programs. But Mondale thought he, like Carter, perceived shifts in the country's mood—away from traditional liberalism, away from expensive social programs. Mondale agreed with Carter that ignoring inflation would be foolhardy. He also recognized the strategic and political necessities of bolstering defense spending. What bothered Mondale was Carter's habit of committing himself prematurely to fixed numerical goals that only enraged the party's special-interest constituencies—like blacks and organized labor—before other steps could be taken to cushion the blow. Mondale felt he needed time to help the administration, and himself, straddle the issues raised by Carter's budget pronouncements. There were certain imperatives to be balanced. Inflation clearly had to be designated as a top concern, but the administration could not allow itself to be seen as callously turning its back on the aged, the needy, the powerless, the sick. Having made that argument in a lengthy December meeting with Carter, Eizenstat, and Budget Director James McIntyre, Mondale won a concession. Some $2 billion in social-service spending would be restored to the administration's budget. But even as he left the room, Mondale was not sure whether that limited victory was due to his advocacy or was a step Carter intended to take anyway.

Whatever Mondale's disagreements, he kept them private. Despite his unprecedented influence as vice president, Mondale sought only limited victories. His attitude about becoming a "kamikaze pilot" had not changed. He was still the same politician who sat on the Finance Committee to seek modest and pragmatic goals—goals that did not include taking on Russell Long or waging highly visible losing crusades for drastic tax reforms. He worked in the present tense, meaning that he was content to go only for goals that were possible. As he had done throughout his career, he sized up the reality of the moment and then devised a strategy that would work—and would not pose undue risks.

And it indeed worked. Contrary to predictions, Mondale did not sink into the customary oblivion of vice presidents. He proved his strength early in the administration during a showdown between himself and CIA Director Stansfield Turner. The Washington *Post* triggered the clash in February, 1977, when it disclosed that the CIA had made secret cash payments to King Hussein of Jordan. Turner subsequently told a Senate committee that he would support criminal sanctions to deter leakers of secret intelligence. Turner, moreover, seemed to be speaking with the president's support. At a session with congressional leaders, Carter described the *Post* story as "irresponsible." Several days later, Carter told State Department employees that the nation's "key intelligence sources are becoming reluctant to continue their relationship with us because of the danger of being exposed in the future."

The fledgling administration seemed headed toward proposing an official-secrets act with criminal penalties for both the official who leaks a secret and the reporter who discloses it. The idea was intolerable to Mondale. A free press was a powerful countervailing force helping to hold the government accountable for its abuses. Mondale had watched the process work in the unraveling of the Watergate and intelligence-agency scandals. He took his case to the president. He also went public, telling the Washington

Post in a March 5 interview, "I would find it very difficult to accept the system of criminal penalties. I don't think it works and I don't think it should work." The best safeguard against the abuse of authority by presidential subordinates, Mondale said, is "the fear that they may be caught and they may read about it in the press." Four days later, Carter told a news conference that he hoped the problem of leaks damaging to the national security could be solved without resorting to criminal penalties.

Indeed, Mondale's intense interest in the practices of national intelligence agencies continued into the vice presidency. He made it his business to insure that the CIA and FBI did not slip back into old lawless habits. A tough executive order, filled with procedural restrictions, bore his specific imprint: No wiretaps, searches, or mail openings without a warrant; no domestic spying on Americans by the CIA; no political investigations by the FBI; no covert FBI harassment of suspicious individuals or organizations.

Mondale was less successful in his initial attempts to persuade Carter not to swamp Congress with legislative proposals. It wasn't just the number of bills that concerned him. It was their complexity—welfare reform, a controversial energy package, an intricate and massive urban-aid program, a plan to contain escalating hospital costs. Mondale tried to tell Carter that he would have better luck were he to pick his fights more carefully and give Congress more time to catch its breath.

By the summer of 1978, Mondale sensed from his extensive contacts on Capitol Hill that the administration was in serious trouble. Carter's presidential authority had become an object of ridicule. One long-time friend and loyal administration supporter even drew Mondale aside and begged him to make sure the president vetoed *something.* "They're laughing at the president," the friend said. "This can't continue. He's got to let them know he's president."

The friend even offered one of his own bills as veto bait. But that wasn't necessary. Mondale had a bill in mind. It was a $37 billion weapons-procurement measure, containing a $2 billion authorization for a fifth nuclear aircraft carrier. The administration had attempted to delete the carrier but Congress insisted. It was, in fact, the latest version of a ship Mondale had opposed since 1969 when he and Clifford Case tried to scuttle funding for the nation's third nuclear carrier.

When Mondale took it up with Carter, he was badly outnumbered. Defense-authorization bills were traditionally considered veto-proof. Almost all of Carter's major advisers—Jordan, Jody Powell, Eizenstat, Frank Moore—were opposed to a veto. An outraged Congress, they argued, would surely override the president, making him look more foolish than ever.

But Congress was Mondale's special area of expertise. He also had learned to become more direct.

"Mr. President, you've got to veto something," Mondale said. "Here's one where you've got a good case. You said you're for a strong defense but wouldn't take a carrier.

"If you don't do it now, you'll never get control."

Carter agreed. The job of persuading Congress not to override the veto was placed in the hands of a task force headed by Dick Moe. The veto was sustained. Easily.

However, Carter's political problems continued to grow. The Ninety-sixth Congress arrived in Washington in January, 1979, even less inclined to follow Carter's lead than the Congress it replaced. The Shah's fall in Iran and a host of other complicated supply problems sharply reduced the availability of gasoline at the pump. The result was long lines of frustrated and angry motorists, particularly on the East and West coasts. Meanwhile, inflation continued to worsen and the economy edged towards recession.

What to do? Carter was in deep political trouble. Each succeeding public opinion poll showed further erosion in his popular support. One of the many shadows lying across Jimmy Carter's—and Walter Mondale's—political future was cast by Teddy Kennedy, who was positioning himself for a possible intraparty challenge to Carter in 1980.

In an attempt to assert leadership, Carter on July 15 delivered a nationally televised speech written to address the concerns that seemed to be at the heart of his political troubles. Half of the speech turned out to be a sermon on the country's "crisis of confidence."

That portion was based on an analysis of the national mood by Patrick Caddell, Carter's pollster. In discussions at Camp David—to which Carter had retreated to contemplate his and the nation's state—Mondale made it clear he thought Caddell's theory about a national "malaise" was silly. Mondale—and Eizenstat—argued that the trick was to offer practical and feasible programs to solve the problems that seemed to be weighing in on the nation. The second half ot the speech reflected Mondale's advice.

Several days after the speech, Carter—while Mondale was on the road campaigning for SALT II—received en masse the resignations of his entire Cabinet and White House senior staff. That, too, was a move opposed by Mondale. When the idea was first raised at Camp David, Dick Moe was reminded that Nixon had done the same thing after the 1972 elections. Mondale also fought unsuccessfully to save Joe Califano's job as secretary of Health, Education and Welfare.

The entire episode—the preachy tone of Carter's speech, the offering of the resignation and the subsequent firings —again underscored the limitations of Mondale's ability to influence the course of the Carter presidency. Yet, the summer's events also underscored the inner strength of the Carter-Mondale relationship. Fighting for his political life, Carter naturally turned to those who had earned his trust through long and loyal service. While Mondale was not consulted on some moves, and disagreed about others, he remained a member of the inner presidential circle whose advice was often sought, if not always heeded.

18

A New Voice on Foreign Policy

When the onetime governor of Georgia and his political partner, the former senator from Minnesota, took over the government, foreign policy had not been a conspicuous concern of either. That did not discourage Jimmy Carter, as a presidential candidate, from promising a sharp break with the policies of his predecessors, who, he said in his second campaign debate with Gerald Ford, had blundered most seriously when "the American people have been excluded from the process." He went on to complain, "Our country is not strong anymore; we're not respected anymore. . . . We've lost in our foreign policy the character of the American people." Walter Mondale embellished his own campaign with similar pieties on the subject. He had told a student audience at Notre Dame University on September 10, 1976, that a Carter-Mondale administration would work for the "restoration of a foreign policy that will enable Americans to see the best of themselves reflected in our actions abroad."

Two months after taking office, Carter told the United Nations that none of its members "can claim that mistreatment of its citizens is solely its own business. Equally, no member can avoid its responsibilities to review and to speak when torture or unwarranted deprivation of freedom occurs in any part of the world."

Few were sure what these ringing words meant in practice. It fell to Mondale during the early months of the new administration to explain to other world leaders what to expect of Jimmy Carter.

And so it was that Mondale found himself on the afternoon of May 19, 1977, seated opposite John Vorster, the blunt-spoken, bulldog-visaged prime minister of South Africa. The setting for their grim encounter was a small, spare room with a single bronze chandelier tucked away in the Hofburg Palace in Vienna. Outside, a team of majestic Lippizaner showhorses was prancing in a dusty courtyard, the clop-clop-clop of their flashing hooves echoing dully through the room's open window. Carter was facing a severe challenge to his human-rights policy by events in the huge racial tinderbox of southern Africa, and part of the political message that Mondale was bearing dealt with the transition to black majority rule in Rhodesia and Southwest Africa. The stakes were extraordinarily high. A Cuban expeditionary force had helped usher a Marxist regime to power in the former Portuguese colony of Angola. The success of that Russian-backed venture was now being repeated in Ethiopia. It required no great strategic insight to guess that Rhodesia might be next if U.S. and British initiatives for peaceful political reform should fail.

The rest of the message involved South Africa itself. It was Mondale's assignment to tell the stubborn Afrikaner politician sitting across from him that his nation's political value system was intolerable. Delivering that message would be a little like telling a stranger that he was morally corrupt and had BO as well.

Mondale prepared himself for the assignment with the same intellectual thoroughness that had characterized his industrious researches as a senator into the problems of migrants, disadvantaged kids in the classroom, and the embattled American family. First, he directed his staff to draw up a reading list covering everything from southern

Africa's geography to its history, social composition, and political development. Then, building on that base, he put himself through an intensive series of briefings with experts, gradually narrowing the focus to a point of intense concentration on the issues that would be on the agenda at the Hofburg Palace, the former seat of the Hapsburg Empire.

As Mondale was about to enter the room, whose spartan appearance contrasted with the baroque elegance of the rest of the palace, he gathered around him the State Department and National Security Council experts who had prepared him.

"You guys have done all you can to help me get ready for this," Mondale told them. "The rest is up to me. If I start going off the beam at any point, just pass me a note."

At this point he paused, a small, ironic smile tugging at the corners of his mouth.

"If I still can't get it right, just feel sorry for your country."

The session lasted through the afternoon of May 19 and resumed the following morning. Aside from detailed discussions of the situations in Rhodesia and Southwest Africa, the talks involved veiled warnings from Mondale that the United States would not come to South Africa's aid if persistent adherence to racially separatist policies were to embroil Vorster's countrymen in internal conflict. Indeed, Mondale said, a failure to assure full political rights for South Africans of all races would cause "our paths to diverge and our policies to come into conflict. . . . In that event, we would take steps true to our beliefs and values."

When Vorster sarcastically chided Mondale for ignoring his own nation's experiment in separate development, as symbolized by the American Indian reservation, Mondale candidly conceded that the United States was not free of disgrace in its dealings with minorities. Indeed, the very urgency of his mission, he said, reflected the extent to which American values had been formed by the national experience of forging a democratic society open to all races.

For Mondale, the moment was filled with emotional tension and drama. His most intimate political values—nourished since childhood by the religious certitudes of his high-minded parents—were at the core of his assignment. Ultimately, the strength of his convictions carried him one step farther than he intended to go.

At a press conference in the Vienna Hilton Hotel after his final session with Vorster, Mondale was asked by a South African journalist whether he saw any compromise short of the one-man, one-vote principle which the South Africans viewed as an immediate and unconditional political surrender to their huge black and mixed-race majorities.

"No, no," Mondale answered softly. "It's the same thing. Every citizen should have the right to vote and every vote should be equally weighted." An awkward silence greeted Mondale's words, and the press conference came to a close.

Inexperienced in the subtleties of diplomacy, Mondale had crossed an invisible line. For the last day and a half, he had been telling Vorster with earnest directness what would happen to relations between the two countries if South Africa failed to heed black demands for political reform. Now he was dictating a solution to an embattled but sovereign nation whose politicians were notoriously sensitive about outside meddling. When it was his turn at the microphone, Vorster said pointedly, "If there is a choice and if that is the only choice—whether I want to be free and independent or whether I want to be recognized throughout the world—then naturally I opt for freedom and independence."

By advocating universal suffrage for South Africans of all races, Mondale in effect was demanding that Vorster's group commit political suicide. The repercussions were felt for months afterwards, as American diplomats labored to assure the Vorster government that the United States had no intention of telling them how—in specific terms—they should solve South Africa's racial troubles. Finally, Mondale disavowed his own words. In an October interview with the Rand *Daily Mail,* one of South Africa's leading newspapers, Mondale said, "I believe that the crucial step is to begin the dialogue among all segments of society. If there is one central suggestion that I made, it was that the leaders of the South African government meet with the legitimate nonwhite leaders of South Africa and develop with them the reforms which made sense to all South Africans." That was a far different message from an unyielding insistence on a one-man, one-vote formula as the only basis for restructuring South African society.

Having helped Carter lay out the grand design of the administration's African policy, Mondale faded from public view on that issue, following his encounter with Vorster in Vienna. It was now time for professional diplomats and area specialists to take over the detailed, day-to-day execution of that policy. There also was another reason for dissociating himself from a direct, personal responsibility for African affairs. Deepening unrest across that continent—the deteriorating situation in Rhodesia, particularly—convinced Mondale that Africa was, as he expressed it to one friend, a political "tarbaby." A no-win issue, in other words. No amount of mediation seemed likely to produce a political settlement that would avert massive bloodshed. As with the migrant issue in the Senate, Mondale felt he had no more to contribute and a great deal to lose by a continuing political association with an inherently intractable problem.

Although diplomatic greenness was at least partly to blame for his misstep at the press conference following his session with Vorster, Mondale also brought a fresh perspective to his foreign assignments. It was the viewpoint of a politician unawed by the imperial trappings of office or the extravagant courtesies that would await him in foreign lands. Three days after Inauguration Day, Mondale and an entourage of personal aides, Secret Service agents, military experts, and diplomatic specialists took off in a refitted silver-and-blue Boeing 707 on a ten-day, 24,508-mile mission to introduce the Carter administration to NATO allies and to Japan. Lavish state dinners, ornate palaces, sleek limousines, police escorts with sirens wailing, crack military units and brass bands honoring his arrival—that was how he traveled now. After a state dinner in a magnificent Roman palace that entombed a priceless and exquisite collection of cultural treasures—tapestries, paintings, candelabra, sculpted marble staircases—Mondale rode back to his hotel in silence. As the motorcade pulled to a halt, he turned to an aide and, shaking his head incredulously, remarked, "Can you imagine how the goddamn nobles who built that thing must have screwed the peasants?"

Mondale had a number of specific assignments, such as trying to persuade West German Chancellor Helmut Schmidt to step up his country's rate of economic growth and to cancel—or at least to scale down—a potential billion-dollar nuclear-power deal with Brazil. His encounters with heads of government and other ranking political leaders of his host countries stamped Mondale as an intelligent and serious politician and an important figure in the new administration. Public impressions of Mondale were also shaped by his breezy informality and sharp wit.

Asked a complicated question in French about Libya, Mondale paused during a Paris news conference for a translation. When no one came to his rescue, Mondale, who speaks only English, said, "I'm glad you asked that question. I've wanted to talk about my program for child development but no one has asked me."

When the reporter persisted, Mondale shrugged. "The question, then, is how can I look so handsome and vital after a long trip," he offered.

After the laughter subsided, Mondale added a final self-mocking grace note: "It's the nobility of my ideals that show through . . . That's your lead for tomorrow."

The high point of the trip undoubtedly was a private dinner at No. 10 Downing Street that turned into a songfest reminiscent of Mondale's beer-drinking sessions with young Labor Party activists during his summer in England twenty-eight years earlier. But instead of ale or stout, throats were now lubricated by a 1912 cognac and a 1948 port from Sir Winston Churchill's private stock, in addition to a 1955 Mouton Rothschild. The singing started when Prime Minister James Callaghan led a chorus of "I Belong to Glasgow." Soon they were singing "Land of My Fathers" in Welsh, "On Ilkley Moor" in Yorkshire dialect, and of course, "It's the Same the Wide World Over."

That trip was followed by other foreign missions—good-neighbor visits to Canada and Mexico, a show-the-flag trek through the Far East, including tough human-rights talks with Philippine President Ferdinand Marcos, and then a swing through the Middle East. The same political impulsiveness that caused him to overstep on the South African question also led to a minor diplomatic triumph when he arrived in Israel in late June, 1978. Over State Department objections, he visited the Wailing Wall in East Jerusalem—a part of the Holy City seized by the Israelis in the 1967 war and regarded by the American government as occupied territory, and therefore off-limits to official U.S. representatives, if accompanied by an Israeli host. After listening to the arguments, Mondale said he would go to the wall anyway—because he wanted to. It would be a personal visit and not change American policy. And so he did, accompanied by Jerusalem's mayor, Teddy Kollek, in a limousine from which the customary American flag was conspicuously absent. Approaching the wall, Mondale encountered about a hundred members of Gush Emunium, an ultra-nationalist organization, carrying signs declaring, "SADAT DOESN'T

BUDGE ONE CENTIMETER BUT THE U.S. PRESSURES HER REAL ALLY, ISRAEL," and "NO APPEASEMENT—U.S., DON'T BETRAY US." On the other side of the path to the wall was a throng of cheering Israelis. When the Gush Emunium demonstrators began chanting abusive slogans in Hebrew, Mondale abruptly left his security force and plunged into the crowd of friendly spectators, shaking hands as if he was working an American political rally. When he found himself at the huge, honey-colored wall, Mondale, wearing a dark suit and black skullcap, shoved a small paper into a crevice between two of the large Herodian stones of the wall, the last remnant of the Second Temple and Judaism's holiest site. The message read, "Shalom, Shalom, Peace."

Mondale's visit was recalled months later as the participants in the Camp David Middle East summit were congratulating each other on what appeared to have been a diplomatic breakthrough. As he was preparing to leave, Israeli Prime Minister Menachem Begin told a small group of Americans that the vice president had been singularly responsible for the apparent success. The process started, Begin said, with Mondale's arrival in Israel aboard Air Force II.

From the beginning, Mondale often found himself playing a dissenter's role in the formulation of Middle Eastern policy. One of Carter's earliest proposals involved reconvening a Geneva conference first constituted under the joint chairmanship of the United States and the Soviet Union after the 1967 Mideast War. The idea was to make a try for a comprehensive settlement, distinguishing the new administration's diplomacy from Henry Kissinger's step-by-step approach under previous Republican presidents. This initiative was strenuously opposed by the Israelis because it would reestablish Soviet influence in the region and be dominated by the issue of a Palestinian homeland. Mondale privately agreed. He also sympathized with growing Jewish concerns over statements by Carter during the spring of 1977 that were ambiguous about the status of the Palestinians but that were very specific in spelling out steps for returning territory captured by the Israelis in 1967. In San Francisco on June 17, Mondale gave a speech billed as a major administration policy statement on the Middle East. In fact, it was a restatement of Carter's earlier positions. The speech angered Mondale's activist Jewish friends, who now began comparing his plight on the Middle East to Humphrey's on Vietnam under Lyndon Johnson.

Three weeks later, Carter addressed a White House meeting of about forty prominent American Jewish leaders, telling them that a future Palestinian homeland had to be tied to the moderate Jordanian regime and not be created as an independent state. Visiting Mondale a short time later, a moderate Israeli supporter expressed pleasure with the president's position. Mondale exploded: "Goddamn it, that's what I wanted to say in my San Francisco speech but they wouldn't let me." Later that year, however, the Russians and the State Department issued a joint communiqué that reawakened Israeli anxieties over the Palestinian question and that contributed to what Mondale described to another visitor as "just a goddamned year of nightmares." The communiqué was buried, however, after Egyptian President Anwar Sadat's dramatic appearance before the Israeli Knesset in November and the initiation of face-to-face negotiations between the two nations.

Mondale's trip to Israel the following summer had been planned as a ceremonial visit to help Israel celebrate its thirtieth anniversary as a nation. It became something more, however, when talks with Sadat were added to his schedule. The centerpiece was a major speech to the Knesset. It was widely viewed as a reassuring policy statement from an American administration that had given Israel many anxious moments over the preceding eighteen months. As cleared by Carter, the address reiterated the

American commitment to United Nations Resolution 242, calling for Israeli withdrawal from occupied lands, but it went on to stress that the final boundaries could emerge only from negotiations. Mondale also firmly rejected the notion of an independent Palestinian state. It was the kind of speech he had hoped to deliver in San Francisco.

Perhaps more important was a private, hour-long talk Mondale had with Begin shortly before leaving for the meeting with Sadat. "I made a strong plea that he trust Carter. . . . I tried to interpret Carter to him," Mondale said. "I believe I made an impact on him because I think he was beginning to doubt us in our commitment to Israel."

By the time Mondale left for home, he had persuaded Sadat and Begin to resume negotiations in England. While those talks produced no immediate breakthrough, the deadlock showed signs of easing. Mondale also wrote a memo to Carter, saying the moment was opportune for progress towards peace in the Middle East, but it would be necessary to bring Begin and Sadat together in an environment shielded from outside pressures. Contacts between the parties at lower official levels would not be sufficient.

Six weeks later, Carter alarmed Mondale by going one step beyond the memo's recommendation: Carter sequestered himself with Begin and Sadat at Camp David and staked his own prestige on finding an exit from the labyrinthian entanglements of the Middle East's biblical rivalries. Mondale privately questioned the wisdom of Carter's dramatic move, knowing that the American president had no prior assurances that the summit would not end up as a dismal failure. His alarm grew with the discovery that one of the U.S. proposals forwarded during early negotiating called for substantial Israeli withdrawal from the captured West Bank lands. Mondale killed the proposal by going directly to Carter and arguing that trying to dictate such a solution to the Israelis would be fatal to Carter's peace hopes. In effect, Mondale told Carter, the administration had to come to the negotiating table with a clean slate and let the solution evolve from face-to-face bargaining between Israel and Egypt.

Later in the summit, talks hit a serious snag over Israel's settlements in the Sinai. Drawing on the rapport he established earlier with Begin, Mondale pleaded with the Israeli prime minister to give ground, to realize that the settlements lacked historic and strategic value to his country. Although others on the U.S. team were making the same argument, Carter counted on Mondale because of the respect he enjoyed among the Israelis.

Mondale's effectiveness as a working vice president was by now well established. Although he had no serious specific diplomatic tasks to perform, his visit to China in late August, 1979, helped strenghten U.S.-Sino relations. In an unprecedented gesture, the Chinese government invited Mondale to address their nation via television and radio from a forum of enormous historical and cultural significance—Peking University. No foreign leader since the mid-1950s—including Presidents Nixon and Ford who visited China in the 1970s—had been offered such an opportunity.

Standing at one of China's revolutionary epicenters, Mondale told the world's most populous nation that any power which "seeks to weaken or isolate you in world affairs assumes a stance counter to American interests." The allusion to China's arch rival—the Soviet Union—was unmistakeably clear.

"The leaders of other nations . . . recognize that Fritz indeed speaks for me," Carter said. "I doubt that this has ever been the case in the history of our nation with another vice presicent."

19

Joan Mondale—Arts Advocate

To get to the Mondales' house from downtown Washington, drive northwest along Massachusetts Avenue until you see the big white house on the hill. There you turn left past the guard and go up the drive. From a distance, the house looks like a feudal manor set apart from the serfs. But, drawing nearer, you realize that its aloofness is quite misleading; it seems a warm and neighborly place, quaintly charming in an odd-angled, creaky—yet cozy—way. It's been public property since Washington architect Leon Dessez was commissioned in the 1890s to design a residence for the superintendent of the Naval Observatory. What Dessez produced was a late Victorian house with a three-story Romanesque turret, a curving wood veranda, a gabled roof, and twenty rooms with eleven-and-a-half-foot ceilings—altogether an admirable house for an admiral, which it was until Sen. Hubert Humphrey prodded Congress into providing the vice president with a home appropriate to his station. In so doing, Humphrey was legislating from personal experience, having done his own entertaining as vice president in the cramped quarters of the apartment where he and Muriel Humphrey lived.

Appropriately, the first to benefit from Humphrey's efforts were his old friends, the Mondales. Betty and Gerry Ford would have been the first tenants, but by the time the house had been cleaned up they had already moved to an even better address—1600 Pennsylvania Avenue. He was succeeded in the vice presidency by Nelson Rockefeller, who preferred his own in-town estate and chose to use the official residence primarily for entertaining and as a showcase for a Max Ernst bed (which he repossessed on leaving office). The Walter Mondale family, whose net worth would barely have covered the upkeep on the Rockefeller estate for a year, did not have that luxury. The vintage white stucco house on Lowell Street in Cleveland Park had nicely suited the Mondales' senatorial lifestyle, but it was clearly not in the vice-presidential class. While her husband was studying how to serve as the president-elect's right-hand man, Joan was preparing to become a semi-absentee landlord. As she had done for years during periods of political widowhood, she washed windows and painted rooms, including the one they rented to a college student. She also would have house-cleaned but a platoon of neighborhood friends, armed with brooms, dustpans and mops, surprised her one day while she was gone. Their going-away present was awaiting her return—a clean, fresh-smelling house, ready for the Mondales' tenant. As moving day neared, she scrounged boxes from a neighborhood supermarket. Finally, the family took up residence in their new hilltop home, surrounded by twelve acres of prime, undeveloped Washington real estate and staffed by six naval stewards. Shortly after Inauguration Day, Eleanor expressed the general family mood by getting up from the dining-room table, walking into the living room, and promptly turning two cartwheels. She returned to the table without a word. Mondale was more understated: "It's the best house we've ever had."

For Joan as well as Fritz, the vice presidency was more than a house. For years, she had carried the burden of the typical politician's wife—putting up the storm windows in the fall, taking them down in the spring; driving carpools;

representing the family at the PTA; bringing up the kids. Yet their marriage showed few of the strains typical of other political couples, in part because Mondale would often cut corners on the job to add hours to his time at home. One day in the Senate during a hearing on the CIA, Mondale grumbled to Sen. Phil Hart about missing a chance to watch William play football that afternoon. "Get outa here right now," Hart said. "When I look back on my life, that's the dumbest thing I ever did—cheating my family out of time." Mondale arrived at the field in time to watch William intercept a pass and get tackled a few yards from where he was standing. "He looked up and I was there," Mondale recalled.

As a couple, they went out sparingly and entertained infrequently. Mondale would often wind up in the kitchen, cooking the turkey for Thanksgiving, baking bread for Christmas ("Fritz's bakery," he would say in answering the phone), preparing meals for the kids.

"What are you cooking?" Eleanor asked on one occasion.

"Pheasant under glass," Mondale replied.

"I could have sworn it was chicken," a friend of Eleanor's said.

He played basketball at a neighborhood playground with Teddy and William, took the family skiing in Colorado during the spring vacations and fishing in northern Minnesota in August; he went Christmas caroling every year and spared no one his constant teasing. He was the father of the family, no doubt about it. The demands on Joan were still enormous, yet she continued to expand her interest in the arts. She worked as a tour guide—docent—at the National Gallery; wrote her book, *Politics in Art;* gave art history lectures; attended board meetings in New York of the Associated Council of the Arts; and kept up with the openings, exhibitions, serious art criticism. In 1975, she started taking lessons from a master potter, Vally Possony.

She seemed to thrive in her role. The goals she set for herself added to the bonds of love, respect and admiration that knit the family together. "I've seen people in public life whose wives hate politics—the fatigue and frustration, the toll on family life. Joan has been just the reverse," Mondale told Mary Lynn Kotz in an interview for an article in *Art News* magazine. "She is a partner in my life. And she has her own interests as well. . . . She is effective. She is organized, prepares well, and knows her subjects inside out. I like the special spark she has—not only with the family but with anything else she's involved in."

As planning for the embryonic Carter administration proceeded during the transition, Mondale prepared to pay Joan back for her wifely support over the years by becoming a partner in her life, as she was in his. By offering Carter his thoughts about becoming a working vice president, Mondale in fact presented the president-elect with a two-for-one plan. He recognized the vice presidency as an opportunity for Joan as well as for himself. As he settled into his chair for the December 9 Blair House meeting with Carter, he was prepared to argue that she was no more interested in being a ceremonial Second Lady than he was in being a ceremonial vice president. Carter did not need to be convinced. He was in full agreement with Mondale that his presidency would be greatly enhanced by giving Joan a substantial role. Thereafter, Joan Mondale became known around the bureaucracy as Carter's arts advocate and, unofficially, as Joan of Art.

The change in her life was sudden and dramatic. Close friends knew that she had a second life, despite her demeanor as the self-effacing, supportive wife who picked up the slack in her husband's absence. During the attorney-general years, she had continued her museum work during the day even while she became an activist in politics at night. But her interest in the arts had always been something that she fitted in as time allowed. Now politics and the arts merged. The fact that she was the vice president's wife carrying out an assignment from the president made her suddenly visible—and newsworthy. She became a functioning part of an activist vice presidency and a force not to be ignored.

During Joan Mondale's earlier Washington years, some who hadn't known her well had been inclined to superficial judgments about her apparent lack of an independent personality. She seemed *so self-effacing, so proper, so wifely.* Her clothes were not particularly fashionable and she only had her hair done once a month. What could such a woman possibly have to offer? For one thing, an open, unabashed exuberance and an often unrestrained impulsiveness that was as much a part of her character as her formal propriety as a minister's daughter and politician's wife. In an art gallery, at a pottery class, among friends, she could sparkle with animation, especially if something pleased her. "Oh, that's so neeeeeat. I just love it," she would say, her voice rising an octave and eyes widening with enthusiasm. Or a tidbit of whispered gossip: "Why, that's terrible," she would gasp, sucking in her breath with a whooshing sound. "I love it. Tell me more."

There were times when she would surrender with mischievous delight to the temptations of candor. Asked by one interviewer during the Senate years whether it wasn't a burden to have a husband who was campaigning all the time, Joan Mondale replied, "Why not at all. If he didn't campaign constantly, why, he'd lose and we'd have to go back to Minnesota." As for her predecessors as Second Lady, she dismissed them during an interview with Maureen Santini of the Associated Press with devastating directness: "What did Happy Rockefeller do? What did Betty Ford do? What did Judy Agnew do? What did Lady Bird do?" Dropping her voice to a whisper, she answered her own question: "Nothing. They went to luncheons, teas, and receptions. They did the social things which I try to avoid as much as possible. I don't have time." She could also be unaffected as well as unpredictable, as when she strolled into a luncheon with some old friends from her Cleveland Park neighborhood, casually accompanied by an unannounced guest—Rosalynn Carter.

As the vice president's wife, she became more conscious of her appearance. That meant having her hair done once a week. It also meant dressing with just the right amount of chic—smartly without being elegant or trendy. What was important was the substance of her role.

One of her first and most helpful advisers was an old friend, Martin Friedman, director of the Walker Art Center in Minneapolis, one of the nation's premier museums of modern art. Together, they sketched the basic outlines of her role over peanut-butter-and-jelly sandwiches amid the packing boxes and wrapping paper cluttering the Lowell Street homestead. They agreed that she should be a "lightning rod" for the arts, attracting ideas and criticisms about government programs and policies. She would use the visibility of her administration position to tout artists and craftsmen. She would attempt to become a "facilitator, a connector." Friedman also agreed to track down representative American paintings and sculptures from Midwestern museums for a six-month display in the vice-presidential mansion's first-floor rooms, which seemed ideally sized and shaped for the project. Art exhibits from other regions were to follow.

Joan Mondale wasted little time in testing her clout. While her husband and Carter were laying out the new administration's agenda at the Sea Island meeting three weeks before Inauguration Day, Joan seized the opportunity to lobby future Interior Secretary Cecil Andrus on behalf of the first of her many schemes to enlarge the federal government's sponsorship of local arts and crafts. With Andrus's enthusiastic backing, she persuaded National Park Service concessionaires to begin stocking locally produced crafts in the souvenir shops of ten national parks as alternatives to the mass-produced trinkets that traditionally cluttered their display cases.

Another early target was Jay Solomon, then administrator of the General Services Administration. After softening up Solomon, an art collector and husband of a photographer, with knowledgeable chit-chat, she hit him with a cold-cash proposal—that GSA increase the percentage of total construction costs set aside for art in new or renovated federal buildings from the current three-eighths of one percent to one percent.

It was a negotiator's ploy. Solomon was interested in her proposal, but the one-percent figure was too steep. He also needed one more encouraging nudge. It was willingly supplied by the vice president. On a late-night flight back to Washington after a political fund-raising dinner in Nashville, Solomon sought Mondale's advice. Mondale enthusiastically endorsed his wife's idea. That led to a compromise under which the GSA increased its Arts in Architecture funding from three-eighths to one-half of one percent of construction costs. It meant that in a $10 million new federal building, $50,000 would be set aside for commissioned works of art as part of the overall design.

"This lady is not just a mouth," reported Al McConagha of the Minneapolis *Tribune*'s Washington Bureau. "She is muscle, and she is exercising a steadily increasing influence over federal policy on the arts."

That muscle was developed in part when the vice president turned over four of his staff slots to his wife to help advance her interests. For one of the slots, she immediately hired Bess Abell, former social secretary of Lady Bird Johnson and an experienced, efficient political aide. The pair had worked well during the presidential campaign, when Joan had her own schedule and national responsibilities to help elect the Carter-Mondale ticket. Fritz Mondale was also an alert scout at the top of the government, surveying the administrative horizon for opportunities and issues that she might exploit. He tipped Joan off about plans by the Domestic Council staff to review administration policies on a number of issues, not including the arts. At her request, he persuaded Stuart Eizenstat, Carter's assistant for domestic policy, to add the arts to the agenda. The review prompted a decision to reactivate the Federal Council on the Arts and Humanities, with Joan as the honorary chairperson. The council soon became a bureaucratic stronghold. Under her leadership, its staff went to work on an inventory of federally funded projects with a cultural focus. No one had the complete picture; without it, Joan could not know the full scope of her opportunities. Before long, her researchers had dug up $100 million worth of projects dedicated to culture, not including the well-known National Foundation with its twin endowments for the arts and humanities.

Her charter as the administration's arts advocate enabled her to open doors. She could plead her case, not as a supplicant but as a presidential agent. When artists complained that the federal tax code treated them unfairly, she won a high-level hearing at which their grievances were spelled out. A "livable cities" project, developed by the National Endowment for the Arts, received a $20 million boost from the Department of Housing and Urban Development, thanks to her efforts. Her lobbying also helped persuade Labor Secretary Ray Marshall to expand a jobs program to help out unemployed artists. Meanwhile, as a partial result of the vice president's personal attention, Carter proposed a record 25 percent increase in 1979 funding for the arts and humanities at a time when funding for most other domestic programs was being cut back. During the intramural jockeying over the 1980 budget, Mondale called James McIntyre, the director of the Office of Management and Budget, to add $5 million to the arts budget.

"What's your reason?" McIntyre inquired.

"Because I wanna stay married," Mondale replied.

"That's not good enough," McIntyre told him.

The vice president persisted, and the money was added to the budget.

Bureaucratic troubleshooting was only part of Joan Mondale's role. At least as important in her eyes were the 70,-000 miles she traveled during the first eighteen months of the Carter administration. Much of her time on the road was spent with artists and artisans, listening to their complaints, learning of their problems—and promoting their work. In political lingo, many of her stops were "quick hits," designed to generate media coverage, dramatizing an issue, a personality, an event. She walked the streets of Houston's old Sixth Ward under a brutal summer sun to plead the cause of the preservationists battling to save the neighborhood's quaint nineteenth-century clapboard houses. There was a crafts center to promote in the mountains of North Carolina, an exhibit of American Indian art to open in Kansas City. She dedicated Claes Oldenburg's "Batcolumn" statute in front of Chicago's new Social Security Building and made pilgrimages to New Mexico honoring painter Georgia O'Keeffe and Indian potter Maria Martinez. When visiting the Craft and Folk Art Museum on Wilshire Boulevard in Los Angeles, Joan found herself sitting at a potter's wheel, apron around her neck, and a ball of wet clay in her hand. As the artists and onlookers pressed forward to watch, she skillfully centered the clay and shaped it into a pot while the television cameras whirred. Afterwards, a sculptor said, "I admire you inordinately for what you just did in front of all those people." Nor did she neglect New York or SoHo where she lunched on stuffed artichokes and fettucine with Jasper Johns, Roy Lichtenstein, Louise Nevelson, Robert Rauschenberg, and other New York art notables.

Inevitably, her role led to controversy, particularly since the parceling out of federal dollars meant that some artists and craftspeople would lose out. There were also over-tones of cultural snobbery. After all, who was Joan Mondale to wield such power over the arts? Did she have *taste?* To leaders in the arts establishment, her fondness for the crafts was cause for alarm. Would she understand that a pot was not a sculpture? Those fears seemed confirmed when Joan Mondale selected the Winter Market of American Crafts in Baltimore for her first visit outside of Washington as Carter's arts advocate. Her democratic instincts were also on display when she persuaded the GSA's Solomon to commission indigenous works—rather than big-name mas-terpieces—for display at regional GSA facilities. Inevitably, perhaps, her interests and activities stirred a sharp debate, pitting the conflicting artistic philosophies of elitism and populism against each other.

Elitists worried about an erosion of artistic quality be-cause of Joan Mondale's interest in helping local artists and promoting crafts. Some of her critics accused the adminis-tration of harboring a quota plan under which museums could qualify for federal dollars only if their trustees and exhibitors were racially and sexually balanced. The endow-ments were being "politicized," elitists charged, with their resources being pirated for crass pork-barrel projects under the guise of creativity. Robert Brustein, former dean of the Yale Drama School, wrote a slashing attack that Joan Mondale interpreted as saying that "I don't know the diff-erence between basketweaving and fine art." McConagha quoted one New York museum official as remarking, "Peo-ple worry that they will blow this dough on silly places. There is a kind of phony populism about it, grass-rootsie. Should federal money go to little boob museums showing local artists?"

Joan Mondale listened to the elitists' laments with impa-tience and indifference. "I think the real concerns are qual-ity and accessibility," she said. "You can have both. Mil-lions of garages have basketball hoops in this country and millions of kids grow up shooting baskets. Does that affect the quality of American basketball?"

Besides, she had more pressing concerns. There was, for example, the mayor of Buffalo, who took one look at plans for a Kenneth Snelson sculpture that had been commissioned for the plaza of a federal building and decided the work would look best at the bottom of Lake Erie. The city, he added, would not pay its share of the sculpture's cost. The mayor, however, finally had a change of heart after Joan arranged a face-to-face interview and lured him to a slide lecture on urban-arts projects.

Other public officials were more appreciative. One Sunday in late October, 1977, she traveled to Atlanta to give her urban-arts slide lecture to a group of city officials and to tour a unique playground featuring intriguingly shaped objects sculpted by Isamu Noguchi with the help of a $50,-000 federal grant. Her guide was Mayor Maynard Jackson, who passed up his fifty-yard-line seat for an important Atlanta Falcons football game. Guiding her back to the car, Jackson told her with quiet sincerity, "You've really made an impact and it's important. I just wanted to say thank you."

20

Looking Ahead

He walked slowly into the lounge at Andrews Air Force
Base, where a handful of reporters, bedraggled from the
stormy January night, were waiting. Walter Mondale had
just capped his first year in office as vice president with an
intensive five-day trip through the West, mending Jimmy
Carter's political fences. But politics was not on Mondale's
mind at this moment. Minutes after landing, Mondale had
received a message that he immediately relayed to the president. He was now about to share the news with the world.

Al Eisele, Mondale's press secretary, said only that the
vice president would make a short statement and answer no
questions. Mondale stood in silence, his head bowed,
fingers clasped tightly in front of him, waiting while a couple of TV crewmen set up. Then, face sagging with emotion, voice barely under control, Mondale said, "I've just
talked to the president to tell him that Hubert Humphrey
has died."

Mondale was not the only one to feel the loss. Humphrey's contributions to the nation as mayor, senator, vice
president, and presidential campaigner raised him above
his parochial origins and made him into a national figure.
His death was mourned in foreign lands as well, but no one
captured the essence of Humphrey's life better than Mondale, whose eulogy on January 14, 1978, in the rotunda of

the Capitol ended on this note: "He taught us how to hope and how to love, how to win and how to lose; he taught us how to live, and finally he taught us how to die."

Mondale's prominence during Humphrey's final days and the leavetaking that followed was appropriate. Their careers had traced remarkably similar upward curves, and it would be easy to describe Humphrey as having been the pathfinder, and Mondale the acolyte, on the trek that led from Minnesota's precinct caucuses to the vice presidency. But that would not be quite accurate; the relationship between these two American politicians was never that easy to define. In the beginning, of course, Humphrey was a big-city mayor, running for the U.S. Senate, while Mondale was content to observe and help out as a kind of back-shop apprentice. Eighteen years later, Mondale also arrived in the Senate, but by a radically different route. Humphrey charted his course by jumping into the middle of a DFL party free-for-all, and then outtalking and outmaneuvering anyone who stood in his way. Mondale was an inside man, moving through channels, making himself useful, thriving on the harmony Humphrey, Freeman, and others, including Mondale himself, had created.

By 1971, Mondale and Humphrey found themselves serving together in the Senate, with Mondale holding the title of senior senator from Minnesota in one of history's ironic quirks. They were now often spoken of in the same breath—Mondale and Humphrey, Humphrey and Mondale, the liberal Minnesota twins. And, in fact, they voted alike on most issues. But Humphrey, restless, ambitious, was constantly seeking the presidency. His aspiration for higher office was an open book, and what Mondale read there contributed to his decision in 1974 not to go after the nomination. The price was too high. The cost could be measured by Humphrey's tinted hair, his mechanical attention to Senate duties when presidential-campaign pressures mounted, the subtle sense that Humphrey was losing touch with Minnesota, the forced separations from Muriel Humphrey and the rest of the family.

Mondale had come to terms with himself, realizing that there were certain goals he couldn't achieve without undue political risks or personal sacrifices. That was true whether it involved the hazards of running for the presidency or challenging the chairmanship of Russell Long.

Humphrey arrived at a similar point when he ruled out an eleventh-hour campaign against Carter for the nomination in 1976, saying, "I don't need any more humiliation, I don't need any more knocks, and I'm not going to run." That decision behind him, Humphrey began living quietly and uncomplainingly with himself and the cancer that he eventually learned would kill him, a public man to the end. In those final moments of Humphrey's life, he and Mondale for the first time became genuinely close, their relationship uncluttered by separate ambitions. Past and future fused in one poignant moment late in the summer of 1977, when Mondale visited Humphrey in a University of Minnesota hospital. Humphrey, so hale and robust for most of his life, was emaciated and wan. He had only a few weeks—months, at most—to live, his surgeons having tried for the last time to arrest the cancer and failed. They were alone when Humphrey looked Mondale in the eye. There was no use pretending, Humphrey said. The malignancy in his intestines was killing him—fast. He reflected for a few moments about the career that carried him, the son of a South Dakota druggist, to the threshold of the White House. It had been a good life, he declared. Then, for the first time in their thirty-three years together, Humphrey reached up and embraced Mondale. Now it's your turn, Humphrey said. You must carry on.

Humphrey and Mondale thereafter were in close touch. "There was no self-pity and no complaining," Mondale would write later. "We kidded each other and laughed a lot, and he counseled me."

They last talked in early January, 1978. Humphrey reached Mondale by phone in the Senate. He was calling from his home in Waverly. They talked only for a few minutes. For the first time Humphrey admitted he wasn't feeling well—that he was in pain. They hung up. Moments later, it hit Mondale: The old man had called to say goodbye.

Mondale's inauguration as vice president and Humphrey's death a year later had a resounding impact on their cherished DFL party. The years of political prosperity diverted attention from the dry rot in the timbers of the political house they had helped build. The profusion of talent drawn into the party during its early birth struggles—Humphrey, Mondale, McCarthy, Freeman, and others—had moved on. Nor did anyone seem particularly alarmed at the rebuilding next door. The Republican party had been the dominant political force during Minnesota's first century after gaining statehood in 1858, and the GOP was quietly reestablishing itself across the state.

When Mondale won the vice presidency, his Senate seat became vacant. Gov. Wendell Anderson, who had named Muriel Humphrey to fill her late husband's seat, violated one of the most stubborn taboos in American politics. He resigned by prearrangement to have his successor appoint him to the Senate as Mondale's replacement. Eight other governors had tried that same ploy but only one—Happy Chandler of Kentucky—was successful in holding the Senate seat in the elections that followed. Anderson also ignored the precedent of former Gov. Karl Rolvaag, who—confronting an identical situation after Humphrey's election to the vice presidency in 1964—had sent Fritz Mondale to Washington instead of himself. Gov. Anderson thought he could defy tradition. He was wrong.

His self-appointment and Humphrey's death uncorked the angry spirits in the DFL's bottle. Bitter fights erupted over the rights of succession in 1978. Scabs were rubbed off old wounds. An opportunist named Robert Short, trucking magnate, hotel owner, former boss of the Washington Senators, exploited the irrational appeal of issues like abortion, gun control, wilderness preservation—and then cynically tried to present himself as heir to Humphrey's healing mantle. The DFL presented an unseemly spectacle of greed, demagoguery, and unbridled ambition. Meanwhile, the Republicans, their spadework now complete, nominated their most impressive ticket in years.

Mondale attempted to help out. He was no more successful than Humphrey had been in 1966, when the DFL tore itself apart attempting to oust Rolvaag from the statehouse. The Republicans in 1978 captured the governorship and the two U.S. Senate seats, and made deep inroads in the DFL's strength elsewhere.

For Walter Mondale, the outcome was a sharp personal disappointment. Whether it seriously hurt him politically was unclear. Certainly his home base was less secure. Also, his standing in the eyes of many erstwhile liberal allies was diminished by his haste in endorsing Short after his heavy-handed tactics had narrowly defeated a popular liberal, Donald Fraser, in the Senate primary election. Mondale's friendship with Fraser dated to their days together in Humphrey's 1948 Senate race. Had Mondale betrayed his friendship with Fraser—or at least the liberal ideals Fraser represented—by embracing Short? To some, that seemed an open question. To Walter Mondale, the results of the Fraser-Short primary represented another episode in the eternal political struggle for survival. Short had won the primary. He was a DFLer. His opponent was a Republican. To Mondale, and to the congressional vote-counters in the White House, the choice was a simple one.

One person who thought the election results fatal to Mondale was Marcus Raskin, a member of the New Democratic Coalition, a caucus of party liberals that grew out of Gene McCarthy's 1968 antiwar campaign. Writing in the

New York *Times* on November 16, 1978, Raskin defrocked Mondale, calling him a "lame duck vice president." That was his opening sentence. About seven hundred caustic words later, Raskin concluded: "What remains clear is that Mr. Carter and his inner group will use the vice presidency as a bargaining chip in the near future so that he might find a way to win reelection."

About the time that edition of the *Times* was being delivered to homes and newsstands in Washington, D.C., Jimmy Carter was casually telling Helen Thomas of United Press International that Walter Mondale would of course be invited back for a second term, assuming that he—Jimmy Carter—ran again.

Mondale's political universe had expanded to a degree that would have been incomprehensible in his shoestring days as a Humphrey vote-hustler in the precincts of Minneapolis and the small towns of the Second District. Huge jet airplanes, platoons of Secret Service agents, an ultra-sophisticated worldwide communications system, the attention of world leaders—all were at his command. Backing him was the confidence of the president of the United States. Mondale did not win that favored niche on the pinnacle of power by accident. Few were as well grounded in the techniques of his profession. He knew when and how to fight, but he also knew when to accept the inevitable. He had done everything he could to elect Democrats in Minnesota, and now he'd have to live with the result. By the same token, there was no way to talk Carter into a 1980 budget that would satisfy the bulk of the Democratic party's liberal wing. Inflation—and the popular apprehension it bred—would not go away, so one had to adapt. That was the pattern of Mondale's earlier career—adapt and adjust, while firmly holding to a set of principles. Mondale never lost his sympathies for the underdogs—the weak, the oppressed, the underprivileged. But he consistently dealt with their problems within the realm of the possible. As a mature, established politician, Humphrey did the same thing, although his earlier years in the Senate were marked by assaults on the established order in pursuit of social, economic, and racial justice. When the strength of his passions caused him to overstep, he was sometimes slapped down.

That never happened to Mondale. While he didn't win every battle, he picked his fights carefully and made sure they did not become personal quarrels or confrontations. He helped produce the compromise that quelled an open floor fight at the 1964 convention over the Mississippi credentials challenge. When he sensed that direct legislative efforts on behalf of migrants would lead nowhere, Mondale did not attempt to build the same kind of coalition that had succeeded on open housing. Instead, he broadened his efforts, although his eye was constantly on the goal of helping the ultimate victims—the migrants and others like them. When the fight over school busing flared, Mondale took a strong and well-documented stand in support of equal educational opportunity—and then sought the most defensible tactical position he could find. That was not a defense of busing per se—as a means of combatting racial isolation—but a defense of the judiciary's constitutional prerogative to order busing as one method of desegregating schools. His tenure on the Finance Committee conformed to the same pattern. He shied from a direct battle with Chairman Russell Long—a fight that would have entailed going over Long's head and appealing to a broader constituency within Congress and outside, as well. What he sought was a pragmatic accommodation with Long that yielded mutual, practical benefits to both.

For much of his political life, Mondale has been a builder of short-term coalitions. An activist, he has pursued objectives persistently—but rarely so single-mindedly that he has foreclosed accommodation. At the same time, he has been a deeply contemplative public official who has conscientiously explored and examined issues in all their complexities. Whether as an attorney general broadening his powers on behalf of consumers or as a senator unraveling the causes of family distress, he has sought original solutions that deal with the causes of problems, not merely their effects. His entire mature life has been devoted to mastering the American political system. His skills have now carried him to a vital crossroads, not only in his own career but possibly in the life of the nation. Indeed, four of the seven presidents to serve since 1948 have occupied Mondale's seat underneath the vice-presidential seal, but none of them ever grasped the levers of national power as firmly in that office as he does now. His place in the constitutional line of succession raises the question of whether a Mondale administration would be guided by a broad strategic vision or whether it would be content to react tactically to specific situations. Would Mondale challenge the country as a bold, venturesome leader? Or would he tinker with the system, tailoring a program to fit the prevailing mood?

Mondale's career points in both directions. But his personal integrity, sincerity, intelligence, and humanity are beyond question. There is no reason to believe that those qualities would change if he became president. After more than thirty years in tough, competitive politics, he has emerged with his personal and political values firmly intact. He never emulated the crude, political macho of Lyndon Johnson and despised Nixon's brand of partisan hardball. Mondale's is a different kind of toughness. It is the basic, unyielding determination of a man committed to solutions that make a qualitative difference. It is a toughness born of an understanding that progress, even in minute, incremental steps, is still progress. Like his father who overcame hardships and disappointments, Walter Mondale is a survivor. Some races have been impossible to win. Sometimes winning has meant knowing when to walk as well as when to run.

Index